MW01634888

Women Writers of Gabon

After the Empire: The Francophone World and Postcolonial France

Series Editor

Valérie K. Orlando, University of Maryland

Recent Titles

Women Writers of Gabon: Literature and Herstory, by Cheryl Toman
Backwoodsmen as Ecocritical Motif in French Canadian Literature: Connecting Worlds in the Wilds, by Annie Rehill
Front Cover Iconography and Algerian Women's Writing: Heuristic Implications of the Recto-Verso Effect, by Pamela A. Pears
The Algerian War in French-Language Comics: Postcolonial Memory, History, and Subjectivity, by Jennifer Howell
Writing through the Visual and Virtual: Inscribing Language, Literature, and Culture in Francophone Africa and the Caribbean, edited by Ousseina D. Alidou and Renée Larrier
State Power, Stigmatization, and Youth Resistance Culture in the French Banlieues: Uncanny Citizenship, by Hervé Tchumkam
Violence in Caribbean Literature: Stories of Stones and Blood, by Véronique Maisier
Ousmane Sembene and the Politics of Culture, edited by Lifongo J. Vetinde and Amadou T. Fofana
Reimagining the Caribbean: Conversations among the Creole, English, French, and Spanish Caribbean, edited by Valérie K. Orlando and Sandra Messinger Cypress
Rethinking Reading, Writing, and a Moral Code in Contemporary France: Postcolonializing High Culture in the Schools of the Republic, by Michel Laronde

Women Writers of Gabon

Literature and Herstory

Cheryl Toman

LEXINGTON BOOKS
Lanham • Boulder • New York • London

Published by Lexington Books
An imprint of The Rowman & Littlefield Publishing Group, Inc.
4501 Forbes Boulevard, Suite 200, Lanham, Maryland 20706
www.rowman.com

Unit A, Whitacre Mews, 26-34 Stannary Street, London SE11 4AB

British Library Cataloguing in Publication Information Available

Library of Congress Cataloging-in-Publication Data Available

ISBN 978-1-4985-3720-9 (cloth : alk. paper)
ISBN 978-1-4985-3722-3 (pbk. : alk. paper)
ISBN 978-1-4985-3721-6 (electronic)

∞™ The paper used in this publication meets the minimum requirements of American National Standard for Information Sciences Permanence of Paper for Printed Library Materials, ANSI/NISO Z39.48-1992.

Printed in the United States of America

Table of Contents

Acknowledgments

This book is the product of eight years of research with the most rewarding part being all of the memorable, warm, stimulating, and insightful conversations with the women writers of Gabon and with numerous literary scholars working on the African and European continents. In March 2011 and January 2015, my work took me to Gabon where I became thoroughly convinced of what I had already gathered through archival research: Gabon is indeed a powerhouse of African literature and its women writers are largely responsible for this.

Above all, I extend sincere thanks to Edna Merey-Apinda who was the first Gabonese author I met in person in February 2010. Thanks to Edna, I was able to discover the profound beauty of her country as she also made monumental efforts to connect me with as many of her fellow authors as possible. Many fruitful exchanges resulted and continue to occur today in Libreville and in Paris, and to some extent, in Cleveland where we have been fortunate to host some of these very authors presenting their work for the first time in the United States at Case Western Reserve University.

In addition to Edna, I am also grateful to Mélissa Bendome, Charline Effah, Alice Endamne, Miryl Nadia Eteno, Justine Mintsa, Honorine Ngou, Sylvie Ntsame, and Nadia Origo who each contributed in a unique way to this project and who are all remarkable women for many reasons. During my most recent stay in Gabon, I had the privilege of meeting several more second generation women authors whose works will also undoubtedly be the subject of further studies of Gabonese literature. Talented writers like Élisabeth Aworet, Muetse-Destinée Mboga, and Pulchérie Abeme-Nkoghe, just to name a few, will surely have an enormous impact on forming a third generation of writers in Gabon.

For the most part, Gabonese women writers have enjoyed the support of their male counterparts and I would also like to thank some of those individuals in particular who brought me interesting perspectives and encouragement while I was undertaking this project—Cyriaque Akomo-Zoghe, Hallnaut Mathieu Engouang, Wilfried Idiatha, Bellarmin Moutsinga, Rodrigue Ndong, and Albert Ngou.

I mustn't forget others who accompanied me in this research in one way or another. I made the first unforgettable trip to Gabon with my longtime friend and colleague, Julia diLiberti, and it was thanks to her optimism that we met against all odds Honorine Ngou. My colleague at Case Western Reserve, Gilbert Doho, could not have been more supportive, especially during the visits of the Gabonese writers and scholars whom we hosted together at CWRU and in Cleveland over the past several years. Most recently, I've been thrilled to discover the work of an ambitious young scholar, Sara Hanaburgh, for whom I had the pleasure of writing the afterword for her superb translation of Rawiri's *Fureurs et cris de femmes* and I am happy to share with her this enthusiasm for Gabonese women's writing, which I'm hoping will soon be contagious in North America. I am also grateful to my students who supported my interest in Gabonese women's writing, especially Beth Johnston who beautifully translated and published Merey-Apinda's *Des contes pour la lune* and my advanced students who have been translating the works of Alice Endamne and Miryl Nadia Eteno. My husband, Carl Kohnhorst, as always, made technical issues seemingly effortless and was an excellent host himself for our guests from Gabon.

Lastly, this book was made possible through generous funding by Case Western Reserve University through the ACES+ Advance Opportunity Grant and the Baker-Nord Center for the Humanities. And finally, I was most honored to be a 2011 recipient of the Brown Foundation Fellowship funded through The Museum of Fine Art–Houston. This fellowship offered me the opportunity to be a resident at the Dora Maar House in Ménerbes, France, and this was one of the most invaluable experiences of my career, enabling me to do a significant amount of writing and research for this particular book.

Quotes from the following works were published with permission:

Introduction

Assessing an "Absence" of Literature in Gabon and the Invisibility of Women

Well into the twenty-first century, the literary histories of certain African nations still suffer from inconsistent if not downright flawed information put forth, at times, by even the most respected writers and critics in the field. The result is devastating for literatures that Western scholars deem "young,"[1] and all too often a potential readership is directed instead toward what is already somewhat "familiar and safe." In African Francophone literature, this "familiar and safe" refers to works emerging from longtime powerhouses of writing such as Cameroon, Côte-d'Ivoire, Senegal, and Congo. Outside of these countries, however, novelists—both male and female—often find their works falling disproportionately and unfairly into what Irène Assiba d'Almeida calls "the empty canon: unknown, unpraised, uncriticized" (*A Rain of Words* xxii).

The central African nation of Gabon finds itself within this empty canon in some respects, but not in others. Gabon boasts several successful publishing houses (Éditions Ntsame, Maison Gabonaise du Livre, and ODEM, among others) and the country's literature is known in France thanks to both Gabonese and French efforts. In 1991, the renowned French literary journal on African and Caribbean literature *Notre librairie*,[2] featured the issue, *Littérature gabonaise*, edited by Honorine Ngou, novelist, professor, and at the time, chair of the Department of French at Omar Bongo University in Libreville. This issue of *Notre librairie* was the first critical work that finally put Gabon on the radar of critics in France. Gallimard, arguably one of Europe's most prestigious publishers of literature, duly took note and inaugurated their Continents Noirs Series in 2000 with the publication of Justine Mintsa's

Histoire d'Awu. Soon after, acclaimed scholar, writer, and Gabonese professor, Grégoire Biyogo, directed several collections for L'Harmattan in Paris between 2005 and 2011, during which he oversaw the publication of hundreds of works on literature, criticism, anthropology, sociology, and indigenous languages by Gabonese authors. Most recently, a younger generation of Gabonese writers finds representation thanks to novelist and geographer Nadia Origo, who founded in Paris La Doxa Éditions as well her magazine *Reflets* highlighting in particular black achievement in literature, arts, and entrepreneurship. Although La Doxa is considered a small press, it has nonetheless managed to lure established second-generation writers away from larger publishers, one example being Edna Merey-Apinda who published her latest novel, *La nuit sera longue*, with La Doxa in 2014. La Doxa and its authors also make regular contributions to literary criticism; the collection *Regards sur les grands thèmes de la literature gabonaise* (2010) is the most notable example and it remains a most useful reference today. New French publishing houses such as Edilivre and Jets d'encre, both established in 2007, have also welcomed several young Gabonese authors among their ranks. In 2010, the academic press Les Éditions Odette Maganga (ODEM) was created by Pierre Ndemby-Mamfoumby in Libreville and has since published several excellent collections of essays that are not only invaluable resources in Gabonese literary criticism but they also help bring Gabon's deserving authors into the spotlight.

Despite this most positive trajectory over the last three decades, however, and the fact that literary production in Gabon continues to increase, Biyogo's departure from L'Harmattan has had a noticeable impact as there have since been fewer newer titles of literary criticism published in France that center on Gabonese works. In addition, the overall study of African Francophone literature in France has suffered enormously following the 2005 retirement of Jacques Chevrier, professor and prolific scholar of African Francophone literature at Paris IV-Sorbonne.[3] The French university system unfortunately has done little to recruit scholars of Chevrier's caliber despite the fact that Chevrier directed dozens of theses by former students who are available and more than suitable for the task.

In the United States and Canada where the African Francophone novel has arguably gained more critical attention than in France, the Gabonese novel—not to mention all other genres of literature—has been relatively unknown and there is a dearth of criticism in English. The first critique of Gabonese women's writing that appeared in English was Odile Cazenave's insightful analyses of Angèle Rawiri's novels included in her study entitled *Rebellious Women* (1999).[4]

There is evidence that this trend of ignoring Gabonese literature is about to change, however. Recently published translations of novels such as Rawiri's *Fureurs et cris de femmes* (1989) as *The Fury and Cries of Women*

(2014) in the CARAF[5] Series of the University of Virginia Press, and Alice Endamne's *C'est demain qu'on s'fait la malle* (2008) appearing in English as *Afropean* (2015) with CreateSpace not only offer the literature itself but these volumes also include critical introductions. Edna Merey-Apinda's *Des contes pour la lune*, a contemporary text based on a reworking of traditional oral tales, has also been recently translated into English under the title *The Moonlight Tales* (2016).[6] This follows the prior publication of Merey-Apinda's poems "Le secret de la nuit" (The Secret of the Night) and "Peu importe" (Little Does it Matter) in both French and English in Kalu, Makuchi, and Nfah-Abbenyi's *An Anthology of New Work by African Women Poets* (2013).[7] These works plus additional forthcoming translations of Justine Mintsa's *Histoire d'Awu*, Alice Endamne's *Garçons et filles* (2010), and Miryl Eteno's collection of short stories and flashbacks entitled *Les doux murmures de mon enfance* (2012) all point to signs that an interest will be rekindled in Gabonese literature—in either its original or translated form—and consequently, many works will finally be attributed their rightful place in Francophone literary criticism worldwide.

The literary history of Gabon is remarkable in many ways, but what makes this national literature especially unique from all others on the continent is the sheer number of Gabonese women novelists and their overall importance in African literary history. Ironically, the very reason for this literature's distinctiveness may also be a factor contributing to its invisibility elsewhere. That is, Gabonese literature conceivably has a "herstory"[8] larger than its "history," making it seemingly less important and invisible to many. Paul Tiyambe Zeleza writes precisely about "invisible women" in his essay, "Gender Biases in African Historiography." He states: "[The authors of African history] are predominantly male and sexist in so far as their texts underestimate the important role that women have played in all aspects of African history. In more extreme cases, women are not even mentioned at all" (208). Zeleza's words most certainly apply to African literary history and specifically to the case of Gabon. As writers, Gabonese women confront double oppression as both Africans and females, which may explain why their works have subsequently been overlooked or underestimated.

One striking example of the effacement of Gabonese women writers came from a 2006 widely read blogpost by Alain Mabanckou, the acclaimed Congolese author who is now also a professor at the University of California–Los Angeles (UCLA) and the 2015–2016 visiting professor of artistic creation at the Collège de France in Paris. In his highly controversial post entitled "SOS: pays africains cherchent désespérément des écrivains" (SOS: African countries desperately in search of writers),[9] Mabanckou had singled out Gabon as a country that suffered from "an absence of literature" claiming: "The Gabonese now seem to be indulging in self-praise as I see no proof that Gabon even has a literature or any major authors."[10]

Mabanckou continued on in his blogpost by launching an attack on two of the country's major women writers—Justine Mintsa and Chantal Magalie Mbazoo-Kassa—faulting Mintsa for publishing at L'Harmattan after her success at Gallimard,[11] and suggesting that Mbazoo-Kassa and others have been the recipient of growing praise from Gabonese critics that is undeserved.[12] While such remarks by Mabanckou can be dismissed as mere personal opinion, his words were far-reaching coming from a celebrated writer of his status and the reaction in Gabon was fierce, with writers forming new organizations promoting their literature and creating their own blogs countering Mabanckou's assertions. Launched at that time and still having considerable impact today, for example, is the Facebook public group entitled "Littérature gabonaise" that, as of 2016, has attracted over 700 writers and followers of Gabonese literature, especially those among the younger generation who are thoroughly media literate. Another example from social media defending and promoting Gabonese literature was created by writer and critic Auguste Moussirou-Mouyama whose well-received 2007 blog addressed Mabanckou's claims directly and offered a forum for Gabonese writers to expose their works online as he proudly declared, "Même si elle n'a pas l'épaisseur de sa fôret, la littérature gabonaise existe" (Even if it is not yet as widespread as its forests, Gabonese literature does exist).[13]

What was most surprising, however, about Mabanckou's blogpost was his lack of knowledge of the most basic facts concerning Gabonese literature, but unfortunately this is characteristic of similar mistakes committed by Francophone studies scholars throughout the years, which have in turn negatively affected African women writers in particular, especially those from countries whose literature is already underrepresented in the field. Mabanckou incorrectly cited Laurent Owondo's 1985 novel, *Au bout du silence*, as Gabon's first novel, omitting either intentionally or inadvertently Angèle Rawiri's *Elonga* (1980), hailed almost unanimously by critics, Gabonese or otherwise, as the country's first novel (Ambourhouet-Bigmann, "Où est le roman gabonais?" 18; Francis 877; Mbazoo-Kassa, "La femme et ses images" 27; Ovono Mendame).[14]

Mabanckou's oversight reveals a disturbing pattern occurring ever since African women began to write novels in French during the 1950s. That is, critics (both male and female, African and non-African) have diminished or erased the importance of the earliest African women writers. In Francophone African literature in particular, this trend is witnessed as early as the *Négritude* period of the 1930s—a movement for which the ultimate goal was to promote solidarity among all African writers and scholars by bringing to the forefront black intellectual thought and identity. In her book entitled *Negritude Women*, T. Denean Sharpley-Whiting asserts that "Negritude is generally studied through the works of Césaire, Senghor, and Damas. For their part, the threesome provide a conspicuously masculine genealogy of their critical consciousness" (12).

Even works from the aforementioned literary "powerhouses" suffered the same fate. The earliest examples of women's writing from Francophone Cameroon—Marie-Claire Matip's autobiographical novella entitled *Ngonda* (1956) and Thérèse Kuoh-Moukoury's novel *Rencontres essentielles* completed in 1956 but first published in 1969—for a long time found themselves in the "empty canon," leaving many critics to cite Anglophone African texts such as Nigerian author Mabel Segun's *My Father's Daughter* and Ghanaian playwright Ama Ata Aidoo's *The Dilemma of a Ghost* as the first works of African women's writing even though both were published in 1965 after Matip and Kuoh-Moukoury had written theirs. Perhaps the least well-known African women writers, however, are Lusophone for the simple reason that the literary history of Portugal's former colonies is even more difficult to document since many of the initial exploits were distributed privately by the authors themselves, with formally published works remaining all but unavailable until the 1980s.[15] Regardless of the language in which they wrote, African women authors knew equally well the challenges of finding a publisher for their earliest manuscripts.

Marie-Claire Matip grew up in a village in the area of Eséka, a region located between Cameroon's two major cities, Yaoundé and Douala. *Ngonda* was published as a result of a writing contest sponsored by Air France and *Elle* magazine; such competitions were common in the former French colonies, their ultimate purpose being to promote literacy in French (Toman 1). A native of Douala, Thérèse Kuoh-Moukoury waited thirteen years to secure a publisher for *Rencontres essentielles*, a novel now widely recognized and studied today in both French and English translation.[16] It is necessary to note, however, that at the same time these women writers were struggling to have their works acknowledged, there were already several well-known African male authors who had been published by the mid-1950s—Léopold Senghor from Senegal, Ferdinand Oyono and Mongo Beti from Cameroon, Camara Laye from Guinea, and Bernard Dadié from Côte-d'Ivoire, among others—gaining critical attention during that same period for their denunciation of colonialism. Ironically, Odile Cazenave and Patricia Célérier claim in *Contemporary Francophone African Writers and the Burden of Commitment*: "There were no women among the early generations of committed writers," further explaining that this was "largely because engagement was tacitly associated with male writers" (33). However, it can certainly be argued that women were indeed present, writing, and speaking against colonialism but they were simply invisible.[17] The manuscript for *Rencontres essentielles* unfortunately was completed at a time of dramatic political change when women had no presumed role of importance and it was assumed they had nothing to contribute in this regard. In "African Women and Feminist Theory," Nalova Lyonga explains: "In the fifties and sixties, due to the fact that male writers were reacting against the emasculating forces of colonization, the literature foregrounded clashing male African and Western interests, to the exclusion of female concerns" (153). As Juliana Makuchi Nfah-Abbenyi reminds us in *Gender in African Women's Writing*: "The study of African literature has long been the preserve of male writers, and despite the enviable position women have occupied as oral artists, African women writers were not given the attention they deserved, even after the advent of the feminist movement" (2). The status of African women writers was slow to improve as their works continued to be overlooked or dismissed well into the 1980s and even into the early 1990s. In the case of Gabon, this situation still has not been rectified entirely.

Considering this history, one comes to understand the enormous responsibility assumed by those conducting research in African literature. Once scholars and researchers promote false assumptions in the field—even unintentionally—these may remain unchallenged for years to come, prolonging the invisibility of certain authors. To cite yet another example, many early critics often cited 1975 as the year marking the true beginning of African women's writing of French expression (Ormerod and Volet 12; Syrotinski 54) since autobiographies *La Vie d'Aoua Kéita racontée par elle-même* and *De Tilène au Plateau* by Aoua Kéita and Nfissatou Diallo, respectively, and Christine Kalondji's novella, *Dernière genèse*, all were published during that year. Such declarations of "firsts" dissuaded a majority of researchers who followed from going back in time to discover other possible gems of women's writing existing prior. The fact that Mariama Bâ's *Une si longue lettre* (1986) appeared on every course syllabus in the many fledging programs being developed in Francophone Studies in the United States, Canada, and France during the 1990s led many students and professors alike to believe that no novel by an African Francophone woman writer ever preceded it. Cazenave and Célérier explain that this type of error is destined to occur regularly because "production by 'young' Francophone African writers living and/or publishing in France has become more predominant in syllabi because of their visibility on the Parisian literary scene" and this fact "has driven canon formation in a certain direction, particularly in the United States where older texts tend to disappear from the curriculum, and literary history is thus affected" (164). These early perceptions began to change only when greater numbers of scholars from Africa entered the field in the late 1980s when a more Afrocentral approach to the field became the norm. Even today, however, we see that the situation that Cazenave and Célérier describe still persists somewhat.

EDUCATION IN GABON, THE EMERGENCE OF WOMEN WRITERS, AND DEFINING 'NATIONAL LITERATURE'

Although there are many, one of the most compelling reasons to study Gabonese literature written in French is precisely because Gabon has the distinction of being one if not the only country worldwide where a woman was the first to publish a novel. Although male authors are certainly present and influential in Gabon, the momentum of building a solid national literature has been and still is driven by women first and foremost and in fact, women overwhelmingly dominate the youngest generation of writers in the country today. Since its inception in 1987, the Union des Écrivains Gabonais (UDEG) has had at least two long-term female presidents, authors Justine Mintsa and Sylvie Ntsame.[18] During a 2011 interview in Libreville, Ntsame, who is also the founder and CEO of the first full-service[19] female-owned African publisher Éditions Ntsame, reported fifty known published authors from Gabon with half of this number being female.[20] Since that time, not only have new women writers appeared—Miryl Nadia Eteno, Charline Effah, Mélissa Bendome, Irène Dembé, Pulchérie Abeme-Nkoghe, Muetse-Destinée Mboga, and Élisabeth Aworet among them—but more established women writers of the first and second generations continue to produce as many if not more novels than their male counterparts. The youngest generation of authors attribute this to the fact that culture and lifestyle in Gabon seem to encourage females more in this regard. Alice Endamne, author of *C'est demain qu'on s'fait la malle* (2008) and *Garçons et filles* (2010), believes that Gabonese society, especially its elite classes, has in mind a particular mold for educating young men. Endamne explains that while boys in Gabon are pressured to focus their attention on acquiring skills that will serve them immediately in the workforce and ensure them employment, girls ironically are left to explore more choices in terms of studies and career paths and are thus freer to develop their writing.[21]

Prolific author of novels, short stories, children's literature, and poetry, Edna Merey-Apinda believes that in Gabon, there is actually more emphasis on educating girls than in other countries in the region and that it is this reality responsible for the increase in the numbers of young women who write. However, Merey-Apinda also admits that producing writers is not the immediate underlying motivation for encouraging girls to stand out in the classroom: "At school, girls are encouraged more than boys in general because girls won't be able to take advantage of male privilege the way boys can; if girls don't excel, they risk living in the street or being stuck in a low-paying job. So you find that girls are rarely held back at school here."[22]

The push to educate girls in Gabon, however, did not start with this newest generation of writers, but can be traced back to the first generation as well. Angèle Rawiri, Justine Mintsa, and Honorine Ngou were all encouraged by their parents to continue their studies at an advanced level; this is true even in the case of Ngou whose mother was never formally schooled and her father completed only three years of elementary school with neither parent knowing how to speak French during Ngou's formative years.[23]

Considering this widespread and longtime desire to educate girls in Gabon coupled with the time that has passed since other pioneering African women authors had to struggle to have their own works published, it is not surprising that Gabon was ready to embrace their first novelist, even though she was female. Jean-René Ovono Mendame explains:

> When *Elonga* appeared in 198[0], Ntyugwétondo Angèle Rawiri's 261-page novel, the Gabonese public greeted with enthusiasm the zeal of the first woman writer to dedicate herself to writing. The event commanded respect especially during those years when few men, academics or otherwise, ventured into writing. ("*Histoire d'Awu* de Justine Mintsa")[24]

Angèle Ntyugwétondo Rawiri, as she was known in her earliest years as a writer, published both *Elonga* (1980) and *G'amèrakano au carrefour* (1983) in Paris with Editaf and ABC, respectively, a few years before Owondo's *Au bout du silence*, the novel that Alain Mabanckou falsely identified in his blog as Gabon's first novel. Although Editaf and ABC were small presses, both novels were adequately distributed and renowned Africanist critics at that time regularly referenced them in their works. To name just a few examples, Kembe Mololo included detailed and lengthy analyses of both *Elonga* and *G'amèrakano* in *L'Image de la femme chez les romancières de l'Afrique noire francophone* (1986), Jean-Marie Volet featured Rawiri's works in *La paroles aux Africaines* (1993) as did Odile Cazenave in *Femmes rebelles* (1996) and Lilyan Kesteloot in *Histoire de la littérature négro-africaine* (2001). *Elonga* and *G'amèrakano* continue to appear, along with Rawiri's third and final novel, *Fureurs et cris de femmes* (1989), in more contemporary literary criticism such as in Bellarmin Moutsinga's *Les orthographes de l'oralité, poétique du texte gabonais* (2008) and in the lengthy afterword of Sara Hanaburgh's English translation of *Fureurs*, *The Fury and Cries of Women* (2014).[25]

The overall positive reception of *Elonga* and *G'amèrakano* led to second editions at Silex in Paris in 1986 and 1988, respectively. However, these subsequent reprints have led to some confusion in the documentation of Gabon's literary history and one therefore commonly sees the latter publication dates erroneously listed as the initial publication dates of these two novels. This is perhaps yet another reason explaining why Rawiri is often not mentioned as Gabon's first novelist.

For being the first female novelist of her respective country, Rawiri arrived relatively late on the scene, and thus she tends to be seen, unfortunately, in isolation from other pioneers of African women's writing. Unlike other African women writers who have been and still are readily associated with their countries of origin, however, Rawiri tended to be considered by critics as a "lone wolf" of sorts and indeed early critical works rarely mention that she was from Gabon at all but rather tend to categorize her simply as a "Francophone" writer. The fact that Rawiri uses fictitious names for African cities and countries without exception in her novels meant that readers were never readily conditioned to associate the author with her country of origin and therefore, Rawiri was not perceived within a continuum of African women writers traditionally classified according to their country of origin. This detail has nothing to do with the overall quality of her work and it actually means little, considering that, as Irène Assiba d'Almeida reminds us, "contemporary nation-states [in Africa] are of course not indigenous but remains of colonial configurations" (*A Rain of Words* xxv) yet such categorizations to which researchers still cling (and which the discipline refuses to give up) ultimately deprive of their due recognition these writers who do not easily fit into such classifications.

Most Gabonese women writers to follow adopted a technique similar to Rawiri's in that they too often preferred creating fictitious names for cities and villages and sometimes even for the country itself although these places are often admittedly identifiable to those in the know. Even if many of these authors are directly inspired by the customs, traditions, and rituals of their own ethnic group, it is clear that they see their audience as extending well beyond readers of the same ethnic heritage. In fact, as the following analyses will demonstrate, Gabonese women are certainly making a conscious effort in their literary works to write against and diffuse any underlying notions of tribalism in their society. Thus, they have found successful ways to write the richness of their individual cultures—about forty in all—while contributing to and creating a national literature all the same. In many cases, writers like Sylvie Ntsame and Edna Merey-Apinda, for example, have intentionally highlighted in their own respective works contemporary versions of tales originating from other traditions. A fascinating reality about Gabonese writers—both men and women—is that they are incredibly united and this is immediately apparent for those who become acquainted with Gabon's literary scene. There is a tight bond and awareness shared by Gabon's first and second generations of writers and while younger writers look up to those who have preceded them, they also recognize the essential role that they, too, play in shaping the national literature of postcolonial Gabon.

The Union des Écrivains Gabonais (UDEG) has excellent records of seemingly all writers of both the first and second generations and regularly hosts a plethora of literary events and meetings in the country, but it is the younger, social media–literate generation of authors in particular who have created numerous websites, blogs, and their own organizations in Libreville and Port-Gentil that serve not only to promote their own published individual and collective work but also to transmit a history of Gabonese literature to the general public beyond the country's borders. The Gabonese writer thus finds a very supportive network of peers and mentors that is unparalleled on the continent or anywhere else for that matter and this undoubtedly contributes to a writer's individual success.

Considering these realities, one can by all means speak of a national literature in Gabon that is authentic because it is the writers themselves who have been responsible for creating the canon while others were not looking. That is, unlike some postcolonial African states whose literary canons had been determined early on almost exclusively by literary critics living outside the African continent whose perspectives were ultimately driven by the colonial configurations to which d'Almeida refers, Gabon's writers and critics have participated in this decision of what belongs in their canon from the beginning, and this, in a strange way, has been an unexpected advantage to being "invisible" for so many years.

With the exception of Émilie Koumba's 1992 novel for adolescents, *Sally de mes rêves*, Angèle Rawiri remained the sole female novelist from Gabon until Justine Mintsa's *Un seul tournant: Makôsu* was published in 1994. As Gabon was far less populated pre-independence than many other former French colonies,[26] it lacked an educational infrastructure on the level of other systems already in place, for example, in Cameroon and Côte-d'Ivoire. Considering this fact, it is only logical then that one sees novelists in Gabon emerging much later.[27] The first secondary school in Gabon, Lycée National Léon Mba, was not established until 1958 and it remained the only *lycée* in the country for several years, forcing many Gabonese students to leave for Brazzaville for their secondary school education during that period (Mba-Zué 48). By comparison, neighboring Cameroon had its first secondary school by 1945. Gabon had even less access to and opportunity for higher education. Even today, Université Omar Bongo in Libreville, founded in 1970, remains Gabon's only university where degrees in literature are awarded and this does not include the *doctorat*, the equivalent of the PhD. Thus, Gabonese students of literature must go outside the country to obtain this highest level of training.[28] Although higher education is certainly not a requirement for being a novelist in any country, statistics confirm nonetheless that in African Francophone countries, rare are authors who do not at least possess the *baccalauréat*,[29] the diploma inherited from the French school system marking the completion of secondary school (Mba-Zué 49) so one can assume that there is a direct correlation between access to higher education and the relatively late literary production in the country.

AN INVISIBILITY OF WOMEN

Another reason that specialists have cited as to why women writers from Gabon have suffered from a lack of visibility is because too few works of Gabonese literature in general have been the subject of literary criticism (Mba-Zué 47). But in her essay, "Women's Transgressional Writings in Gender and Body: (Con)texts in Gabonese *Afra* Writings," Gladys Francis points out a contradiction: "The scarce critical exploration of Gabonese literature is in total opposition to its flourishing production. As a matter of fact, for the last 30 years, the Gabonese novel has been predominant within the sub-Saharan literary space" (877). Can the veritable omission of Gabon from general literary criticism early on be explained by the fact that the discipline has traditionally focused more on the male writer and there does not seem to be enough of them in Gabonese literature? Gladys does point out that Gabonese male authors have suffered a similar fate as their female peers: "very few reviews or articles offer an exploration of the Gabonese male writer" (877). Because critics have viewed Gabonese literature as dominated by women overall, is it perhaps more accurate to conclude that this fact makes Gabonese literature less appealing in general? Or can one say that literature scholars have merely constructed a notion that there is a lack of criticism, somehow refusing to see the numerous studies on Gabon's writers?

If Gabonese literature has not only survived but flourished in spite of its perceived lack of critical attention, it is because Gabonese women authors have had from the beginning the support of their fellow writers, scholars, and intellectuals, male and female. Other pioneering women writers from Africa such as Thérèse Kuoh-Moukoury not only felt excluded from the *Négritude* movement, but they were unable to rally support from male writers in their respective countries at that time.

Although published in France, the aforementioned 1991 special issue of *Notre librairie* devoted entirely to Gabonese literature was a homegrown project of Francophone literature scholars at Omar Bongo University featuring an impressive list of contributors from Gabon including renowned novelist Laurent Owondo, the *mvet* master Tsira Ndong Ndoutoume, and novelist and essayist Honorine Ngou among other scholars and authors. As Angèle Rawiri had already published all three of her novels by the year the issue appeared, in-depth analyses of her works were included in every one of the scholarly articles that treated the subject of the novel. It must be noted that two essays in the collection seem to challenge Rawiri's status as first novelist, as Ambourhouet-Bigmann and Mba-Zué cite Robert Zotoumbat's autobiographical novella *Histoire d'un enfant trouvé* (1971) as Gabon's first novel and Rawiri's *Elonga* as the second (Ambourhouet-Bigmann, "Naissance d'une littérature" 39; Mba-Zué, "De la société précoloniale" 43). However, both these scholars emphasize in yet another essay appearing in the same volume that *Elonga* was clearly the "début de création imaginaire" or in other words, a first in fiction (Mba-Zué, "Une littérature en quête" 47) and that Rawiri's novel holds a unique place in Gabonese literary history nonetheless.[30] The *Notre librairie* issue also includes an analysis of the image of women in the oral traditions known as the Olendé among the Obamba (Mve Ondo 70) and the famed epic poetry of the Fang known as the *mvet*[31]—a genre of oral literature to be discussed at length later in this study since women writers have managed to appropriate and then incorporate this exclusively male tradition into their contemporary works.

Ever since the publication of this first groundbreaking critical analysis of Gabonese literature, a trend of general support has continued for the country's women writers especially within Gabon and among Gabonese of the diaspora. Critical works that dedicate substantial analyses to Gabonese women writers include Chantal Magalie Mbazoo-Kassa's *La femme et ses images dans le roman gabonais* (2009), Bellarmin Moutsinga's *Les orthographes de l'oralité, poétique du texte gabonais* (2008), Clerc and Nzé's *Le roman gabonais et la symbolique du silence et du bruit* (2008), and Nicolas Mba-Zué's *L'œuvre romanesque de Sylvie Ntsame* (2011) in addition to several collections of essays such as the volume *Ces espaces littéraires sans frontières: de la critique gabonaise aux études francophones actuelles* co-edited by Pierre Ndemby-Mamfoumby and Pierre-Claver Mongui (2013). Such works affirm that Gabonese women writers are not a mere curiosity but rather recognized and essential contributors to a national literature, to African literature, and to *francophonie*. As Ovono Mendame stated in *Africultures*:

> After years of still being considered in its early stages, Gabonese literature and the novel in particular have seen remarkable progress since the 1980s. In the midst of this intellectual awakening, women have clearly exhibited their determination to promote their national and cultural heritage through literature which up until now has been virtually unknown to an African Francophone public. (2006)[32]

Of course, distribution remains a serious problem for the promotion of Gabonese literature both within Gabon's borders and beyond. Naturally, since the majority of Gabonese writers publish in Libreville or in Paris, titles are more readily available in these cities and while books published in France are more and more accessible worldwide, this is not yet the case for texts published in Gabon. It must be noted that European and North American book vendors are the major problem in this regard as they make little effort to order works from Gabonese publishers citing potential problems with billing, currency conversion, and customs, in addition to the fact that unsold merchandise cannot easily be returned to suppliers.

Even within Gabon's own borders, however, some books on the national program for secondary schools prove difficult to find outside of the capital.

During my numerous interviews in Libreville in March 2011 and January 2015, author and publisher Sylvie Ntsame, poet and critic Hallnaut Mathieu Engouang,[33] and novelist and scholar Honorine Ngou all pointed out in independent discussions how a Gabonese writer can have a book published in Libreville that never actually sees the interior of the country. Indeed, writers Justine Mintsa, Honorine Ngou, Sylvie Ntsame, and Edna Merey-Apinda have all cited the numerous campaigns to promote reading in Libreville, in Port-Gentil, and even in the interior of the country, and each one has taken it upon herself to drive copies of her works and those of other Gabonese writers via 4 x 4 vehicles to local schools in villages that remain unlinked to major cities by highway.

It is difficult to ascertain just how many manuscripts, not to mention works of oral literature, have remained unacknowledged in African literature due to cultural, social, historical, economic, or political factors, a lack of critical interest, prejudice and discrimination, or a host of additional obstacles hindering publication at any given time. In light of these oversights that burden the past, the next generations of African writers are sure to challenge our reliance on the Western critical eye in our "discovery" of African literatures and Gabonese women writers will be especially vigilant in this regard. The purpose of this book is not only to assert that Gabonese women writers have earned a rightful place in the history of African literature, but also to show what is unique about their writing and their approach that distinguishes them from other women writers of the continent. What this study reveals will confirm the contribution of Gabonese women writers not only to African literature but also to a body of women's writing worldwide. Consequently, the goal is to stimulate more critical analyses of this literature not only to make up for lost time and to fill a void in the field, but also to establish Gabonese women's writing's rightful place alongside other powerhouses of African literature.

This book focuses primarily on the first generation of Gabon's women writers who all continue to produce literary works today with the obvious exception of Angèle Rawiri who passed away in 2010. This is not to suggest, of course, that Gabon's youngest writers have nothing to offer or that their works lack quality. In fact, Alain Mabanckou's infamous 2006 post on the lack of Gabonese literature is now overshadowed by his glowing 2015 review in *Jeune Afrique.com* of Charline Effah's most recent novel, *N'être*. Revisiting his comments of 2006 in this latest reevaluation, Mabanckou states: "I had said several years ago that Gabonese literature 'did not exist': Gabon now has a voice, a writer who is to be included among the most talented in contemporary African literature."[34] Mabanckou continues to laud Effah's second novel in his review, calling it one of the best to be published since Mariama Bâ's *Une si longue lettre* (1981), although one assumes here that Mabanckou is most likely referring to works written by women authors specifically as opposed to comparing Effah's novel with all works of African literature.[35]

Indeed, many of Gabon's youngest women writers making up the second generation have been mentioned throughout this study. However, the need to present a solid early history of Gabonese women's writing has taken precedence, not to mention that the sheer number of Gabonese novels published by female authors in the last decade prohibits them from all being included in just one study. Gabon's second generation of women writers also duly deserves an additional volume devoted exclusively to them.

Chapter 1, entitled "Emergence of the Gabonese Novel: The Works of Angèle Rawiri," focuses on Rawiri's three critically acclaimed works all written in the 1980s. The chapter includes biographical information important to understanding the complexity of Rawiri's novels and discusses her rather mysterious disappearance from literature soon after publishing her last work, *Fureurs et cris de femmes*, in 1989. Rawiri's "trilogy," as some critics refer to it, is comprised, in fact, of wildly different works that were written with various degrees of feminism, as debated by various African feminist scholars in the field. These three works, *Elonga*, *G'amèrakano*, and *Fureurs et cris de femmes*, all introduce issues that were not commonly found in novels by African women writers at the time and in *Fureurs*, Rawiri even takes on the subject of lesbianism. This is remarkable for the period considering that any discussion of homosexuality in the African novel is still highly taboo and risky for the author even today.

While *Elonga* is Rawiri's only novel with a prominent male protagonist, she still managed to present readers of the 1980s with one of the first portraits of a successful African female entrepreneur. Rawiri's second novel, *G'amèrakano*, shows a clear pronouncement of African feminisms in an increasingly globalized, capitalistic, and individualistic society where specific challenges are presented in so-called underdeveloped countries. Although it is perhaps the least optimistic of Rawiri's three novels, *G'amèrakano* illustrates the complexity of male/female relationships in contemporary urban environments in Africa, discussing globalization well before the term became widely used. Finally, the chapter on Rawiri concludes with an analysis of *Fureurs*, the trilogy's crown jewel and the one work of the three that is unanimously hailed as a feminist novel. Here, Rawiri's Émilienne is the rebellious and disobedient woman like few have seen in African women's writing before. Although her position and salary allow her to control many aspects of her life, Émilienne still leads readers to ask whether it is possible for women even in the most favorable of conditions to simply "have it all." Arguably Gabon's very first novelist, Rawiri has a unique influence on her country's national literature like no woman author to follow. Treating new subjects like underdevelopment, tribalism, HIV/AIDS, and homosexuality but also bringing to the forefront new perspectives on motherhood and infertility in contemporary African society, Rawiri's writings still have the ability to capture the interest of a new generation of readers and here lies the originality of her work.

The next two chapters of the study highlight the works of Justine Mintsa and Sylvie Ntsame, two writers whose origins are Fang, the ethnic group comprising forty percent of Gabon's population. With creative styles that are highly distinctive, Mintsa and Ntsame each plays a major role as both a Fang diaspora writer and a Gabonese one. The infusion of Fang culture and language into the contemporary Gabonese novel is a way that both Mintsa and Ntsame decolonize African literature written in French while aspiring at the same time to contribute an important piece of a multi-ethnic national literature defined by African writers and intellectuals themselves. Their rewriting of Fang oral literature—especially the celebrated art of the epic poetry known as the *mvet*—set these particular authors apart from their peers.

Chapter 2, "Justine Mintsa and Gabonese Writers of Fang Heritage: Orality, Culture, and Tradition," is dedicated to Justine Mintsa and two of her four literary works, *Histoire d'Awu* and *Larmes de cendre*, which bring to light the harsh treatment to which Fang widows are subjected during traditional mourning rituals. *Histoire d'Awu* is actually Mintsa's second novel, but its publication gave Mintsa the distinction of being the first African woman writer ever to be published by the prestigious French publisher Gallimard. Awu is perhaps the most well-known protagonist internationally in all of Gabonese women's writing thus far.[36] Beautifully written, Mintsa's *Histoire d'Awu* makes an indelible mark on any reader. In addition to its courageous and insightful characters in general, the novel is loaded with references to Fang oral traditions, especially its rewriting of Fang creation myths and the *mvet* with Awu recast as its principal warrior.

Like *Histoire d'Awu*, Mintsa's *Larmes de cendre* also reevaluates various Fang traditions and criticizes those that are particularly oppressive to women. Mintsa points out, however, that traditions are often used as a tool of manipulation and thus their oppressiveness stems not so much from the traditions themselves but rather from persons who choose to interpret them in their favor to gain power over others. Thus, both of Mintsa's novels address the willingness—or lack thereof—exhibited by individuals, families, and ultimately society to keep what is empowering about tradition while disposing of those aspects that are detrimental. One of the most powerful sentences in *Histoire d'Awu* is a simple reminder by Awu to her brother-in-law who has inherited her, "La coutume, c'est les gens" (106; The custom is people).

The concentration on Fang culture in selected works of Gabonese women writers continues in chapter 3, entitled "Fang Culture, *Bwitifang* Spirituality, and the *Mvet* in the Novels of Sylvie Ntsame." While the chapter offers at least a brief analysis of all of Ntsame's works to date—four novels and a collection of traditionally inspired tales—the most profound analysis is paid to Ntsame's first novel, *La fille du Komo*, for its clever use of Fang words and expressions within the text written in French, for its presentation of Fang spirituality and the Bwiti indigenous religion practiced equally by the Mitsogo as well as the Fang in Gabon and Cameroon, and for Ntsame's appropriation of the *mvet*, an art form from which women are traditionally excluded. There is unequivocally no other work in African literature written by a male or female who incorporates the *mvet* into the novel in the manner that Ntsame does and this is perhaps her greatest literary achievement. This chapter also provides biographical details about Ntsame's accomplishments as founder of one of the first female-owned African publishing houses and her former role as president of UDEG, the official organization founded for Gabonese writers.

Chapter 4, "Gender and Sexuality in Selected Works of Honorine Ngou," takes an in-depth look into Ngou's first novel, *Féminin interdit*. Although Ngou can also be considered a Fang diaspora writer, her works differ from those of Mintsa or Ntsame in one obvious way. While Fang culture might serve as a source of inspiration, specific traditions and rituals do not have a central place in Ngou's novel as they do in Mintsa's *Histoire d'Awu* or Ntsame's *La fille du Komo*. *Féminin interdit* is a book about the African woman, gender, and sexuality in no uncertain terms even though the actions and reactions of the protagonists—especially those of Dzibayo, the daughter raised like a son—can be interpreted in a variety of different ways depending on the reader. The novel challenges Western constructs of gender and sexuality uniformly applied to African societies but demonstrates nonetheless how such notions have indeed had an impact on contemporary Africa to the point where gender constructs there have become a veritable *mélange* of both African and Western ideas since the colonial era. This chapter relies heavily on theories concerning gender systems put forth by Ifi Amadiume and Oyèrónkẹ́ Oyěwùmí who both claim that while gender and biological sex are inseparable in Western cultures, many African societies move beyond such a *bio-logic*.[37] Oyěwùmí interestingly attributes this fundamental difference to the fact that Westerners privilege the visual in their conceptualization of society—interpreting their environment according to a "worldview"—whereas a number of African societies exist that favor senses other than or in addition to the visual and thus use as a point of reference what Oyěwùmí calls a "world-sense" (2–3).

In addition to the novel's fresh perspectives on the realities surrounding the conceptualization of gender in contemporary African society, *Féminin interdit* is also innovative in how it chooses to present the relationship between the protagonist, Dzibayo, and her friend Suzanne Molet. Although there are remarks from other characters and from Dzibayo herself that have the reader guessing about the protagonist's sexuality, in the end, Ngou leaves the nature of the relationship between the two women open to interpretation and debate and imposes no judgment unlike Rawiri had done in *Fureurs* in the 1980s. Homosexuality is still a highly taboo subject in the African novel and rare are works that depict same-sex couples at all, let alone do so in an objective fashion. Of course, the novel leaves open the possibility that the relationship between Dzibayo and Suzanne is a profound friendship and nothing more, proving Oyěwùmí's theory that when it comes to understanding gender and sexuality in Africa, Westerners tend to "inject Western problems where such issues originally did not exist" (9). This chapter also includes a discussion of theories on homophobia in Africa as posited by Ayo Coly and Signe Arnfred among others.

Finally, Gabon produces a considerable amount of literature intended first and foremost for children and/or adolescents and this is discussed at length in chapter 5, "Taking Literature to the Schools: Gabon's Children and the Contribution of the Woman Writer." In addition to analyzing selected works by Justine Mintsa and Edna Merey-Apinda who write inspiring texts infused with aspects of traditional culture and oral tales of the Fang and the Myènè, respectively, this chapter also highlights the extraordinary activism of Gabonese women writers to promote reading in the country, a reality that clearly explains why children's literature in Gabon is so abundant. Such engagement also sends a message that Gabon's women writers do not accept "invisibility"; by ensuring that Gabonese literature becomes part of school curricula on all levels, these authors play an essential role in educating and motivating future writers and scholars throughout the country while creating their own legacy and affirming their peers. As this book is devoted mostly to Gabon's first generation of women writers, it is appropriate to end the study with analyses of the works of Edna Merey-Apinda who is clearly the leader of Gabon's second generation of woman writers. If this second generation's accomplishments thus far prove anything, it is that they are as potentially strong as the first in fighting invisibility as they do their best to ensure that Gabon remains well outside of the "empty canon."

NOTES

1. African literatures are described as young literatures because literary history often tends to start from the publication date of a country's first novel. Not only does this tendency sweep away into oblivion any poetry, theater, or novellas that may have been published prior, but most notably, it denies any and all oralities from being considered "literature."

2. The journal *Notre librairie* was founded in Paris in 1968 and still exists today in electronic form under its new name, *Cultures sud*.

3. Jacques Chevrier first published *Littérature nègre* in 1974, one of the first books of its kind on African Francophone literature. Published by Armand Colin, the work received many prestigious awards, including the Académie Française's Prix Broquette-Gonin. This title has been updated and reprinted several times, most recently in 2003. Chevrier's other important works include his essay on African oral literature, *L'arbre à palabres* (1986) and his most recent book, *Litératures francophones d'Afrique noire* (2006).

4. Cazenave provides excellent analyses of Rawiri's works in her book *Rebellious Women: The New Generation of Female African Novelists* (1999), which is her English translation of *Femmes rebelles: naissance d'un nouveau roman africain au féminin* (1996).

5. CARAF stands for "Caribbean and African Literature Translated from the French." Rawiri's novel was translated by Sara Hanaburgh and published in 2014.

6. *The Moonlight Tales* was translated by Beth Johnston.

7. These poems in English appear on pages 17–19 (translated by Cheryl Toman) and the original poems in French are included in the book's appendix on pages 169–171.

8. "Herstory" is defined as history rewritten to include women that were effaced from it. The term was coined by American feminist Robin Morgan, and it appeared for the first time in Morgan's essay "Goodbye to All That" included in a 1970 issue of the underground New York newspaper *Rat*.

9. See www.congopage.com/SOS-pays-africains-cherchent.

10. All translations from the French found throughout this book are mine except where noted. The original French reads: "Chez les Gabonais, au contraire, l'heure est à l'autosatisfaction même si je ne vois rien qui puisse me dire que le Gabon a enfin une littérature et quelques écrivains majeurs."

11. In his blog, Mabanckou refers to L'Harmattan's 2004 republication of Mintsa's very first novel, *Un seul tournant: Makôsu*, that had been originally published in Paris by La Pensée Universelle in 1994. However, Mabanckou does not acknowledge in his blog that the edition to which he refers is indeed a reprint and therefore implies the novel is a newly published work. Mabanckou almost seems to punish Mintsa by diminishing her status and favoring instead short-story writer Ludovic Obiang. The full quote by Mabanckou reads: "Pour le reste, si vous voulez mon avis, le voici: il est clair que Ludovic Obiang, auteur de nouvelles, semble le plus sérieux espoir des lettres gabonaises tandis que Justine Mintsa—auteur d'*Histoire d'Awu*, roman paru en 2000—a créé une grande déception en regressant de la collection Continents noirs de Gallimard à l'Harmattan!" (As for the rest, if you want my opinion, here it is: it is clear that short story writer Ludovic Obiang seems to be the most serious hope for Gabonese literature whereas Justine Mintsa (author of *Histoire d'Awu*, her novel that appeared in 2000) created much disappointment downgrading herself from Gallimard's Continent Noirs series to L'Harmattan!)

12. Referring to Jean-René Ovono Mendame's 2006 essay in *Africultures* entitled "Gabon: Naissance d'une littérature: Chantal Magalie Mbazoo-Kassa une romancière en pleine croissance," Mabanckou writes, among other things, "Ah bon? C'est à croire que les années 80 nous sont passées par-dessus la tête au point que nous n'avons pas remarqué ces fameux écrivains gabonais qui ont contribué louablement 'au progrès remarquable' comme le souligne ce chroniqueur vraisemblablement averti" (Really? The 1980s sailed right by us to the point where we didn't even notice these famous Gabonese writers who contributed laudably "to such remarkable progress" as this informed critic credibly points out).

13. The blog *La plume et les mots du Gabon* began in October 2007 and currently shows archives up until May 2013. This quote was taken from a post from 14 October 2007: azokhwaunblogfr.unblog.fr/2007/10/14/les-romans-ecrits-par-des-gabonais-en-2007/.

14. Gabon's very first work of written literature in French is actually Robert Zotoumbat's *Histoire d'un enfant trouvé* (1971), yet many critics have argued that both the work's highly autobiographical nature as well as its brevity disqualify the 59-page text from being considered a novel.

15. For a somewhat complete bibliography, consult aflit.arts.uwa.edu.au/FEMECalireLU.html. It is necessary to note, however, that most of the earliest writers listed here were not natives of African Lusophone countries at all but rather Europeans who wrote their works while living in Africa as wives or children of those with responsibilities in the colonial political and economic structure.

16. After numerous reprintings in France, *Rencontres essentielles* has been simultaneously published in both the original French and also in English translation by Cheryl Toman as *Essential Encounters* in the MLA Texts and Translations series (2002).

17. Kuoh-Moukoury's *Rencontres essentielles*, in fact, made several references to colonialism and its ill effects on Cameroonian society starting with the very first paragraph, which

speaks of the French and Greeks as "occupants" (3). The very next pages take the reader to the Cameroonian protagonist's school as a child, describing a curriculum dominated by the French language and French subjects while Cameroonian revolutionary figures were only spoken about underground (4–6).

18. UDEG was founded in 1987 by a group of writers and poets led by Maurice Okoumba-Nkoghe.

19. What is meant by "full-service" here is the fact that all aspects of publication are done on site including the managing of peer reviews and editorial issues plus printing. Created in 2003 by Chantal Magalie Mbazoo-Kassa, La Maison Gabonaise preceded Éditions Ntsame but Mbazoo-Kassa sent out her manuscripts for actual printing.

20. This information stemmed from a personal interview with Sylvie Ntsame at Éditions Ntsame in Libreville on March 4, 2011.

21. Personal interview conducted on August 13, 2011, in Paris.

22. Personal interview conducted on January 5, 2015, in Libreville. Merey-Apinda's comments reflect a change in Gabonese society with families (especially those living in urban areas) realizing that women can no longer assume they will be taken care of by a husband or by other male members of the family and thus they must prepare themselves to live independently out of necessity but also as a lifestyle choice.

23. Personal interview conducted on January 4, 2015, in Libreville.

24. The original French reads: "Quand paraissait en 198[0] *Élonga*, roman de 261 pages de Ntyugwétondo Angèle Rawiri, le public gabonais saluait avec enthousiasme l'ardeur de la première femme à s'investir sur le champ de l'écriture. L'événement forçait l'admiration surtout en ces années où peu d'hommes, universitaires ou autodidactes, se hasardaient à écrire."

25. The afterword to Hanaburgh's translation is written by Cheryl Toman and appears on pages 195–223 of the volume.

26. According to the United Nations, Gabon's population today is approximately 1.7 million people and it is ranked 146 out of 193 countries in terms of population. When the first *lycée* opened in 1958, the country's total population was a mere 487,000.

27. Gabonese children, of course, had access to education through traditional schooling methods based on the cultural teachings of their ethnic group but the formation of a standardized and centralized system of national education occurred much later. We find an example of such traditional schooling in Honorine Ngou's essay *Mariage et Violence dans la société traditionnelle Fang au Gabon* (2007) in which Ngou has quoted one interviewee whose parents enrolled her at the age of seven in an "école Fang" in 1933 (169) and another who credited the *école Fang* for teaching her how to sew (138). Gabon is comprised of over forty ethnic groups, with each having its own forms of traditional teachings.

28. Ironically, the Gabonese government provides scholarship assistance to pursue the *doctorat* even though there have been many Gabonese literature scholars who have returned to Gabon after their advanced studies, ready and willing to develop such a program in their own country.

29. The Cameroonian author Werewere Liking is often singled out as one of the only authors from Francophone Sub-Saharan Africa to have benefited solely from traditional African structures of education (in Liking's case, Bassa) in addition to being self-taught later on in French language and literature.

30. In a 2001 issue of *Africultures*, Ambourhouet-Bigmann wrote about how literary specialists were split over the veritable first novelist of Gabon with most choosing Rawiri's novel but with a few still claiming that Zotoumbat's work should have this honor (18). In 2009, Gladys Francis reiterates what is more or less accepted today; Zotoumbat's text was later unanimously classified by experts as a novella, "thus Angèle Rawiri emerges as the first novelist" (877).

31. See "L'image de la femme dans l'épopée gabonaise" in this same issue, 70–72.

32. The original French reads: "Après de nombreuses années de balbutiements, la littérature gabonaise, en particulier le roman, connaît de progrès remarquables depuis 1980. Dans ce mouvement d'éveil intellectuel, les femmes affichent nettement leur détermination à promouvoir par l'écriture le patrimoine culturel national jusque-là mal connu du public africain et francophone."

33. Engouang is a writer, literary critic, and professor at Lycée Immaculée Conception in Libreville.

34. Mabanckou's exact quote in French is as follows: "J'avais dit il y a plusieurs années que la littérature gabonaise 'n'existe pas': le Gabon a désormais une voix, une plume qui comptera parmi les plus talentueuses de la littérature africaine contemporaine." *Jeune Afrique*. 30 June 2015.

35. Mabanckou states in the same review: "Depuis *Une si longue lettre*, de Mariama Bâ, je n'avais plus rencontré ce regard pointilleux sur les travers des sociétés africaines et à ce titre, Charline Effah pourrait être considérée comme la 'petite-fille' de cette immense romancière sénégalaise qui a marqué les lettres du continent" (Not since *So Long a Letter* by Mariama Bâ have I seen such a fastidious look on the failings of African societies and in this regard, Charline Effah could be considered as the "granddaughter" of the great Senegalese novelist who left her mark on the literature of the continent).

36. During a January 2015 interview in Libreville, Mintsa recounted how she originally believed that her central character was Obame, Awu's husband. But Gallimard's editors were the ones who pointed out to her that the novel was very much "the story of Awu," thus the title of the novel was born.

37. Oyĕwùmí uses the term "bio-logic" in the introduction to *The Invention of Women* on page ix and it is introduced again in chapter 4 of this study.

Chapter One

Emergence of the Gabonese Novel

The Works of Angèle Rawiri

Angèle Rawiri has played quite a unique role in the development of a national literature in Gabon and historically speaking, she has set herself apart from other pioneering women authors of any time period or tradition. Angèle Ntyugwétondo Rawiri was born in 1954 in Port-Gentil, the economic capital of Gabon and home to its largest petroleum companies. Port-Gentil is also long considered Gabon's epicenter of political opposition and growing up in such an environment perhaps inspired Rawiri's rebellious spirit as a novelist. Even though her father, Georges Rawiri, was not only president of the Gabonese Senate but also a dear friend of Omar Bongo who was Gabon's president for 42 years, this did not jade Rawiri or blind her from seeing the corruption inside political systems, African or otherwise. Rawiri never used the names of actual political leaders, and in fact, the cities and even the country about which she wrote all assume other identities in her texts. As Gabonese society was the one with which she was most familiar, things she observed there of course provided some of the seeds for a larger discussion on corruption and oppression but Rawiri also aimed to address a much larger African audience. Thus, her use of the fictional name "Kampana" in *Fureurs et cris de femmes*, for example, is less about masking Gabon's identity and more about Rawiri going beyond borders of a homeland similar to others on the continent. Although the political and social climate of Rawiri's semi-fictitious country is important for readers to understand not only in *Fureurs* but in her other two novels, *Elonga* and *G'amérakano au carrefour* as well, what is most obvious in all of her works is the rebelliousness of her protagonists as shown in their words, actions, and everyday lives.

Although her father was active in political life and a published poet,[1] Angèle rarely spoke about her private life in public. It is well known, however, that her mother's death when Angèle was just six years old had a devastating effect on the rest of her childhood if not on her entire life. As to be expected, her father eventually started another family, and it has been widely said that Angèle suffered profoundly from this, battling feelings of isolation and exclusion from her father's new life and family. Traces of these emotional wounds are obvious in all three of the families she creates in her novels.[2] As Rawiri left Gabon to complete her *baccalauréat* and her post-secondary studies in translation in France, these feelings may have been exacerbated by her separation from her homeland. After a short stint as an actress and model in Great Britain, Rawiri returned to her native Gabon and to her hometown of Port-Gentil at the end of the 1970s where she accepted a position with a major oil company as a translator and interpretor of English. As Rawiri was still looking for a way to expunge her demons of childhood upon her return home, it was her brother who encouraged her to write her first two novels, *Elonga* and *G'amérakano*. But by the end of the 1980s, however, Rawiri left Gabon definitively and headed for France where she finished and published her third and final novel, *Fureurs et cris de femmes*.

Interestingly, Rawiri used her given Omyènè name, Ntyugwétondo Rawiri, to sign her first two novels, and thus only on the cover of *Fureurs* is she identified as Angèle Rawiri, having dropped Ntyugwétondo which in Omyènè translates as "the beloved day."[3] This modification of self-identification may have been a reflection of how Rawiri felt torn between continents, cultures, and families. In a 1988 interview for the African women's magazine, *Amina*, Rawiri recalled this sense of alienation that she was never able to shed entirely. She considered herself a "déracinée" (uprooted woman), explaining "I never felt at home on African soil and at the same time, I didn't feel at home in Europe either" (13).[4] Writing was obviously cathartic for Rawiri, a means of dealing with sentiments of perpetual exile that followed her since childhood. Only through writing did Rawiri manage to find an outlet for exploring aspects of culture and society that bewildered or enraged her.

Rawiri's disappearance from the literary scene at the height of her career has never been explained, and it is even mysterious given the fact that she apparently had several projects in the works at the time. In the aforementioned *Amina* interview, Rawiri referred to a manuscript in progress that was to become her fourth novel (16), and while she alluded to material she had written for three others (12), these novels, if completed, were unfortunately never published. Her three published novels continued to attract a respectable amount of critical attention well into the 1990s from influential Francophone Studies scholars in Europe, North America, and Australia such as Jean-Marie Volet and Odile Cazenave, among others.[5] Although Rawiri had been out of the public eye for years at the time of her death in the fall of 2010, those who followed her work were nonetheless shocked to learn of her premature passing at the age of 56.

Rawiri encountered relatively few obstacles if any in becoming Gabon's first novelist, unlike other aforementioned African women writers from neighboring countries of Francophone Africa. In the same *Amina* interview, Rawiri explained, "I must admit that it was rather easy. Friends who were journalists helped me out by putting me in contact with an editor" (10).[6] It also appears that she became Gabon's first novelist without ever intending to be, and it is obvious from the following comments from the same interview that she wrote for herself first and foremost: "I hadn't thought about [becoming Gabon's first novelist]. I was rather taken up by my reflections, my doubts, my worries, my fears. When the novel came out, I found out that I was the first" (10).[7]

A DECADE OF NOVEL WRITING AND A BUDDING NATIONAL LITERATURE

Often described as a "trilogy" even though they have little in common, Rawiri's three novels, *Elonga* (1980), *G'amèrakano au carrefour* (1983), and *Fureurs et cris de femmes* (1989), are the hallmarks of an important decade for Gabonese literature written in French. Rawiri's first novel, *Elonga*, opens with the scene of young male professor, Igowo, and his Spanish father whose dying wish is for his bi-racial son to leave Spain to reconnect with the country of his already deceased mother's birth, the fictitious African country Rawiri names Ntsémpolo.[8] Despite his best friend Alberto's wariness of this situation and his father's ominous comment about the "nombreux mystères" (numerous mysteries) that he would inevitably discover in Africa (13),[9] Igowo decides to respect his father's wish, and plans to seek employment at a university in Elonga, the city in Ntsémpolo where Igowo's estranged uncle lives.

Igowo's arrival in Elonga marks his first visit to the country said to be a former colony of Spain (34), and he is mesmerized by all that he sees at first. After settling in at a hotel, Igowo soon takes a taxi to the address of his mother's brother, Mboumba. When he arrives, he is taken aback by the fact that his uncle, aunt, and nine children live in miserable conditions in an impoverished area of the otherwise vibrant city (28–29).

Igowo receives a frosty reception from his uncle and aunt. He realizes that they have little formal schooling and their lifestyles are worlds apart—so much so, that Igowo doubts their ability to have a close relationship as he begins to understand what his father was trying to convey to him from his deathbed. Even the taxi driver who drops him off felt compelled to warn him:

"Ici, les gens sont jaloux" (35; People are jealous here). Igowo declines an insincere offer to stay with his uncle's family and returns to his hotel aiming to make a life for himself in Elonga on his own.

At the bar of his hotel, Igowo meets Ziza, a young, beautiful fashion designer and entrepreneur who has started up her own trendy line of African clothing with a friend in Elonga (38–39). A relationship develops between Igowo and Ziza, and the couple soon have many mutual friends. Igowo keeps contact with his uncle's family to a minimum. Although he maintains he is not interested in their affection, Igowo feels he is morally obligated nonetheless to help them financially (55). During one visit, Mboumba refuses the money Igowo offers him, only to have his wife, Pemba, snatch it from his hand. The reader senses that the humiliating circumstances of this encounter coupled with a profound sense of jealousy regarding his nephew's wealth and success will incite Mboumba to use sorcery as a means of revenge. Despite warnings from those around him, however, Igowo cannot believe his uncle would ever harm him (57).

Igowo and Ziza finally decide to marry, leaving her parents concerned about Igowo's uncle's reputation; it is already believed that Mboumba's sorcery had a hand in Igowo's mother's death although the young couple is unaware of this suspicion. As a precaution, Ziza's parents seek the protection of a *ganga* or spiritual healer who assures them that if Mboumba ever harms the young couple, he would have to pay for his deed at the price of his own life (68).

Ziza soon gives birth to a daughter, Igowé. All goes well until one day, Igowo's aunt and uncle decide to visit their nephew's house for the first time since his arrival in Elonga. Shortly after the visit, two supernatural events disturb the couple in their sleep. Igowo's best friend, Pierre Henry, removes the family temporarily from their house and takes them next to a *ganga* who determines Igowo's uncle has unleashed a vengeful spirit of his dead sister in the house (103). They are able to return home only with the protection of the talismans the *ganga* provides them (107). Igowo's aunt and uncle hear from their own son that they are suspected of causing the supernatural events, which they vehemently deny in a second visit to Igowo's home (127).

Soon after, Igowo becomes deathly ill and when all forms of Western medicine fail, the family consults the *ganga* as a last resort at which time it is revealed that it is, in fact, the jealousy of another acquaintance of the couple, the boyfriend of Ziza's business partner, Elombo, who is responsible for Igowo's debilitating disease (148). After a harrowing period, Igowo eventually survives his illness and life returns to normal for the family with the exception of unexplained incidents of devastating weather that plague Elonga.

As time progresses, disaster strikes; a truck hits Ziza as she is getting into her vehicle and she succumbs to her severe injuries a few hours after the accident (212), leaving the entire family in shock. Pierre Henry urges Igowo to find a new house for himself and his daughter, but he refuses, reasoning that abandoning the house would be like renouncing all the happiness he had there with his wife (214). Another *ganga* informs the family that the misfortune was brought on by Ziza's earlier encounter with Igowo's cousin Mpira, the means through which his uncle Mboumba sent the "fantôme destiné au malheur de l'un des époux" (215; phantom destined to bring misfortune to one of them).

Shaken up by this news, the family considers several options. Ziza's mother, Ayila, insists on consulting a faraway *ganga* to seek revenge by calling for the death of Mboumba. Her husband Ossany forces her to reevaluate this decision, pointing out that this action would not bring their daughter back (219). Igowo considers moving, but first settles on a two-week vacation with his family and friends (226) after painfully packing away Ziza's possessions in an unoccupied room of the house (227). It is determined that Ziza's business partner will continue on alone with the clothing company the two women had founded together (229).

After returning from vacation, Igowo gives the impression he is able to put his life back together as he and his daughter move into a new apartment near Pierre Henry (233). At the university, however, Igowo soon begins to notice changes in the attitudes of his students and colleagues toward him (245). His friends try to tell him he is imagining this ill treatment. However, when the dean dismisses him from his duties, his fears are confirmed (250). Igowo reacts to this situation by initially shutting himself up in his new residence, choosing to talk to a very limited number of people besides his daughter.

The last ten pages of the novel bring a few more surprises, including a direct message to the reader, a technique Rawiri uses in no other novel she has written. Oddly, she chooses to use the more familiar "tu" form in French, signaling an intimacy with the reader that purposely puts him or her in an uncomfortable position. The purpose of the message is to challenge the reader's understanding of the events in the novel up to that point. It serves to disorient the reader in a way, much like what Igowo experiences throughout the novel albeit for much different reasons:

> Lecteur, tu as suivi Igowo depuis son départ d'Espagne jusqu'à ce jour. Tu es donc à même de le juger et de dénoncer ces erreurs au besoin. Si tu le trouves innocent, il va falloir alors chercher ailleurs qu'en lui-même la source de ses ennuis. Il est évident que s'il était resté dans le pays de son père, il se serait bien entendu avec ses congénères pour la bonne raison qu'ils avaient été formés par la même culture, la même civilisation, cette civilisation occidentale qu'il avait rejetée au profit d'un autre qu'il trouvait moins avancée, mais plus riche et plus hétérogène à cause de cette amorce de symbiose du monde noir et

> du monde blanc. Aurait-il été heureux pour autant? Avait-il sa place dans ce monde nouveau? (251)
>
> Reader, you have followed Igowo since his departure from Spain until today. You are thus able to judge him and to point out his mistakes if need be. If you find him innocent, he'll have to look elsewhere for the root of his problems. It is clear that if he had stayed in his father's country, he would have gotten along well with others for the simple reason that they had all been molded by the same culture, the same civilization, this Western civilization that he had rejected in favor of another that he found to be less advanced, yet more rich and more homogenous just as a symbiotic relationship between a Black world and a White one was beginning. Would this have been enough to ensure his happiness, however? Did he actually have a place in this new world?

After a couple more paragraphs directed at the reader, Rawiri refocuses her attention on the protagonists in this final chapter where in just a few last pages, Igowé develops a frightening abscess on her back, undergoes surgery, and after some initial improvement, finally takes a turn for the worse and dies (258). Igowo then feels compelled to leave the hospital in a hurry to drive to a place in the woods where he used to spend happy moments with his family. Despite the fact that night has already fallen, he finds the exact location easily and while there, he sees the faces of his dead wife and child and hears their laughter. When he reaches out to touch them, however, the faces withdraw as he chases them deeper and deeper into the forest shrouded in darkness (258). He finally retreats to his car and returns home. There, the remaining members of his family await him in the presence of yet another *ganga* who reveals that Igowo himself is ultimately the cause of the tragedies that have befallen his family, not only because he had become a target due to the jealousy of others, but also because he had ignored or scoffed at several warning signs. The *ganga* reveals that while he had been away on vacation, his uncle Mboumba had buried in Igowo's courtyard the head of a white rooster, announcing the misfortunes to come (259). Although Igowo had subsequently moved away, it was already too late; he had brought the malefic spirit with him to his new home.

Igowo asks the *ganga* if they can return to his former home to unearth the rooster head in order to free himself of evil once and for all. Upon doing so, he finds the head to be in its original state before burial, fresh blood still seeping from the neck. The sky suddenly turns red and the novel ends with Igowo uttering, "Il faudra que je sois solide" (261; I have to stay strong). The reader understands this to be a reaffirmation of Igowo's will to remain in his mother's country, as he has stated throughout the novel, in spite of all that he has lost. It is logical that he stay at this point; this ultimately has to be the reason why Igowo ends up being the only surviving member of his family.

Elonga is perhaps not only the least feminist but also the least woman-centered of the three novels Rawiri had written, which may explain why this work suffers from a lack of critical attention compared to the other two; critics simply were at a loss as to how to categorize it since women novelists from Gabon, like other African women writers, do tend to give the spotlight to female protagonists. That said, it is clear that there are additional obstacles the African woman writer confronts if she does not choose to write an overtly feminist novel; it is even more likely that her work will fall into the "empty canon."

Although it is consistently mentioned in chronologies of Gabonese literary history, *Elonga* is rarely profoundly analyzed with the exception, perhaps, of Jeanne-Marie Clerc and Liliane Nzé's *Le roman gabonais et la symbolique du silence et du bruit* (2008) and Jean-Marie Volet's chapter on Rawiri that he includes in his book, *La parole aux Africaines* (1993).[10] Volet states, however, that there is no real need to bring in the plot of *Elonga* in order to do a feminized analysis of Ziza.[11] What Volet essentially means, then, is that Rawiri's discussion on sorcery and development can be ignored. Rawiri herself came to the realization early on that the trend was for readers and critics to avoid this element of the novel:

> [A]fter my first novel, *Elonga*, was published, I experienced a sense of failure. [W]hat bothered me the most was the lack of interest most people showed concerning the troubling problems that I was exposing. But I was realistic. I didn't expect that my writing of this novel would change my fellow citizens. It just confirmed for me that people were going to see witch doctors as much as they did before. (Bikindou and Baker 1988)[12]

One can argue, however, that *Elonga* clearly did inspire later works by Gabonese women writers such as Justine Mintsa and Sylvie Ntsame. Death is pervasive in *Elonga*—to the point where even the title in Omyènè evokes death,[13] much as one sees in the title of Mintsa's *Histoire d'Awu* where "Awu" is not only the protagonist's name, but it is also a Fang word meaning "death." One could say that Rawiri began a trend in Gabonese literature of using words from an author's native African language as a form of literary decolonization of the French language in the text, a concept that will be further demonstrated in the following chapter.

Mintsa's *Histoire d'Awu* refers to death both literally and figuratively and thus, this becomes a more nuanced subject when compared to how it is presented in *Elonga* since Mintsa deals with specific rituals and more oppressive aspects of tradition and not with sorcery per se. However, in Mintsa's first novel, *Un seul tournant Makosû* (1994), some characters insinuate that sorcery has played a role in the death of the protagonists' son and that the son's life was the price of the couple's upward mobility. In her latest novel,

Larmes de cendre (2010), Mintsa also references powers of the occult but once again ties them to rituals and the negative aspects of tradition.

Sylvie Ntsame who, like Mintsa, can also be classified as a writer of the Fang diaspora, uses a similar technique in her novels by infusing Fang words throughout the texts, but perhaps *Elonga*'s greatest influence on Ntsame is obvious in the way that she presents sorcery specifically in her novel *Malédiction* (2005). In fact, Clément Moupoumbou and Pierre Ndemby-Mamfoumby make all of these connections in their collection of essays entitled *La mort dans l'espace littéraire gabonais* (2012). More specifically, they claim that Rawiri, and later Ntsame, both portray sorcery in their novels as a reappearance of throwback culture used to crush and/or kill society's values (9).[14]

While it is common for African authors to deal with sorcery in their works—with some even glorifying traditional healers—few have been so openly critical of this aspect of African society as Rawiri. First of all, Rawiri states categorically that such beliefs are pervasive regardless of social class: "Les Elongais sont tous des clients assidus des féticheurs, guérisseurs, et charlatans; mais personne ne veut l'admettre" (62; Everyone in Elonga is a regular customer of shamans, traditional healers, and quacks; but no one wants to admit it). Ziza's parents even claim that the spiritual world is part of the "patrimoine culturel" (159; country's cultural heritage). Throughout her novel, Rawiri warns of a co-dependence that exists between the "malade" (patient) and the *ganga*[15]—the word she uses most often to refer to a spiritual healer. She ridicules the thought that *gangas* are demigods merely in a human form (64) and that they are sought as a means of protection against the evil harbored by one's enemies. She attributes the *gangas*' success to an "industrie d'exploitation de la condition humaine" (64; industry of exploitation of the human condition) that results from African societies that have a taste of rapid and sudden development (65). The co-dependence stems from the fact that it is not in the best interest of the *ganga* to heal all his patient's troubles once and for all since it would mean risking a decrease in revenue (129). In this manner, he can take advantage of the contemporary man who is incessantly seeking a way to be relieved of his pain, worry, or annoyance. "Ils savent que l'homme, en général, est un perpétuel insatisfait" (64; They know that man is in general perpetually unsatisfied)—and the *ganga* counts on this fact to survive financially. Rawiri is harsh and relentless in her criticism, even likening the relationship between a *ganga* and his patient to that of parent and a whiny child:

> Il joue un peu le rôle d'un père ou d'une mère vis-à-vis d'un enfant malheureux qui demande à être consolée lorsqu'il pleure, guéri lorsqu'il montre une écorchure. (65)

> His role is a little bit like playing a father or a mother faced with an unhappy child who asks through his tears to be consoled but who is healed the moment the child shows the parent his tiny scratch.

Rawiri blasts the hypocrisy of this supposedly secret world of the *ganga*, pointing out that is "un monde fermé mais où tout le monde entre" (124; a closed world open to everyone).

Of course, this angle of discussion does not consider more philosophical questions such as what constitutes a belief system and its limits. Through Igowo's conversations with minor characters in the novel, the reader is allowed additional insights on this particular subject. What is exactly this impediment to development to which Rawiri alludes? Does Rawiri include animism in "sorcellerie" (witchcraft) and if so, does her criticism extend to religion and other spiritual philosophies as well? At one point in the novel, Igowo has a conversation with Akewa, the wife of the traditional healer who is treating him. He asks her: "Étant donné que l'Africain est prisonnier des croyances qui font partie de sa vie quotidienne, ne pensez-vous pas que cela représente un danger réel?" (175; Given that Africans are prisoners of their beliefs that are part of their daily lives, don't you think there is a real danger in this?). Akewa's answer is rich in information and reveals exactly how complicated the subject matter Rawiri attempts to tackle truly is. The exchange demonstrates that this debate concerns not only Africans, but extremism in all of its forms in any given society. Akewa explains that belief systems are the "nourriture de l'âme" (175; food for the soul) with a potential to help humanity survive:

> Sans ces croyances, qu'elles soient religieuses ou mystiques, beaucoup d'entre nous ne sauraient pas comment faire pour affronter ce parcours semé d'embûches qu'est la vie qui nous attend. L'homme, où il soit, croit au plus profond de lui-même en une force qu'il ne peut que rechercher et adorer. Il n'est donc pas dangereux de croire à quelque chose. Le danger provient du mauvais emploie de cette force, maîtresse de nos pensées et de nos sentiments, qui règne aussi sur nos sens. (175)

> Without these beliefs, whether they be religious or mystical, many of us would not know how to take on this journey that is life, full of pitfalls that are in store for us. Wherever he is, man believes with all of his heart in some kind of force that he seeks and admires. It is therefore not dangerous to believe in something. The danger hails from the misuse of this force, letting it master our thoughts and feelings and take over our senses.

The reader understands now that categorically rejecting African spiritual beliefs may also be dangerous, leading to "cultural alienation":

> Vous, les jeunes de l'ère du développement, vous trouvez de bon ton de condamner nos croyances sous prétexte qu'elles manifestent notre infériorité par rapport aux Blancs (175).
>
> You, the youth in the age of development, you find it in good taste to condemn our beliefs on the grounds that they indicate our inferiority when compared to White society.

Thus, here lies the originality of Rawiri's criticism; the impediment presented by witchcraft in regard to development is created by those who embrace it excessively as well as by those who deny it categorically. Allowing sorcery to become so powerful that it can be manipulated to purposely inflict harm on others is as devastating to society as those who refuse to acknowledge the positive aspects of African belief systems that can aid in the continent's development by inspiring African solutions to African problems. Western thought has brought no remedies to African society and at times, has engendered more chaos. Rawiri reminds the reader that the West is perhaps enchanted by its progress in science and technology whereas Africans are just as enraptured by witchcraft (175). The comparison is indeed meaningful, with Rawiri implying that all of the positive elements stemming from advances in Western civilization should not allow us to forget that its science and technology can also be held accountable for the destruction and exploitation of colonized peoples and their societies. Similarly, the overwhelmingly negative effects of witchcraft on African society has not only hurt Africa's perception in the West by fueling racist ideas that African societies are primitive but it has also caused some Africans, intellectuals and professionals in particular, from extracting the progressiveness and wisdom embedded in African belief systems and philosophies.

Elonga must be recognized equally for its two major contributions to African literature; it offers an essential commentary and analysis on sorcery and its impact on development in addition to providing one of the first portraits of a successful African female entrepreneur. Ziza's tragic death should be framed in a discussion about witchcraft and development and in no way deters from Rawiri's positive message about where the contemporary African woman was headed in 1980. Furthermore, the fact that Ziza creates a company to promote African fashion at a time when Western-style clothing was infinitely more popular in Africa is meaningful. Rawiri's attack on witchcraft as an impediment to true development should not be taken as an overall condemnation of traditional values and culture and her insistence that Ziza's line of clothing be African shows Rawiri's appreciation for certain aspects of tradition that still have their place in contemporary society.

There are additional details that cause some to question if *Elonga* qualifies as a feminist novel. At times, Ziza tries to gain the affection of Igowo in the most traditional ways expected of a woman; she cooks for him, washes and irons his laundry, and dusts his furniture (59). The reader also learns that Ziza is involved with a married man at the time she meets Igowo, and she justifies the relationship by stating that love is uncontrollable (47) and that "une jeune célibataire ne peut être tout à fait seule, surtout lorsqu'elle cotoie une multitude de gens" (44; a young woman cannot really be alone, especially when she frequents so many people). Igowo also seems quite possessive of her early on and admits feeling "violently jealous" at the thought of her in another man's arms (46). Volet points out that despite his otherwise liberal views, Igowo can nonetheless be very accepting of patriarchal values (129) and he applies these quite often in his relationship with Ziza.

However, Rawiri's first novel is often not given enough credit for the feminist ideas that it does present and Ziza and her business partner, Elombo, are clearly the portrait of the new African woman of the 1980s for whom education, career, and family are all important, if not essential.

Early on in the novel, Rawiri uses symbols representing motherhood and Mother Africa to bring out her underlying feminist message conveyed through Ziza. Judging from Igowo's first encounter with Ziza at the hotel bar, the reader is not convinced he is seeking an equal partner; in fact, despite the fact that Ziza is attempting to discuss with him issues concerning employment and development, Igowo can only focus on his desire for her and Ziza is without a doubt objectified: "Physiquement, elle est parfaite, décide Igowo avec satisfaction. Tout à son examen, il a oublié la question qui lui a été posée" (38; Physically, she is perfect, Igowo decides with satisfaction. Completely taken in by her appearance, he forgot the question asked of him). The reader has already learned that Igowo is *métis* or bi-racial and it is confirmed later that his African mother died giving birth to him. After Igowo becomes hesitant to form a bond with his uncle, Ziza becomes his link to Africa and to his lost mother. Amid the physical qualities that Igowo admires in Ziza, there is a curious observation, "On croirait qu'elle n'a jamais connu d'autres aliments que le lait maternel" (38; One would think that her only nourishment had come from mother's milk). Throughout the novel, there is no doubt that Ziza embraces African ideals and puts forth an African form of feminism for the contemporary woman. Her insistence on creating African fashions as opposed to Western ones which may be more lucrative for her company is representative of this commitment to promote African ideals: "Notre but n'est pas réellement de nous enricher, mais de contribuer au succès de la mode africaine" (42; Our goal is not really about getting rich, but rather contributing to the success of African fashion).

Ziza's confession that she has made an independent decision in choosing not to avoid a pregnancy while the couple was still dating is telling. Upon revealing that she is four months pregnant, Igowo wonders why she had not informed him sooner. Ziza explains:

> Tu aurais peut-être pensé que j'en profitais pour te forcer la main. Non! Il fallait que ce soit toi qui, en toute liberté, m'offre le mariage. Bien sûr, j'aurais pu éviter cette grossesse. Mais vois-tu, je désirais vivement un enfant de l'homme que j'aime. Si nous ne nous étions pas mariés, j'aurais élevé moi-même cet enfant. Voilà, chéri. Tu sais tout. (75)

> You would have perhaps thought that I was taking advantage of the situation to force you into marrying me. No! It had to be you freely asking to marry me. Of course I could have avoided this pregnancy. But you see, I so much wanted a child from the man I love. If we hadn't gotten married, I would have raised this child myself. There you have it, dear. You know everything.

Ziza clearly reveals the importance of motherhood which for her, outweighs marriage; Ziza was prepared to live without a husband but not necessarily without a child and thus she considers the decision what to do with her body to be hers alone. Ziza's excellent education, her training in one of the most renowned fashion houses in Dakar (66), and her general resourcefulness in business have empowered her to the point where she can comfortably make this decision, knowing she does not have to depend on a man to be able to raise her child. Rawiri sends here a profoundly feminist message to her readers. Ziza self-identifies as belonging to a category of women in her country who have become "exigeante" (demanding):

> Elle n'accepte plus de lier son existence, même temporairement, à un homme dont la mentalité lui déplaît ou qui est, socialement et intellectuellement, très au-dessous d'elle. (46)

> She no longer accepts to link her existence, even temporarily, to a man who is of an unappealing mind-set or who is socially and intellectually very much beneath her.

Although Ziza is speaking in this quote about an elite class of women, who, like herself, come back to Ntsémpolo after spending time abroad, she also makes some generalizations about all Ntsémpolonaises; they refuse polygamy and the idea of becoming a co-wife, scoffing at the "advantages" that are believed to come with this arrangement, namely the duty the husband has to his wives financially. Ziza claims these kinds of marital relations are no longer necessary as almost all women, rich or poor, work and can thus take care of their own needs (48). Ziza tells Igowo that if men today are unhappy with women, they need only to look at themselves to identify the problem; it is not women who push men to take on mistresses or to frequent prostitutes. "Si vous voulez que les femmes changent, alors changez vous-mêmes vos mœurs" (48; If you want women to change, simply change your own ways). Apparently Ziza's words have some effect; even Pierre Henry realizes his friend, Igowo, has become "un grand défenseur de la cause féminine" (53) (a big defender of the feminine cause).

Rawiri's feminist message is carried through to the end of the novel as Ziza's parents entrust their daughter's share in the company not to her husband but rather to her business partner, Elombo, with provisions made for Ziza's share of the profits to be given later to the couple's daughter, Igowé (227). Elambo continues in their tradition of hard work and dedication to the company's goal, even using time away on vacation as an opportunity to promote and distribute her clothing line and to meet new African designers with whom to collaborate (229–231). Despite all of the tragedies provoked by sorcery in the novel and even the uncertainty surrounding Igowo and how he will reconstruct his life, this woman-centered project is never threatened or even hampered; its innovation, progress, and future are all ensured through a strong and reliable chain of women.

READING *G'AMÈRAKANO: AU CARREFOUR*

Rawiri takes a more decisive feminist approach in her second novel, *G'amèrakano*, the story of Toula, a dismally paid secretary who succumbs to her mother's badgering and is further convinced by her best friend and colleague, Ekata, that she should dramatically modify her appearance if she ever hopes to find her way out of the poor neighborhood of Igewa. Such a physical change would provide Toula more avenues for attracting wealthy businessmen as potential husbands or lovers. Reluctantly, Toula takes draconian measures to chemically lighten her skin (using Western brand-name products) and to lose weight. Although Toula is soon physically transformed, she remains mentally torn and even frustrated and unhappy by these choices and she ends up rejecting the first executive who makes advances toward her (112). Yet, despite her apprehension, Toula perseveres, and is especially determined to better her life in any way possible after two suitors from her neighborhood, Mebalé and Ipéké, end up coming to blows over her, leaving Mebalé dead and Ipéké fleeing Igewa for fear of being accused of murder even though he had acted in self-defense.

While on a short vacation with friends in the interior of the country, Toula meets Angwé, a young, dynamic, up-and-coming bank executive who, despite being orphaned at a young age, has forged his own career path, even with his very modest resources (158). The two eventually fall in love (perhaps Angwé more so than Toula), but Moussiliki is candid about her disapproval of the match (145). Although Angwé seemingly has a bright future ahead of him, this is all he has for the time being; with an entry-level position at the bank, he essentially lives no differently than Toula and her mother (150). Later in the novel, Toula makes Angwé wait for an answer to his marriage proposal not necessarily because of her mother's influence, but simply because she is not sure herself about getting married purely for love: "Mais quelque chose en elle se rebelle devant cette perspective" (151; But something inside of her is making her rebel against this notion).[16]

While waiting for Angwé to finish work at the bank one evening, Toula encounters Eléwagnè, Angwé's superior, and he immediately shows an interest in her (149). Eléwagnè is already married, but he desires Toula as a mistress and proposes to take care of her and her family in exchange (153). He even offers to construct a magnificent villa in Toula's neighborhood in place of Moussiliki's crumbling, failing bistro (174). Of course, the offer does not come without compromises, and Toula is expected to leave Angwé for good knowing that Eléwagnè would assure him stability, upward mobility, and additional financial perks allowing him to purchase a car and a decent home (172). Toula knows that if she refuses Eléwagnè's conditions, however, Angwé's position would be terminated and he would be blacklisted, preventing him from pursuing a career in banking anywhere else in the country. Toula proposes to Angwé, however, that they continue to see each other in secret and with time, she hopes that Eléwagnè will eventually lose interest in her and the young couple will be free to pursue their dreams together (167). Angwé rejects this idea at first, citing that it would be too difficult imagining her in the arms of his superior, but eventually he comes to terms with the arrangement so as to not lose Toula entirely (170).

The lavish villa—the only one of its kind in Igewa—tips off Toula's neighbors to her potential resources and incites jealousy. One of Toula's acquaintances, Ozoumet, begins extorting large sums of money from her by threatening to reveal details about the cover-up of Mebalé's death that would potentially incite ethnic conflict in the neighborhood (104). Ozoumet's plan succeeds for a bit before Toula finally stands up for herself (191–192). In revenge, Ozoumet tips off Eléwagnè that Toula is still seeing Angwé. Ozoumet urges Eléwagnè to go to Angwé's house to see for himself as she knows the approximate time Toula and Angwé would be there together (195).

Realizing what Ozoumet has told him is true, Eléwagnè promptly fires Angwé, provoking the young man to commit suicide; Toula learns about Angwé's death from the radio. When Eléwagnè learns of the suicide, he informs Toula he can no longer see her or care for her since he would not want to be implicated in such a controversial situation. Toula's life immediately spirals out of control without her love and her rich lover; she soon gains back all of the weight she had lost and becomes careless about her beauty regimen, allowing her skin to darken (196). As Chantal Mbazoo-Kassa succinctly describes this evolution in her book *La femme et ses images dans le roman gabonais*: "la 'fausse Toula' meurt" (81; The "false Toula" dies). Impoverished once again, Toula turns to the streets to make money as a prostitute, but even there she is rejected and left standing alone while all the other young women around her are chosen (197). She asks herself, "Non, non, comment en suis-je arrivée là? Est-ce bien moi qui suis réduite à ça? Oh! mon Dieu, comment suis-je tombée si bas?" (197; No, no, how did I end up like this? Have I really been reduced to this? Oh my god, how have I fallen so low?).

As she heads back toward Igewa, Toula remembers all the same what her grandmother Okassa once told her:

> Ton cœur, ton âme, ton esprit ont plus de valeur que tous les artifices dont les hommes s'entourent. Ces choses qui sont en toi et qu'on ne peut voir, c'est cela qui fait la personnalité. Améliore-les et tu seras plus forte. (197)

> Your heart, your soul, your mind have more value than any device these men can possess. These things within you that are invisible make you who you are. Improve these things and you will be the stronger for it.

G'amèrakano readily fits the Westernized description of a feminist novel, although interestingly, Mbazoo-Kassa reserves the distinction of "feminist novel" exclusively for *Fureurs et cris de femmes*. Concerning *G'amèrakano*, Mbazoo-Kassa describes the work as one that "emphasizes the problematic relationships between men and women in African society." She continues by explaining that the word "carrefour" (crossroads) in the full title of the novel refers to the complexity of relationships impacted by notions of gender-appropriate roles that often lead to dysfunction within society (28–29).[17] Those who refuse to "play the game" and to follow such prescriptions assigned to one gender or another are left to pick up the pieces of their shattered lives. Instead of formulating a more feminist analysis, Mbazoo-Kassa analyzes the text from a perspective that man and woman are complements, emphasizing in particular the impact of traditional male/female roles on modern African society. From this point of view, one understands her distinction between *G'amèrakano* and *Fureurs*. In Mbazoo-Kassa's view, *G'amèrakano* is more of a critique of society as a whole—where men and women both ultimately find themselves in powerless positions, and Toula is the lens through which we see a society in trouble. Mbazoo-Kassa emphasizes: "In other words, to study woman is to study the society to which she belongs" (12).[18] In direct contrast to certain ideas within Mbazoo-Kassa's analysis, however, Jeanne-Marie Clerc and Liliane Nzé state emphatically in their book, *Le roman gabonais et la symbolique du silence et du bruit*, that certain declarations within *G'amèrakano* smack of "radical American feminism" (263) and Toula's words such as "Je veux vivre mon corps par tous les pores de ma peau" (Rawiri 176; I want to feel my body with every pore of my skin) are indeed "rare in African women's writing" (Clerc and Nzé 263).[19] Yet Clerc and Nzé fail to see that Toula's claiming of her right to sexual pleasure is what makes this novel so unique, especially for the period in which it was written, making the debate as to whether this belief is "Western" (and particularly feminist) or not a moot point. Toula is not merely saddened by Eléwagnè's disinterest in satisfying her sexually, she is angered by it: "Il n'a pas le droit de me laisser dans cet état" (176; He has no right to leave me [unfulfilled] in this way). Later in the novel, Toula refuses him sex outright, still fuming from their last unsatisfying encounter. "Ne crois-tu pas que j'ai moi aussi le droit de ne pas être à tes ordres?" (187; Don't you think that it's my right not to be at your beckoning call?). Clearly Toula believes, despite their arrangement, that she owes Eléwagnè nothing. She affirms this by stating: "Cette partie de moi qui se réveille aussi brutalement est certainement plus importante que ma nouvelle apparence, que tous mes autres désirs" (176; This part of me that has been so brutally awakened is certainly more important than my new appearance and all my other desires).

Jean-Marie Volet likens *G'amèrakano* to *Fureurs* in that both novels contain examples of young women in society who "have sold off their youth to married men" (136). Indeed, Toula tells her grandmother in *G'amèrakano*:

> Je côtoie un monde qui n'a d'yeux que pour l'instruction, l'argent, et même l'apparence. . . . Les femmes ne sont plus les mêmes. Elles travaillent. Elles deviennent plus libres et cherchent à plaire aux hommes. Oui, Yaya, les hommes commandent encore aux femmes. (18)
>
> I live in a world that sees only how you act and how much money you have, and looks are everything. . . . Women are no longer the same. They work. They are becoming freer and they are looking to please men. Yes, Yaya, men still hold the reins.

What is interesting in the novel is that "becoming freer" also implies a woman's freedom from the authority of her parents under which she feels restrained well into adulthood until she is married. Even after marriage, true freedom escapes her, since in a patriarchal society, this authority once held by her parents is simply "transferred" to her husband.

Rawiri illustrates repeatedly in *G'amèrakano* that there has yet to be a simple, realistic, and enduring solution to women's problems in contemporary society and one of novel's obvious purposes is, in fact, to document in six pages in particular (35–41) a history of the "problematic relationships between men and women in African society," to which Mbazoo-Kassa has thus referred. In the end, the state of African male/female relationships in contemporary society seems not so different from unions of long ago with one obvious exception—today young people meet in the streets of the city instead of in the fields. Rawiri reveals this through the words of Toula's grandmother, Okassa:

> La femme était libre de disposer de son corps. Elle n'appartenait pas à un seul homme mais à tous. Les parents, qui n'étaient pas informés de ces unions, n'intervenaient jamais dans les disputes des amants. C'est cette situation instable des couples d'autrefois qui réparait aujourd'hui. (35–36)
>
> Woman was free to use her body as she wished. She didn't belong to one man but to all of them. The parents, who were never informed about these unions, never got involved in lovers' disputes. It's this unstable situation of couples in the past which is reappearing again today.

In the following pages, Rawiri continues to outline how she sees traditional male/female relationships with the aforementioned union evolving to become similar to what is now defined as marriage; a man would inform a father or a maternal uncle of his desire to live with their daughter. Upon the parents' approval, the man would move in with the family and have limited rights over his spouse (36). Eventually, dowry became an accepted practice and was even expected for marriage; this marked a time when authority over a young woman was split between parents and husband:

> La partie inférieure du corps de la femme, à partir du nombril, appartenait au mari. Il pouvait en faire ce qu'il voulait. La partie supérieure était la propriété des parents. L'homme n'avait pas le droit de maltraiter cette partie de la femme. En cas de faute grave commise par l'épouse, l'époux devait s'en rapporter à ses beaux-parents. (36)
>
> The lower part of a woman's body, from the navel down, belonged to the husband. He could do what he wanted with it. The upper part was the property of her parents. The man had no right to mistreat that part of the woman. In case of a grave error committed by the wife, the husband was supposed to take it up with his in-laws.

Toula's friend, Ekata, eventually leaves her parents' home for good after a heated confrontation and this part of the novel provides an opportunity to reflect on Rawiri's earlier discussions. In analyzing her own decision, Ekata states:

> Je regrette de quitter mes parents à la suite d'une querelle. Mais j'ai choisi la liberté. Voyez-vous, il faut que m'assume entièrement, loin d'eux. Plus tôt je serai livrée à moi-même, mieux je m'affirmerai et préparerai mon avenir. Un avenir qui ne leur devra rien à eux. Tout ira bien. Mes amants, en particulier le vieux se chargent du loyer et de ma nourriture. Mon salaire me servira d'argent de poche. (135–136)
>
> I regret leaving my parents because of an argument. But I chose freedom. You see, I must take full control of my own life, far away from them. The sooner I am on my own, the better I will be able to assert myself and prepare my

> future—a future for which I will owe them nothing. Everything will be all right. My lovers, the oldest one in particular, will take care of my rent and food. My pocket money will come from my salary.

Odile Cazenave suggests that *G'amèrakano* illustrates the "semi-prostitution" (75–76) that young, African urban women who lack sufficient resources must exercise in order to survive.[20] According to Cazenave, young adults as well as their parents have lost faith in formal education and diplomas as the keys to success for women; likewise, traditional values espoused by those like Toula's grandmother no longer hold importance in contemporary society to secure upward mobility. What is of prime importance is to appear successful and to be seen in the right places and with the right people. In a sense, as Cazenave rightfully points out, *G'amèrakano* almost reads like a "documentary" of sorts in which the main characters represent countless other women like themselves all confronting the same social malaise (Cazenave 79–80).[21] Clearly in agreement with Cazenave's perspective, Mbazoo-Kassa claims that the female protagonists in *G'amèrakano* are all "victimes de l'inhumanité de cet espace" (36; victims of the inhumanity of this space).

Alluding to the subject of semi-prostitution, Rawiri's characters, Ekata and Onanga, engage in a debate about polygamy in modern African society. Although polygamy is increasingly denounced in all social classes and especially in urban environments, the mistreatment of mistresses who have seemingly no rights in a relationship even when children are involved has led to many African women writers to ask—even if sarcastically—whether or not women were actually better off in polygamous marriages where at least they enjoyed some protection. What is particularly interesting in African women's literature—Francophone or otherwise—is the presentation of professional and well-educated protagonists who consider polygamy as a viable option for maintaining or improving their situations. Readers encounter such a protagonist in Esi, in Ama Ata Aidoo's *Changes: A Love Story*, a novel that will be discussed more in detail in the following section on *Fureurs*. Rawiri's *G'amèrakano* presents a similar scenario presented in *Changes*, this time with Onanga considering becoming Lemiat's second wife in order to please her parents by having the advantages and protection of marriage. Ekata is shocked by this reasoning, claiming: "C'est bien la premiere fois qu'une intellectuelle se proclame ouvertement en faveur de la polygamie" (148; This is really the first time an intellectual has declared herself openly in favor of polygamy). She wonders if her friend is really a modern woman or simply one who is still influenced by tradition (148). But it is the dysfunction in other aspects of African society—namely economic—which makes Onanga consider such a possibility in addition to the fact that a "union libre" or cohabitation without marriage is still uncommon and even unacceptable in many contemporary African societies, especially noting the period in which *G'amèrakano* was written (146). Onanga states:

> Il vaut mieux accepter de partager légalement un homme avec une ou deux rivales que d'être une maîtresse déconsidérée. Que pouvons-faire de mieux? Une épouse ne peut empêcher son mari de s'intéresser à d'autres femmes et on ne peut pas continuellement blâmer les femmes célibataires d'accepter une liaison avec ces hommes qui ne sont pas libres. . . . Les hommes polygames n'ont pas beaucoup de temps à consacrer à une ou plusieurs maîtresses lorsqu'ils ont déjà plusieurs épouses à la maison. Ils sont tenus de satisfaire en premier lieu celles qui habitent chez eux. De leur côté, les épouses se trouvent dans une situation maritale régulière, avec tout ce que cela comporte comme avantages. . . . Croyez-moi, nous ne pouvons pas rêver de mariages heureux si nous excluons systématiquement la polygamie. (147–148)

> It's better to accept to legally share a man with one or two other rivals than to be forever the discredited mistress. What choice do we really have? A woman cannot prevent her husband from being interested in other women and we cannot continually blame single women for accepting relationships with men who are already taken. . . . Polygamous men don't have a lot of time to devote to one or several mistresses when they already have several wives at home. It is their duty first and foremost to satisfy those whom they have at home. As for the women involved, they have an official marital status for themselves with all the advantages that entails. . . . Believe me, we can't even think about happy marriages if we categorically reject polygamy.

Toward the middle of *G'amèrakano*, there is no doubt that Rawiri makes a clear pronouncement of African feminisms, embedding it in a passionate three-page discussion among a group of friends, male and female, taking place in the car as the group travels together to Inanga for vacation (121–123). Rawiri seems well aware that any debate on the status of African women will ultimately be deemed by some as "Westernized" thought, as demonstrated even in Clerc and Nzé's aforementioned claims that Rawiri's writing displays ideas of Western radical feminism. Tabassou, one of the male characters present, is critical of Onanga's recitation of a poem entitled, "Le retard de l'homme noir" (black man behind the times). The poem is undoubtedly written by Rawiri for the novel itself and it seems to be a hostile response to one of Léopold Senghor's most famous poems, "Femme noire" (*Chants d'ombre* 1945), in which he refers to the African woman as his mother: "J'ai grandi à ton ombre; la douceur de tes mains bandait mes yeux" (Shapiro 130–131; I grew in your shadow, and the softness of your hands covered my eyes)[22] and later in this same poem, as his lover, as shown in these lines in particular: "Gazelle aux attaches célestes, les perles sont étoiles sur la nuit de ta peau" and "Délices des jeux de l'esprit, les reflets de l'or rouge sur ta peau qui se moire" (Shapiro 130–131; Heaven-limbed gazelle, the moist drops are stars on the night of your skin) and (Delights of mind's caprice, reflections of red gold on your rippling skin).

Senghor's "*femme noire*" remains but a body throughout and he concludes the poem with an expression of his fear that she will be forever changed with the progression of time: "Je chante ta beauté qui passe, forme que je fixe dans l'Eternel avant que le destin jaloux ne te réduise en cendres pour nourrir les racines de la vie" (Shapiro 130–131; I sing your disappearing beauty, fixing it in an Eternal shape, before an envious Destiny transforms you into ashes to nourish the roots of life).

"Femme noire" was not without criticism, however, especially from feminist scholars who saw nothing but the objectification of the black woman (d'Almeida 1994; Stratton 1994; Larrier 1997; Dolisane 2009). Although superficially he praises her, Senghor's *femme noire* never speaks but she is rather spoken about; an idealized woman that can only exist in myths.

In Rawiri's "L'homme noir," the narrator is presumably female and is critical of this same African man, the one reminiscent of Senghor's poem, who considers woman as his possession. In Senghor's poem, man was clearly fearing an inevitable progression that would ultimately change his relationship with her. In Rawiri's version, this time has already come as man laments his loss of power and feeling of superiority. Rawiri's man, in fact, both rejoices when woman is dependent on him yet criticizes her at the same time for not being able to keep up with him even though it is he who has attempted to keep her from advancing all this time. Rawiri writes:

Quand sa campagne ne savait ni lire ni écrire
Il se plaignait de ses lacunes intellectuelles
Les indépendances la projetèrent sur les bancs de l'école
Très vite elle s'affirma par son acharnement
Et sa volonté d'assimiler des connaissances nouvelles
Elle avança si rapidement si résolument
Qu'elle se mit à raisonner et à oser désobéir
A revendiquer elle aussi son droit de se faire plaisir
Elle voulut violemment s'affirmer s'identifier
Etre d'abord avec elle-même avant d'être avec lui
Voilà que l'homme noir maître absolu
S'indigna de sa libération inattendue
Il revendiqua son autorité pour
Sauvegarder ses privilèges menacés
L'évolution de la femme au lieu de la réjouir l'horripila
Aujourd'hui il veut bien qu'elle travaille
Mais refuse d'accorder sa voix à la sienne
Il veut bien se mettre au pas du progrès
Mais ne tolère pas qu'elle soit à ses côtés
Quel retard chez l'homme noir (121)

When his companion did not know how to read or write

He complained of her lack of intellectual prowess
With independence she was sent to school
In no time at all, she affirmed herself through her perseverance
And her willingness to acquire new knowledge
She advanced so quickly and resolutely
That she began to argue and dared to disobey
She too claimed her right to happiness
She violently wanted to affirm herself, to be known
She put herself first ahead of him
And so this is how the black man, the absolute master
Became indignant over her unexpected emancipation
He claimed his authority
To preserve his endangered privileges
Instead of rejoicing, he was infuriated at how woman had come into her own
Today, he is willing to let her work
But he refuses to regard her words as highly as his
He indeed wants to find himself at the cutting edge of progress
But he does not accept her to be at his side
How behind the times the black man is!

One of the male travelers in the car, Rembayo, labels the poem as "âneries" (122; bullshit). Tabassou says exasperatingly, "C'est encore une de ces féministes qui a écrit ça. . . . Si encore elle ne s'identifiait pas ses désirs à ceux des Occidentales, ça irait" (121; It's another one of those feminists who wrote that. . . . If only she wasn't linking her desires to those of Western women, it would be all right). Onanga answers "violently" (121):

> Vous ne comprenez rien. . . . Sachez bien que nous ne revendiquons pas de caprices mais des droits. Notre lutte ne se limite pas à des revendications d'égalité sociale entre hommes et femmes. Nous combattons aussi le sous-développement, le racisme et les différentes formes d'impérialisme. (122)

> You don't understand a thing. . . . You must know that these are not just whims but we are claiming actual rights. Our struggle isn't limited to claims of social equality between men and women. We are also fighting against underdevelopment, racism, and imperialism in all its forms.

Rembayo defends his stance by attempting to prove feminism is unnecessary in African society since women have always held important roles traditionally as reproducers, beholders of history, and preservers of culture. He further points out that women have always been consulted by village elders in times of conflict (122). Onanga retorts that this power was illusory, citing that even within so-called African matriarchal societies, power is often relegated to a mother's brothers. "Veux-tu me dire où est l'autorité et la propriété de la femme?" (122; Would you mind telling me where is women's authority and ownership in all of that?). Ekata in turn agrees with Rembayo's view that African women traditionally held more power than today, but admits that this power has been whittled away if not destroyed by contemporary social structures. In the end, the friends all come to the same conclusion—that it is this lack of authority and ownership in modern society that perpetuates women's inferior status to men (123).

It is clear that Rawiri's *G'amèrakano* provides readers with interesting points of discussion regarding women's roles and status in African society in the past, present, and future. Rawiri's second published novel has a definite link to her third, *Fureurs*, in which readers encounter some familiar debates amid new subjects presented. *Fureurs* is arguably Rawiri's best known and most highly acclaimed work, which makes it all the more perplexing as to why Rawiri disappeared from view after its publication, at the very height of her career.

FUREURS ET CRIS DE FEMMES: REBELLION AND THE DISOBEDIENT WOMAN

While literary critics tend to debate whether *Elonga* and *G'amèrakano* should even be considered feminist novels, all concur that *Fureurs et cris de femmes* falls into such a category. Mbazoo-Kassa, for example, does not hesitate to label the work as a feminist novel (30). In her analysis of *Fureurs*, Mbazoo-Kassa posits:

> Man is no longer master. It no longer suffices that man merely possesses the attributes of power to rule, he still needs to exercise it effectively. Thus, Joseph's wife places him in a situation of inferiority. . . . Just as man defines himself through the phallus, it matters for a woman to possess an attribute that is just as important: having a child. . . . Motherhood for Émilienne is thus a sign of power and achievement. . . . Here, sexual and economic power is no longer masculine but feminine (34–35).[23]

Unlike early Western feminism that tended to view motherhood as enslavement for women, based in part upon interpretations of theories brought forth by Simone de Beauvoir in *Le deuxième sexe* (1949),[24] one finds the opposite in Rawiri's novel—the empowerment of women through motherhood—and this idea is essential to African feminisms and is pervasive in virtually all of African women's writing. These conflicting ideologies provide ample reasons as to why African and Western feminisms have traditionally clashed. It is not surprising that Rawiri accentuates this fundamental difference within feminism through Émilienne's voice, describing what she perceives to be a threat to women's exclusive power:

> Si les médecins réussissent leurs essais en laboratoire et si les gouvernements donnent leur accord, les hommes pourront dans une dizaine d'années porter des grossesses et accoucher. Comme si leur règne dans le domaine de la

> politique et des affaires ne suffisait pas, ne voilà-t-il pas qu'ils essaient sournoisement de ravir à la femme son unique pouvoir. (111)[25]

> If doctors' laboratory experiments proved successful and if governments gave their okay, in a dozen years or so, men would be able to carry pregnancies to full term and give birth. As if their reign in politics and business not being enough, they were attempting, on the sly, to rob women of their only power. (Hanaburgh 191)[26]

Fureurs opens with a painfully graphic scene of Émilienne's miscarriage. The reader soon learns that the protagonist is a successful career woman with a coveted government position as Director of Administrative Affairs. However, she and her husband, Joseph, are in a failing marriage. The couple already has a pre-teen daughter, Rékia, but Émilienne is desperate to have more children to please her husband, family, and society. To add to the tension, several pregnancies have all ended in medically unexplained miscarriages.

Émilienne is clearly the breadwinner of the household since Joseph is a civil servant with a meager salary. Thus, Émilienne takes care of her own immediate family in addition to her mother-in-law and two nephews—everyone except Rékia appears relatively ungrateful, but the novel becomes even more complex when Rékia goes missing and is later found murdered. Émilienne realizes that Rékia was the final bit of cement holding the failing couple together as their situation continues to steadily worsen after their daughter's death. Deprived of love, respect, and appreciation, Émilienne is lured into a same-sex relationship with her secretary, Dominique, who is not genuinely seeking Émilienne's companionship but rather she is looking for a way to blackmail Émilienne's husband, Joseph, who is her lover and father to her two children, unbeknownst to Émilienne. By the end of the novel, however, Émilienne realizes that everyone around her has turned against her and she thus decides to rid herself of such toxic relationships in order to pursue her own happiness.

There are few female protagonists in African literature like Émilienne. Despite her inner turmoil, Émilienne still manages to be relatively in control of her situation within her family and society. Often Émilienne does not realize how much power she really has, but admittedly, this does not mean that everything can come easy for her without sacrifice or feelings of isolation. One of the few protagonists in African women's writing worthy of comparison to Émilienne is perhaps Ama Ata Aidoo's Esi found in the novel *Changes: A Love Story*. Like Émilienne, Esi is a well-educated and career-oriented woman, in addition to being a wife and mother, who has more than sufficient finances to take care of herself and her family. Émilienne and Esi both earn more than their husbands, and both harbor feelings of guilt at times concerning their daughters, Rékia and Ogyaanowa, respectively, whose affective needs may not have been met because of the time-consuming positions their mothers hold.

Like Émilienne and Joseph, Esi and her first husband, Oko, have grown distant over time. In *Fureurs*, Émilienne herself tries to understand this "drifting away" a couple can experience (74): "Comme c'est étrange que des êtres qui s'estiment, s'aiment, ne puissant cohabiter longtemps sans que leurs rapports ne se détériorent" (121; How strange it is that people who have such high regard for one another and who love each other cannot live together for long before their relationship starts to deteriorate). In *Changes*, Esi eventually divorces Oko after he resorts to marital rape in an attempt to show her who is boss, a scene reminiscent of *Fureurs* in which Rawiri describes one of Joseph's rare nights spent at the house (29): "Il lui fait l'amour comme un ivrogne se jetant sur une prostituée ramassée sur un trottoir obscur" (38–39; He had made love to her like a drunkard throwing himself on a prostitute he'd picked up off some obscure roadside).

Having always felt that her monogamous marriage takes away too much time from her professional responsibilities, Aidoo's Esi eventually decides to enter into a polygamous marriage as a second wife, reasoning that this might allow her to love a man while simultaneously reserving time for her career and for herself. Émilienne's and Esi's experiences make them both realize in the end that marriage and the presence of an extended family offer no guarantee as a cure for loneliness. In such a case, both women come to the conclusion that it may well be preferable to continue on one's own in a pursuit of true happiness. Concerning Émilienne in particular but certainly applicable in theory to Esi as well, Odile Cazenave states in her book, *Femmes rebelles* (1996; *Rebellious Women*, 1999): "Rather than put up with an unhappy marriage and suffer her husband's infidelities and her mother-in-law's rebuffs, the young woman opts for a new beginning, alone and without marital constraints, a new life in which she can be committed to her own professional development" (33).[27]

Both Rawiri and Aidoo send a most realistic message—unfortunately, even successful professional women may not be able to "have it all." After a particularly trying day with her family, Émilienne recalls a citation from an article in a women's magazine that speaks to her:

> Une femme n'est jamais totalement comblée. Certaines réussissent leur carrière professionnelle, d'autres par contre font un mariage d'amour sans fissures, d'autres encore font des enfants qui leur donnent pleine satisfaction. Aucune femme, pourtant, ne parvient à réunir ces trois conditions. Et s'il existe des femmes parfaitement heureuses, c'est-à-dire réunissant ces trois critères, elles sont rarissimes et à notre avis, la réunion de deux d'entre eux constitue déjà une réussite (93).

> A woman is never completely satisfied. Whereas some enjoy professional success, others build a solid marriage based on love, and then there are those who have children to feel fulfilled. No woman, however, manages to enjoy all three. And if there are women out there who are perfectly happy, who have brought these three together, they are extremely rare and, in our opinion, if they have even two of these, that is a great achievement. (154)

In addition to societal pressures that every woman faces, it is also the human being's ultimate need to be loved and the fear of living and dying alone that explains why women like Émilienne and Esi feel obliged to make compromises regarding their feminism. Rawiri and Aidoo do not wish to diminish the power of their protagonists by uncovering this truth, but rather do so to paint an accurate picture of what life really holds for the modern African woman, a reality which is not unlike one lived by any successful, career-oriented woman from any culture.

Émilienne is more than a rebellious woman, however. She is disobedient, a protagonist who does an about-face and ultimately does what she wants, disregarding or circumventing reactions from family and society and deciding that she cares little in the end about appearances for she realizes that the impressions of others have been for too long a determining factor of her behavior. During the most troubled times in their marriage, Émilienne's general disobedience leads her husband, Joseph, to reevaluate their future together: He reasons:

> C'est une femme d'intérieur remarquable et une mère parfaite quand tout va bien. Mon rêve serait qu'elle élève tous les enfants que je ferai avec d'autres femmes. C'est ce que font certaines épouses dans cette situation. Seulement voilà, je suis tombé sur une intellectuelle qui refuse de franchir certaines barrières. (95)

> She is a remarkable homemaker and a perfect mother when all is well. My dream would be for her to raise all the children I have with my lovers. That's what some wives do in her situation. Only here's the problem, I fell for an intellectual who refuses to break certain barriers. (158)

Émilienne refuses the traditional family of her modern society—that is, the extended family plus the mistress—even in the context of her infertility in which case even her own mother agrees it would be acceptable for Joseph to find another woman to give him children (147). As Émilienne does not consider her infertility to be the prime source of conflict in their marriage, she refuses to see polygamy as justifiable in this or in any case. She attempts to explain to Joseph just how flawed such reasoning is, shouting in frustration:

> C'est ça! Si j'ai un enfant, tu quitteras ta maîtresse. Si j'ai un enfant, tu m'aimeras de nouveau. Si j'ai un enfant, ta mère m'adoptera et ma famille sera comblée. En en mot, tout rentrera dans l'ordre. (97)
>
> Is that it! If I have a child, you will leave your mistress. If I have a child, you will love me again. If I have a child, your mother will adopt me and my family will be satisfied. In a word, everything will be back to normal. (163)

The distinction between a rebellious woman and a disobedient one is indeed intriguing and worth analyzing here. In literature, one can cite countless examples of the rebellious woman who may seem more defiant in thought than in action. In Simone de Beauvoir's *La femme rompue* (1967; *The Woman Destroyed*, 1969) Monique appears to be a subservient housewife, but we see her displeasure with what society dictates for women through notes in her personal diary.

Similarly, by means of a series of letters written to a friend in *Une si longue lettre* (1986; *So Long a Letter*, 1989), Senegalese author Mariama Bâ allows her protagonist, Ramatoulaye, to explain her shock at her husband taking on a much younger second wife after 25 years of monogamous marriage together. Few protagonists, however, can earn the distinction of "disobedient" in the way Rawiri's Émilienne does. The rebellious woman struggles against certain realities and nearly always gains the respect of the reader in doing so. The disobedient woman goes a step further, setting herself apart from the rebellious woman in that the former ultimately chooses to opt out of the lifestyle that will gain her respect or make her existence in society more comfortable. The disobedient woman is strong, but she is not necessarily a winner. She may not even win over the reader in all cases, he or she who is the ultimate interpreter of her life. Ultimately, readers will not cast negative judgment upon Monique or Ramatoulaye for being devoted mothers. However, the same readers may be disappointed in Émilienne for linking her affection for Rékia to the status of her relationship with Joseph (44)[28] or they may be shocked when Émilienne physically assaults her elderly mother-in-law (94), even though the latter is a character with whom the reader can hardly sympathize. The disobedient woman is perceived as aggressive, frank, distant, and unforgiving at times, and while these characteristics may be interpreted as signs of strength and determination in men, history proves that women who exhibit these traits are not privy to the same positive impression from society.

It is the Martinican writer, Fabienne Kanor, whose protagonist, Louise, in *Anticorps* (2010) gives us two important reasons as to why this is so. First, when it comes to any relationship within the family, woman is simply not allowed to be "fundamentally selfish" (37), and secondly, even if she manages to be, "ce n'est qu'une femme rudement courageuse qui pourra le trouver facile de finir sa vie sans personne" (117; only the most terribly courageous of women will be able to find it easy to finish her life alone). Perhaps this is why Rawiri chose to end her novel with the revelation that her protagonist is pregnant (174), as this leaves the reader somewhat relieved that Émilienne no longer risks ultimate loneliness after evicting her husband and extended family from the house. The pregnancy thus spares Émilienne from additional failure and pity.

Odile Cazenave also offers an interesting interpretation of the ending of *Fureurs*. That is, failure lies not with Émilienne but rather with Joseph and Eyang who are ultimately thrown out of the house (Cazenave 32). Ironically, they will never enjoy the child Émilienne is carrying; she will see to it that they are deprived of this for all the suffering they have imposed upon her. Cazenave also concludes that closing the novel with a pregnant Émilienne is indeed significant: "According to tradition, [Émilienne's] pregnancy means that she has returned to normal" (32).[29]

Although Émilienne's disobedience is most apparent at the end of the novel, she has exhibited throughout signs of intolerance of family and societal values that she has deemed oppressive and archaic. Émilienne imposes the same standards of behavior for in-laws as for her own parents, as all were initially against her interethnic marriage with Joseph. Of course, she is the most disappointed in her own mother's reaction about this and she insists:

> Je suis navrée de te désobéir, mère. Je ne m'attends pas non plus ce que père m'approuve. Lorsque vous changerez de jugement, vous saurez bien où me trouver si je ne suis pas retournée en France! Adieu! (18)
>
> I am saddened to have to go against you, Mother. I don't expect Father will approve either. When you change your minds, you'll know where to find me, if I haven't gone back to France. Good-bye! (19)

Émilienne's relationship with her parents improves only because they come to accept and respect her choice of husband, something that her mother-in-law Eyang at no time is sincerely willing to do.

According to Jean-Marie Volet, Émilienne chose the man whom she was to marry and would have continued to love him unconditionally if only he had continued to treat her with respect and dignity (135). Likewise, Émilienne's abysmal relationship with her mother-in-law, Eyang, has at its core the elder woman's disappointment that Émilienne does not conform to her vision of a suitable wife for her son. Émilienne remains unapologetic for this, however, and refuses to treat her mother-in-law with respect if this is not reciprocated. The only time this happens is when Eyang agrees to a brief truce with her daughter-in-law, one that ironically becomes threatening to Joseph who fears for his power in the household if both his wife and his mother join forces in solidarity against him (76). His fear is short-lived, however, as Eyang's dislike for Émilienne soon resurfaces as before.

At the end of *Fureurs*, Émilienne overhears a conversation between Joseph and Eyang during which she is made aware of just how much her mother-in-law has been involved in the couple's private affairs. Although Joseph defends his decision to stay with Émilienne instead of conceding to his mother's wishes (that is, living exclusively with his mistress and their two children), this conversation proves more than Émilienne can tolerate (173). As a final act of ultimate disobedience, Émilienne gives the entire family (Joseph, his mother, and her nephews) until that same evening to vacate her home (174)—that is, the home she owns, purchased thanks to her salary alone.

African literature has provided many portraits of women in vulnerable positions, especially widows who stand to lose their home and belongings to the family of their deceased husband, or worse yet, face being "inherited" by a brother-in-law as if they were a possession, as is the case for Awu in Justine Mintsa's *Histoire d'Awu* (2000).[30] But relatively early in African women's writing, *Fureurs* provided us with the rare example of a female protagonist who makes the decision to "repudiate" her husband (Mbazoo-Kassa 135). The novel ends with a triumphal image of Émilienne returning home to an empty—but finally peaceful—house (174).

The power that Émilienne exhibits at the end of *Fureurs* has many dimensions and therefore, it is difficult to define. Émilienne's professional and financial success automatically accords Rawiri's protagonist some power, even though it may not be exactly all that Émilienne had hoped for after so many years of work and marriage. As Jean-Marie Volet explains:

> If one considers power to be not only the simple ability to impose one's will to achieve a predetermined goal, but rather the ability to challenge others and their limited vision of numerous and contradicting forces that influence and justify exchanges and social behaviors, Rawiri's heroines in this case have considerable impact. (145)[31]

Volet further elaborates in the chapter on Rawiri in his book *La parole aux Africaines* (1993), that Émilienne's power is a defensive one that protects her from her husband's selfishness and from his need to dominate (149). Volet states: "Her power represents rather her right to speak: her capacity not only to be heard but to be listened to; and also to withdraw and to pull out of the game when the other players try to lock her into a discourse that works to their advantage alone" (149).[32]

So the question remains, is *Fureurs* pessimistic or is Rawiri's novel quite simply an example of African realism? If a self-declared feminist in words and actions cannot manage to have a near-perfect life despite her financial and intellectual advantages, what hope is there for women from lower social classes who will never enjoy such a status? Why does Rawiri exhibit this desire to remind us, as Volet explains it, that "even at the top of the pyramid, the possibilities are limited" (133)?[33]

Presenting an interesting comparison, Phil Powrie emphasizes in his essay "Rereading between the Lines: A Postscript on *La Femme rompue*," that feminists had criticized Simone de Beauvoir for giving "such a pessimistic view of women's situation" (328). In *Tout compte fait* (1972; *All Said and Done*, 1974), Beauvoir responds to this criticism by explaining "I did not feel compelled to choose exemplary heroines. To describe failure, error, insincerity, this, as it seems to me, does not betray anyone" (145).[34] Powrie continues by saying that Beauvoir "could not have done other than present a pessimistic view, given the absence of a strongly articulated tradition of women's writing" (328), a context that can certainly apply to Rawiri as the first female novelist of Gabon. Powrie then explains how contemporary fiction is problematic and therefore doubly so for the woman writer, making her "no less entombed than her heroines" (329).

Rawiri raises important questions in *Fureurs* and speaks frankly about issues that had never been touched upon before in African writing, especially by a female author. Even when Rawiri does bring up subjects that have been commonly discussed such as infertility, she comes at these from new angles, adding to the innovativeness of the novel.

The consequences of infertility for an African woman regardless of the social class to which she belongs was a subject first presented in Kuoh-Moukoury's *Rencontres essentielles* in 1969. The fact that Rawiri also chose to contribute to that discussion some thirty years later merely shows how timely and urgent the matter has remained.[35] Indeed, there are some similarities in the handling of the subject by these two authors. Both Kuoh-Moukoury's Flo and Rawiri's Émilienne are highly educated, progressive, and urban-dwelling African women. Yet, all these advantages do not necessarily prevent these contemporary women from perceiving their infertility as catastrophic. By all appearances, Flo and Émilienne have abandoned traditional roles and thinking. Yet, their desperation causes them to pursue every possible avenue of traditional and modern medicine to fix what they perceive to be a problem. Flo and Émilienne are persuaded by family members to seek out traditional healers, although both women are embarrassed by this decision in the end. The rituals associated with these consultations are described in great detail in both novels, leading readers to wonder what these two authors had to gain by reinforcing stereotypes that make African practices appear "primitive." However, it must be pointed out that Kuoh-Moukoury and Rawiri also show repeated failures of modern medicine in each protagonist's individual case. In fact, at the end of *Fureurs*, Émilienne's sister, Eva, dies in labor due to the incompetence of the hospital staff and her doctor.

Although the novel closes with the revelation that Émilienne is pregnant, the reader is not so certain that this is to the credit of the expertise of her renowned gynecologist whose final suggestion to her ironically was that she should consult with a hypnotist. Thus, far from reinforcing negative stereotypes about Africans, Kuoh-Moukoury and Rawiri are merely pointing out the imperfections of both the traditional and the so-called modern worlds. This idea in turn demonstrates the weight and influence of customary beliefs and traditions in any given contemporary society and how individuals may resort to these cultural references especially in times of hopelessness and crisis, seeking a solution to problems from within instead of from outside. Flo and Émilienne are constantly reevaluating the old and the new, trying to extract what is positive, and it is this mentality in particular that makes these protagonists forward-thinking.

Despite the similarities found in *Rencontres* and *Fureurs*, Rawiri's discussion of infertility goes a step further. Initially, Émilienne's infertility seems as tragic as Flo's in *Rencontres*. In Kuoh-Moukoury's novel, the conclusion drawn is that motherhood takes precedence over any relationship with a man in the end. However, as *Fureurs* progresses, the reader eventually starts to question if, in an ideal world, Émilienne really would have bothered with children at all. Her desire for children may actually be a mere longing for power. In this case, especially when visits to the gynecologist reveal no somatic problems to explain Émilienne's infertility, the reader realizes that it is perhaps Émilienne's true, subconscious desire not to have children for the sake of others that makes her body rebel, provoking miscarriages and making it difficult for her to conceive. Émilienne gives readers much to consider in her reflection on her own infertility and its true consequences on her marriage with Joseph:

> Est-ce ma stérilité qui le fait fuir? Pourquoi ne peut-il m'aimer même sans enfants? Ma maladie, si c'en est une, n'est pas contagieuse et ne devrait pas nous voler notre amour. Non, je ne peux pas croire que Joseph m'ait aimée pour les enfants que j'étais supposée lui donner après notre mariage. Je ne veux pas croire qu'il n'ait vu en moi que cette femme qui deviendrait la mère de ses enfants. Non, cette idée m'est insupportable. Je suis une femme et je le resterai quoi qu'il advienne. (81)

> Is it my infertility that is making him run away? Why does he need me to have children to love me? My illness, if that's what it is, is not contagious and should not rob us of our love. No, I cannot believe that Joseph loved me for the children I was supposed to give him after our wedding. I don't want to believe that all he saw in me was this woman who was to become the mother of his children. No, that idea is unbearable to me. I am a woman and I will be a woman no matter what happens. (134–135)

Perhaps the only element of *Fureurs* that may be labeled a possible shortcoming is Rawiri's handling of the subject of lesbianism as depicted through Émilienne's relationship with her secretary, Dominique. As the author of one of the first African novels to touch upon this subject that is still taboo for many African writers even today, Rawiri had the potential to go well beyond the stereotypes of a lesbian relationship and unfortunately, at times, it seems Rawiri's own moral judgments prevented her from doing so.

Émilienne's homoerotic relationship with Dominique is complicated, and even troubling on many fronts, especially because it is part of an elaborate strategy crafted by Eyang. Citing Émilienne's infertility as a primary motivation for wanting her son to divorce, Eyang devises a plan for Dominique to secure Émilienne's trust so that Eyang's primary objective to separate the married couple can be realized. However, Eyang is not specific in terms of how Dominique should go about gaining her boss' trust. Eyang only tells Dominique to become friends with Émilienne so that she in turn can put the second phase of her plan into motion (62).

In the end, however, Eyang has very little to do with the homoerotic nature of Émilienne and Dominique's relationship. In fact, it is uncertain as to whether Eyang even knows about the specifics of the relationship, since at the novel's conclusion, Eyang only tells her son that Émilienne is not worthy of his devotion because she spends all her time with witch doctors and in particular, consults "un sorcier blanc" (305; a white witch doctor)—her preferred term for the hypnotist. Believing her son is rejecting her by rejecting the mother of his children, Eyang finally issues an ultimatum to her son, saying she will leave the house if Joseph does not apologize to Dominique for their break-up (173).

Thus, Dominique is seemingly the only one responsible for initiating an intimate relationship with Émilienne. While Émilienne is attracted by Dominique's physical beauty early on in the novel (21)—the first reference to this being her description of "cette jeune femme au visage et au corps presque parfaits" (24; this young woman whose complexion and body were so nearly perfect)—she never exhibits overtly a hint of interest sexually toward her secretary nor is she the first one who makes her desires known. The relationship seems to have an identifiable starting point, however, and this occurs, strangely enough, as the two women witness together the capital punishment of five men just below Émilienne's office window. Although Émilienne and the reader are both unaware of Dominique's insincerity at the time, the secretary takes advantage of the horrifying scene to become physically close to Émilienne:

> Dominique se jette sur elle, l'agrippe par les épaules. Les deux femmes s'enlacent. . . . Les deux corps unis des jeunes femmes frémissent du même émoi. (101)

> Dominique threw herself on her, grabbing her by the shoulders. The two women embraced. . . . The two women's bodies intertwined and shuddered. (172)

Although there is nothing particularly homoerotic in this first physical interaction between the two, it marks a clear turning point in the relationship since Émilienne always maintains a strict level of hierarchy with regard to her employees so any physical contact with them is uncharacteristic. Dominique cannot win over her boss, however, without such an initial interaction. Although the reader suspects Dominique's malicious intentions more and more throughout the novel, her true motivations are not revealed until her ultimate confrontation with Joseph near the end (168): "J'avais établi un plan bien précis pour te récupérer, un plan que ta femme a précipité sans le savoir" (297; I had a very carefully devised plan to win you back, a plan that your wife hastened without even knowing it). Dominique sees this plan as a weapon to blackmail Joseph into leaving his wife completely so that she will have him exclusively for herself. Dominique adds (168): "J'exige que tu quittes ta femme dans les 24 heures. . . . Si tu refuses, sache que je déclare au monde que ta femme est une lesbienne" (296; I demand that you leave your wife in the next 24 hours. . . . If you refuse, know that I will tell the world that your wife is a lesbian).

At first, Émilienne seems to treasure her relationship with Dominique, viewing it like a new beginning as she concludes that she has never lived such intimately fulfilling moments with a man. However, the relationship seems less about a sincere love for a woman, and more about three things—revolt, a "psycho-sentimental awakening" (167), and narcissism—but not a healthy narcissism that is associated with and essential to romantic love. Although Émilienne may seem more genuine about the relationship than Dominique, realistically, both women are using each other selfishly and each has little consideration for the feelings of the other in the end. Rawiri writes about Émilienne:

> La masturbation n'est pas son truc. Elle a toujours eu besoin d'un contact physique. Et le corps de Dominique, semblable au sien, lui permet non seulement de se redécouvrir, mais également lui procure un certain équilibre. Cette liaison interdite est comme une drogue dont elle sait que l'arrêt brutal la rendrait complètement folle. (146)

> Masturbation was not her thing. She always felt the need for physical contact. And since Dominique's body was similar to her own, it allowed her not only to rediscover herself, but also to provide her with a certain balance. This forbidden relationship was like a drug and she knew that sudden withdrawal would make her completely crazy. (255–256)

Indeed, Rawiri's words, "liaison interdite" (forbidden relationship), reflect the taboos associated with homosexuality in African society, but considering the fact that Rawiri presents Émilienne as a rebellious and even disobedient protagonist in terms of what society dictates, the reader is left to ask himself or herself at the end why Rawiri did not seize the opportunity here to defy yet another taboo. It is surprising actually that Émilienne comes to feel ashamed about her relationship with Dominique, calling it "cet épisode salissant de ma vie" (this dirty chapter in my life) and asking herself, "Comment ai-je donc pu tomber si bas?" (284; How could I have fallen so low?). These sentiments seem inconsistent with the character that Rawiri has presented to the reader thus far. At the point where Émilienne decides to break off her relationship with Dominique, the former is still completely unaware of her secretary's ruse. Yet, Émilienne's manner of breaking up is far from sensitive. She immediately reinstates the former social hierarchy between superior and secretary and basically gives only minimal, matter-of-fact reasons for the break-up, stating that the relationship in general is not appropriate and that it negatively affects others close to them (166): "De toutes manières, pour les êtres qui nous sont chers, nous ne pouvons plus entretenir notre liaison" (293; In any case, for those who are dear to us, we can no longer keep our relationship going). When Dominique protests, Émilienne treats her as an insubordinate employee (166): "Écoute, petite, ce problème me regarde. Je t'interdis de t'en mêler dorénavant. Tu m'entends!" (294; Listen, little girl, this problem is my business. From now on I forbid you to meddle in it. Do you understand?).

If one looks at other examples of intimate relationships between women in African writing, such as in Cameroonian author Calixthe Beyala's earliest works, *C'est le soleil qui m'a brûlée* (1987; *The Sun Hath Looked Upon Me*, 1996) and *Tu t'appelleras Tanga* (1988; *Your Name Shall Be Tanga*, 1996), one finds that Beyala's style of writing offers a more objective view of these relationships and leaves the freedom of interpretation to the reader without imposing the author's own moral judgment. This does not imply, however, that Beyala has no strong feelings about the subject. In fact, Beyala has often categorically denied that relationships between Irène and Ateba in *C'est le soleil* and between Tanga and Anna-Claude in *Tu t'appelleras Tanga* are examples of lesbianism. In an interview with Eloise Brière and Rangira Gallimore,[36] Beyala stated with conviction:

> I think that those who see lesbianism in my writings are quite simply perverted because tenderness between women doesn't necessarily imply lesbianism. How can one explain to Westerners that in traditional Africa, intimate relationships between people of the same sex are not defined in terms of homosexuality?" (199)[37]

While there is no shortage of scholars who have spoken about lesbianism in Beyala's two works (Ndinda 1994; Bjornson 1991), others such as Rangira Gallimore (1997), Nicki Hitchcott (2000), and Ayo Coly (2010) have placed Beyala's writings within Adrienne Rich's "lesbian continuum," which, according to Rich, is "to include a range—through each woman's life and throughout history—of woman-identified experience, not simply the fact that a woman has had or consciously desired genital sexual experience with another woman" (317). Rich claims that this definition can be expanded further "to embrace many more forms of primary intensity between and among women, including the sharing of a rich inner life, the bonding against male tyranny, [and] the giving and receiving of practical and political support" (317). In the analysis of Beyala's *C'est le soleil qui m'a brûlée* in her book *The Pull of Postcolonial Nationhood*, Ayo Coly states, "Throughout the novel, heterosexuality is produced, channeled, and monitored for the purpose of reproducing patriarchal structures of power" (49). Indeed, one can apply these same analyses to understand the nature of Émilienne's relationship with Dominique in *Fureurs*, and considering the circumstances and these aforementioned points of analysis, it seems that the homoerotic encounter between the two women was almost inevitable. That is, Émilienne was able to perceive of a sexual relationship with Dominique precisely because of its promise to be potentially free of such embedded patriarchal structures of power, allowing for true intimacy. The fact that Émilienne rejects and belittles Dominique in the end can also be interpreted as a reassertion of power and a dominant role and a return to this hierarchical, patriarchal environment from which they are ultimately unable to escape for good.

Unlike Beyala who never specifically uses the term "lesbianism" in either of her works, Rawiri takes away this ambiguity by having her characters state unequivocally, to cite just one example (168): "Je déclare au monde que ta femme est une lesbienne" (296; I will tell the world that your wife is a lesbian). Scholars as well as general readers are thus forced to address Rawiri's precision in terms in their analyses. Mbazoo-Kassa, for example, labels the relationship "circumstantial lesbianism" (139). Clerc and Nzé once again cite the inspiration of radical American feminism that motivates Rawiri to take on the "problem of feminine homosexuality" in *Fureurs*, but they claim that more than anything else, such intimacy is "a way of compensating for a loss of tenderness on the part of the husband" (263).[38] Cazenave also speaks of a "lesbian relationship" between Émilienne and Dominique, stating: "Lesbian love is presented as a dead-end, since the liaison is shown only in its relations to social taboos and mechanisms" (32).[39] However, Annie-Paul Boukandou provides perhaps a multi-faceted interpretation of this particular relationship and what it contributes both to *Fureurs* and to the African feminist novel in general. In her essay "Personnages et discours féminin dans le roman gabonais," Boukandou applauds novels like *Fureurs* that are open to change. Women, in fact, can and do have loving relationships with each other (122–123). That is, despite the shortcomings one may find in the way Rawiri chooses to handle the homoerotic relationship between Émilienne and Dominique, such a novel "produces a new type of woman free in her emotions, and free in the way she uses her body" (122).[40] The fact that Rawiri can touch upon such a subject in her novel at all proves that there is some kind of shift in thinking in a new, more modern age that allows taboos to at least be debated and no change toward acceptance can occur without this step. Although every reader may not be pleased with the end result of this initial discussion, the fact that Rawiri has introduced the topic was in itself radical, especially in 1989.

RAWIRI'S OVERALL CONTRIBUTION TO AFRICAN LITERATURE

Angèle Rawiri's three novels continue to ignite debate and passion. As Rawiri's works are true representations of the African novel, they nonetheless have an international appeal that will continue to grow especially with the reintroduction of *Fureurs* in English translation to a twenty-first-century audience. *Elonga* offers a rare insight into witchcraft and its continued influence on African society, a first for a work by an African woman writer. All three of Rawiri's novels can certainly be analyzed from a feminist perspective and in fact, contribute much to the formulation of African feminisms in literature.

On a personal level, readers can easily relate to depictions in the three novels of complicated relationships within couples and families and how these can be further marred by infidelity, love triangles, poverty, and jealousy. The stories of Toula in *G'amèrakano* and of Émilienne in *Fureurs* in particular prove to readers that education and career do not necessarily guarantee personal happiness and emphasize the often superficial interactions of the *nouveaux riches*. In an increasingly globalized world, government and corporate corruption, favoritism and nepotism, violence against adults and children, malpractice, extortion, and blackmail are ever-present, universal realities of which readers are also aware. The ability to capture the interest of a new generation of readers thus attests to the originality of Rawiri's three novels.

Finally, Rawiri must be applauded for her detailed commentary on the problem of tribalism in former African colonies. Tribalism is more commonly the domain of male writers, but in this instance, Rawiri has once again distinguished herself among female authors along with her countrywoman, Honorine Ngou, author of the essay "Le tribalisme: le virus qui tue la paix" (2003). The interethnic marriage of Émilienne and Joseph serves as the backdrop for this serious discussion that takes up the better part of the first chapter in *Fureurs*, but readers also see the tension of ethnic conflict in Toula's neighborhood of Igewa in *G'amèrakano*. Rawiri draws many conclusions throughout her novels, most lauding the richness of multiculturalism and praising those citizens "motivated by the same spirit in the interest of our country" (*The Fury* 19).

Admittedly, Rawiri's works announced a promising start for Gabonese literature. *Elonga* quickly followed by *G'amèrakano* and *Fureurs* made Rawiri not only Gabon's first novelist but also the most prolific Gabonese author of the 1980s. As these three works in particular are an important influence on Gabonese women's writing to follow, a decision was made to present all three of her works in this chapter. Regrettably, it is impossible to analyze every work of every author to whom the following chapters are dedicated. Many of the most important titles of Gabonese women writers are included in this study, however, since they merit further critical analysis. These particular novels have been chosen for the uniqueness their contribution provides to African Francophone literature overall.

NOTES

1. Georges Rawiri published a collection of poetry in 1975 entitled *Chants du Gabon*.
2. To cite just one example, Moussiliki's words in *G'amèrakano* painfully echo Rawiri's inner pain in feeling a sense of abandonment when her own father remarried after her mother's death: "Lorsque ton père est mort, j'ai tout de suite trouvé un autre homme. Je regrette qu'il n'ait pas voulu de toi" (32; When your father died, I found another man right away. I regret that he wanted nothing to do with you).
3. Gabonese writer Edna Merey-Apinda who also speaks Omyènè explained that Rawiri's name, Ntyugwétondo, translates into French as "le jour qu'on aime," which I in turn translated here as "the beloved day."
4. Rawiri's comment in the original French reads: "Je ne me sentais pas chez moi en terre africaine et, en même temps, je ne me sentais pas non plus chez moi en Europe."
5. Jean-Marie Volet's book, *La parole aux Africaines ou l'idée de pouvoir chez les romancières d'expression française de l'Afrique Sub-Saharienne* (1993), and Odile Cazenave's *Femmes rebelles: Naissance d'un nouveau roman africain au féminin* (1996) were arguably the two earliest and most important analyses of Rawiri's work.
6. The original quote in the *Amina* interview reads: "J'avoue que ça a été plutôt facile. J'ai été aidée par des amis journalistes qui m'ont mise en contact avec un éditeur."
7. The original quote in French reads: "Je n'avais pas pensé à cela. J'étais plutôt accaparée par mes réflexions, mes doutes, mes angoisses, mes inquiétudes. Quand le roman est sorti, j'ai appris que j'étais la première romancière."
8. Although Ntsémpolo is fictitious, Rawiri nonetheless adds some of her native language, Omyéné, to the text; Igowo's uncle greets him by asking, "Itchango?" (30; How are you).
9. All quotations from *Elonga* have been cited from the 1986 edition published by Silex. Many thanks to Paul Dakeyo, Director of Éditions Silex (now known as Panafrika/Nouvelles du Sud/Silex), for permission to cite the French version of *Elonga* as well as *G'amèrakano* also published by Silex in 1988. English translations that follow the citations are mine.
10. See pages 125–154.
11. Volet's quote reads: "Plutôt que de nous pencher sur le roman dans son ensemble, nous concentrerons notre attention sur Ziza, un des personnages principaux car il est inutile de connaître le détail de l'intrigue pour étudier le pouvoir de la jeune femme" (126; We will

concentrate on Ziza, one of the main characters, rather than on the novel as a whole since it serves no purpose to know the details of the plot when analyzing the young woman's power).

12. The original quote from the *Amina* interview with Rawiri reads: "Après la parution de *Elonga*, mon premier roman, j'ai éprouvé un sentiment d'échec. [C]e qui me gêna le plus, ce fut le manque d'intérêt manifesté par la plupart à l'égard des problèmes inquiétants que j'abordais. Mais bon, je ne rêvais pas. Je ne croyais pas changer mes concitoyens en écrivant ce roman. J'ai pu constater que les gens allaient chez les sorciers autant qu'avant la parution d'*Elonga*."

13. The translation is provided by Magloire Ambourhouet-Bigmann in his essay, "Une littérature du silence" (45). Hallnaut Engouang also confirms this translation in his essay in *Regards sur les grands themes de la littérature gabonaise*, volume 1 (96).

14. The original quote by Moupoumbou and Ndemby-Mamfoumby in French is: "Angèle Rawiri (1980) et Sylvie Ntsame (2005) procèdent à la mise en scène de la sorcellerie pour la faire apparaitre comme atavisme culturel qui tue et écrase les valeurs." Although Moupoumbou and Ndemby-Mamfoumby mention *Elonga* in the first paragraph of their study (arguably it is a work that is essential to their study on death in the Gabonese novel), the novel is unfortunately not analyzed any further in the collection.

15. A *ganga* is a Bantu term used by the Fang and the Myènè, among others, to signify a spiritual healer.

16. Paul Dakeyo, the Director of Panafrika/Nouvelles du Sud/Silex, has graciously granted permission to cite all the material quoted in this chapter from *G'amèrakano*, originally published by Silex in 1988. English translations are mine.

17. The full quote in French reads: "*G'amèrakano* met l'accent sur la problématique des femmes dans leurs rapports avec les hommes dans la société africaine. Le sous-titre 'au carrefour' suggère bien la complexité de ces relations sexuées, et le malaise qui souvent en découle."

18. Mbazoo-Kassa's full quote in French reads: "Autrement dit, étudier la femme, c'est étudier la société à laquelle elle appartient."

19. Clerc and Nzé's full quote in French reads: "Proclamation de foi digne du féminisme radical américain, et que l'on trouve rarement dans la littérature féminine africaine. "

20. Mbazoo-Kassa also refers to "semi-prostitution" in her 2009 study, but it is obviously written much later than Cazenave's and furthermore it is less developed on this particular point.

21. The full citation from Cazenave's *Femmes rebelles* reads: "Par le ton de la narration, le roman fait l'effet de documentaire, de chronique. Toula, Onanga, Ekata sont seulement un exemple parmi tant d'autres, représentatrices d'un problème social grave, que lecteurs et lectrices doivent rencontrer" (79).

22. The original and the translation of this poem were transcribed from the anthology *Négritude Black Poetry from Africa and the Caribbean* (1970) edited and translated by Norman Shapiro (pages 130–131). Permission to cite these lines was granted by Dr. Shapiro who now holds the copyright for this volume.

23. The original French quote from Mbazoo-Kassa reads: "L'homme n'est plus le maître. Il ne suffit plus qu'il possède les attributs du pouvoir pour gouverner, encore faudrait-il qu'il l'exerce effectivement. Or Joseph est mis en situation d'infériorité par sa femme. . . . La maternité d'Émilienne est alors signe de puissance et d'achèvement . . . l'homme se définissant par le phallus, il importe que la femme se manifeste par un attribut tout aussi important: l'enfant. . . . Ici, le pouvoir sexuel et économique n'est plus masculin, mais féminin."

24. In *Le deuxième sexe*, Simone de Beauvoir speaks of "la servitude de la maternité" (56; the servitude of motherhood).

25. Permission granted for all quotes from the following text in French that are found throughout this chapter: *FUREURS ET CRIS DE FEMMES*, Angèle Rawiri, Collection Encres Noires, © Editions l'Harmattan, 1989.

26. Rawiri, Angèle. Translated by Sara Hanaburgh. *The Fury and Cries of Women*. pp. 19, 24, 34–35, 38–39, 121, 134–145, 146, 154, 158, 163, 167, 172, 191, 255–256, 284, 294, 296, 297, 305. © 2014 by the Rector and Visitors of the University of Virginia. Reprinted by permission of the University of Virginia Press.

27. Cazenave's quote in French reads: "Plutôt que de supporter un mariage malheureux et de souffrir des infidélités du mari et des rebuffades de sa belle-mère, la jeune femme choisit un

nouveau départ, seule, sans contraintes maritales, où elle peut se consacrer à son développement professionnel" (51).

28. When only one page number is given, as is the case here, the reference is from the original 1989 text written in French (*Fureurs*) and not from the English translation.

29. This discussion paraphrases Cazenave's quote from *Femmes rebelles* that reads: "Or Rawiri rajeunit le thème en lui donnant, outre une intensification de l'hostilité des relations entre belle-mère et belle-fille, un nouveau tour, à savoir que le dénouement signale l'échec non pas d'Émilienne, mais de sa belle-mère et de son mari, l'un et l'autre étant sommés de quitter son foyer, et ce alors qu'elle est finalement enceinte, donc d'après la tradition, rentrée dans la normale."

30. In his essay, "L'impossible absoluité du pouvoir," Pascal Binene points out that in cultures where wives are considered part of a husband's assets and property, it makes perfect sense that according to tradition, a wife would be inherited by her husband's brothers (29).

31. Volet's original quote in French reads: "Si l'on considère le pouvoir non plus comme la simple capacité d'imposer sa volonté pour atteindre un but fixé à l'avance, mais plutôt comme la capacité de mettre au défi les autres et leur vision restreinte des forces multiples et contradictoires qui influencent et justifient les échanges et comportements sociaux, alors l'impact des héroïnes de Rawiri a une portée considérable."

32. Volet's quote in the original French reads: "Son pouvoir représente plutôt son droit à la parole; sa capacité d'être non seulement entendue mais écoutée; et aussi d'avouer forfait et de se retirer du jeu quand les autres joueurs essaient de l'enfermer dans un discours ne garantissant que leur seul avantage."

33. Volet's quote in French reads: "même au sommet de la pyramide, les possibilités sont limitées."

34. In Powrie's essay, de Beauvoir's statement is also quoted as it reads in French: "Je ne me sens pas astreinte à choisir des héroïnes exemplaires. Décrire l'échec, l'erreur, la mauvaise foi, ce n'est, me semble-t-il, trahir personne."

35. I say "thirty years" here since Kuoh-Moukoury's book was finished in 1956 but not published until 1969—thus, there is indeed a thirty-year gap between these two novels.

36. In the same interview, Beyala quite aggressively denies the existence of homosexuality in traditional African societies, and her comments represent a very common reaction among African writers especially at the time of this interview in the late 90s. When pressed about her implying that traditional African society excluded all homosexual activity, Beyala's reponse was "Comme je vous l'ai déjà dit, je ne prétends pas détenir la vérité universelle par rapport à certaines données. Je ne puis donc savoir si les autres sociétés africaines s'adonnent à l'homosexualité. Je suis cependant convaincue que la mienne ne la pratique pas" (199; As I already told you, I can't claim to hold universal truth in regard to certain data. So I wouldn't know if other African societies indulge in homosexuality or not. I am convinced, however, that my own doesn't practice it).

37. Beyala's quote in the original French reads: "Je pense que ceux qui voient du lesbianisme dans mes écrits sont tout simplement des pervertis car la tendresse entre femmes n'implique pas forcément le lesbianisme. Comment expliquer aux Occidentaux qu'en Afrique traditionnelle, les rapports intimes entre personnes du même sexe ne se définissent pas en termes d'homosexualité?"

38. The partially translated paragraph in French reads: "Elle abordera sans plus de complexes le problème de l'homosexualité féminine. Mais il s'agira moins d'une revendication affirmée que d'une façon de compenser la perte de tendresse, de la part du mari repris par le carcan traditionnel de l'union ethnique et de la polygamie."

39. Cazenave writes: "L'amour entre femmes apparaît donc comme un pis-aller, la relation étant utilisée par rapport aux mécanismes et tabous de la société."

40. Boukandou writes: "un nouveau type de femme libre de ses sentiments, et de l'utilisation de son corps."

Chapter Two

Justine Mintsa and Gabonese Writers of Fang Heritage

Orality, Culture, and Tradition

Shortly after Angèle Rawiri's last novel had been published in 1989, new women writers of Rawiri's generation emerged in Gabon. The 1990s brought the novels *Un seul tournant: Makôsu* (1994) and *Premières lectures* (1997) by Justine Mintsa who is today arguably one of the most highly acclaimed Gabonese women writers internationally.[1] The new millennium proved to be a particularly productive period for Gabonese women authors such as Sylvie Ntsame, Chantal Magalie Mbazoo-Kassa, and Honorine Ngou, among others. All of these authors follow in a creative path established first by Rawiri, but each author contributes a uniqueness all her own to Gabon's national literature. The majority of the most influential and prolific women writers of Gabon are either of Myènè heritage (Rawiri, Merey-Apinda, Eteno, and Aworet, among others) or of the Fang ethnic group. The ethnicity of the Gabonese author, however, is not necessarily apparent to the general reader. Of the numerous Gabonese writers of Fang heritage, perhaps Justine Mintsa and Sylvie Ntsame make the most culture-specific references in their works and the originality of how they present this will be the focus of the next two chapters. However, even if the writing of Mintsa and Ntsame is peppered with Fang oralities, culture, and traditions, it has never been the intention of these authors to limit their audience to readers sharing the same roots.

An interesting point of note is that the Fang ethnic group is scattered among four countries in Central Africa. Outside of Gabon, the largest numbers of Fang live in Cameroon where they are known as the Ewondo, the Beti, and the Bulu (Mba Abessole 15), and populations also exist in Equatorial Guinea, Congo, the Central African Republic, and São Tomé and Principe. Angèle Christine Ondo claims that despite the geographic divides, the Fang culture is rather homogenous with all members claiming to be descendants of the same ancestor, Afiri Kara, the founder of the Fang people (11).[2] Thus, in addition to contributing to a Gabonese national literature, we can also speak of these same authors as writers of the Fang diaspora.

Well into the twenty-first century, it is still common to hear African literatures described as "young" despite the recognition long ago that African oralities are indeed literary genres; Western literary critics continue to devote more attention to published novels, poetry, theater, and short stories and tend to ignore, dismiss, or diminish oral genres, even those that have been meticulously recorded. In Gabon, oral literature is rich with all ethnic groups having their own origin myths and stories. These oralities recount the existence of indigenous groups in Gabon and Central Africa since time immemorial and thus studying such oral literature leads to a better understanding of the published African literature of the same region. By blending new literary forms with old ones, Mintsa and Ntsame have managed to produce the most significant Fang literature since the introduction of the celebrated epic poetry known as the *mvet*. Fang oral literature, like any oral literature, is an attempt to understand a universe, a society, and even oneself and it reflects a tradition as old as its people, for humans have always sought to understand for themselves and for their descendants not only their purpose and personal philosophies, but also the world around them and beyond.

Overall, Gabon has documented oral literature better than many other African countries. Archives include "lullabies, nursery rhymes, games, stories and fables, proverbs, riddles, musical rounds for children, mottoes, genealogies, myths and legends, songs, and epic poetry" (Nang Eyi Obiang 29).[3] It is typical for all of these oralities to convey some sort of lesson or moral whether they are aimed at children or adults.

Gabonese epic poetry—or the *épopée* as it is referred to in French—is perhaps the most sophisticated and culturally complex form of oral literature with each ethnicity in Gabon having its own cultural context and specific name: Fang *mvet*, the Obamba *olendé*, the Punu *mubwang,* and the Apindji *mossodoué* to cite a few. Of these traditions, the *mvet*[4]—the epic poetry of the Fang ethnic group—is the most well-known and widely researched inside and outside of Gabon. The *mvet* as oral performance can be traced to the arrival of the Fang in northern Gabon over two centuries ago, and although studies often give the impression that there was no written literature in Gabon before Zotoumbat's 1971 autobiographical novel *L'histoire d'un enfant trouvé,* a translation and transcription of this art form was actually published in 1970—one year before Zotoumbat's text appeared—by one of the great masters of the *mvet*, Tsira Ndong Ndoutoume.[5]

Upon studying the *mvet* in depth, the art form appears very rigid in terms of theme, instrument used, and how it is performed and by whom. While there is technically no discrimination in terms of the age or sex of the *conteurs* or professional storytellers in Gabon (Monsard 59), the *mvet* is distinct, however, in that traditionally the *mbom mvet* or *mvet* performer is exclusively male and has been initiated into the art form.[6] In fact, in many interpretations, women are explicitly sent away at the beginning of the performance.[7] Can the *mvet* therefore be challenged and introduced in a more contemporary form that includes women as either central characters or interpreters of the art form? Interestingly, Tsira Ndong Ndoutoume gave us the following insight and a possible answer to such a question:

> Lorsque je chantais le *mvet*, quand je jouais du *mvet*, quand je disais le *mvet*, je dansais, je vivais, je m'exprimais en toute tranquilité, en toute liberté. Mais quand je me suis mis à l'écrire, je me suis figé avec un crayon sur un bout de papier. . . . Savez-vous que [vos langues] ne sont pas le français et que le français n'est pas ces langues? Je ne vous jette pas l'anathème. Je vous comprends, parce que ceux qui sont tentés d'écrire, de faire de la littérature à la française, ceux-là n'ont pas tort. Ils vivent leur époque. Ce qui ne veut pas dire que notre littérature ne peut pas s'adapter à cette époque-ci. Elle s'adapte à tout. ("Notre littérature" 36)

> When I was singing the *mvet*, when I was playing the *mvet*, when I was telling the *mvet*, I was dancing, I was living, I was expressing myself in total peace, in total freedom. But when I started to write it, I was stuck with a pencil and a piece of paper. . . . You do realize that your languages are not French and that French is not these languages? I'm not throwing an anathema at you. I understand you, because those who are tempted by writing, by making literature the French way, those individuals are not wrong. They are living the times. This does not mean that our literature cannot adapt itself to these times. It adapts to everything.

Tsira Ndong's words imply one of two messages: either he uses his authority as a revered master of the *mvet* to welcome the contributions of others—including women—into the art form, or rather he is simply stating that change is inevitable and beyond anyone's control; literature in Gabon will continue to evolve, and the *mvet* is no exception. Although Bellarmin Moutsinga admits that the *mvet* in written form loses its sacredness and musicality, he maintains that writing it "is more than necessary" since few are the spaces in Gabon today where oral literature alone can still survive (9). In her article "Personnages et discours féminins dans le roman gabonais," Annie-Paule Boukandou also points out: "The Gabonese novel is a product of oral tradition and it serves to perpetuate it, but can we say that archaic discourse about women has stayed the same? Has it not evolved? Currently, the problem is no longer to denounce male hegemony but rather to have woman's voice heard on all fronts" (114).[8]

Although it is indeed quite common to see the myths and traditions of the ethnic group of an African writer influencing contemporary writing, only the Fang women writers of Gabon have skillfully and artistically infused elements of their indigenous culture, language, and even the *mvet* into the Francophone novel and this is indeed original as this is not evident in other Fang diaspora literatures found in Cameroon, Equatorial Guinea, or Congo. In this regard, novels such as Mintsa's *Histoire d'Awu* (2000) and *Larmes de cendre* (2010) as well as Ntsame's *La fille de Komo* (2004), *Malédiction* (2005), and *Mon amante, la femme de mon père* (2007) teach us about Fang oralities and traditions while providing a window on contemporary society in Gabon at the same time.

To cite one pertinent example, Arnold Nguimbi, author of the essay "De la mort du maître à la mort symbolique de l'école: pour une pratique stylistique dans *Histoire d'Awu* de Justine Mintsa," brilliantly interprets Mintsa's rewriting of the *mvet* epic in the novel through her protagonist schoolteacher Obame Afane who is, according to Nguimbi, the reincarnation of Oyono Ada Ngone, a fifteenth-century Fang elder of great respect and wisdom. Legend has it that the Fang encountered many enemies and numerous battles during their migration from north to south, and Oyono Ada was badly injured during one of these conflicts and left in a comatose state. His people never abandoned him, however, and when Oyono Ada awoke from his coma, he recounted the story of how he was visited while unconscious by a spirit who described to him how to create a divine instrument that would serve to awaken and motivate his people and inspire music and words for the Fang to follow (Nguimbi 144). This is generally believed by the Fang to be the origin of the *mvet*—both the instrument and epic poetry. Christine Ondo also confirms that Oyono Ada is recognized by all *mvet* musicians/interpreters as the creator of the literary genre (14).

Instead of the typical weapons held by the fifteenth-century warrior, Mintsa writes of her modern Fang hero in *Histoire d'Awu*, "Dans sa main droite, Obame Afane tenait un long crayon, arme de son temps" (102; In his right hand, Obame Afane was holding an imposing pencil, the weapon of his time). Nguimbi further explains in his analysis:

> The oration made by Obame Afane's father is presented by the narrator as the modern version of the origin myth of his clan. Born of a line of warriors and priests (an obvious reference to the *mvet*), Obame Afane updates the legend or the Fang epic known as the *mvet* with the "weapon of his time" such that Oyono Ada, the spirit of Obame Afane, constitutes the blood that runs through the veins of all those who belong to the Fang culture. (143)[9]

Tsira Ndong Noutoume's remarks about the novel as Gabonese literature *à la française* are interesting juxtaposed with a study by linguist Kwaku Gyasi. Although an African text may be written in French, it is not to be assumed that the author employs no strategies of "literary decolonization" within it as Gyasi explains in "The African Writer as Translator: Writing African Languages through French": "the European language is pushed and forced to the position of 'minor' language and in that sense ceases to be an instrument of domination" (156). Therefore, novels like Mintsa's *Histoire d'Awu* and others contain cultural and linguistic references that add supplemental meaning that may escape the non-Fang reader who can nonetheless come away fulfilled from the reading despite not being able to grasp some of these underlying references.

This study will cover a significant number of Gabonese women writers of Fang origin. Before more specifics are given about the cultural, historical, and linguistic aspects of the Fang transmitted through these novels, it is perhaps necessary to situate this particular ethnic group demographically. Gabon is a nation of just over 1.5 million people with the Fang comprising nearly forty percent of the population. The Fang live in great numbers in five out of the nine provinces in the country (Mba Abessole 15). In the north of Gabon is where the heaviest concentrations of Fang live, centered around the city of Oyem, considered to be the Fang capital. It is not surprising then that we also find the Fang in the three nations closest to those northern borders—in Cameroon, Congo-Brazzaville, and Equatorial Guinea. Fang peoples were and continue to be separated by colonial borders that Europeans had imposed upon them. The migration pattern of the Fang to their present home in Central Africa has been constructed not only by anthropological research but perhaps most importantly and most recently by oral histories which tell of the Fang's journey and the ancestors common to all of its people. Although there is still a debate among anthropologists over the exact migration route of the Fang, most are in agreement, however, that the Fang are distinct from other indigenous groups in Gabon (Minko Mve 34). Political scientist Paul Mba Abessole supports one of the beliefs concerning Fang migration in his book *Aux sources de la culture Fang* (2006). That is, that the Fang have Egyptian and Sudanese roots, having traveled along the banks of the Red Sea until reaching the Dead Sea where they had settled for approximately 300 years (66). Anthropologists located them in the plateaus and valleys of the Nile between the 15th and 16th centuries (Minko Mve 34). Mba Abessole and other Gabonese contemporaries maintain that the Fang then crossed Egypt, Libya, and Algeria before heading south across Niger, Nigeria, and Cameroon, eventually reaching Gabon by the mid-ninteenth century (66). However, other scholars such as socio-ethnologist Bernardin Minko Mve question why the Fang, a people known to be highly organized and homogeneous, would assume such an erratic path (35) and he believes this theory was likely propagated by ill-informed Western missionaries and anthropologists. Minko Mve posits that the Fang most likely have Central African roots either in the Congo valley or in the region east of Adamaoua, Cameroon (31), in which case they may have been pushed out across the forest by the Peuls (also known as the Fulani). African linguists also confirm this latter theory through the study of languages in the region. Oral histories likewise authenticate this presumption, for Minko Mve cites one Fang myth in particular that describes a people who had to dig their way through a colossal tree trunk that served as a long tunnel, a symbolic reference to a long trek by the Fang across the equatorial forest (33).

In her book *Mariage et violence dans la société traditionnelle Fang au Gabon* (2007), Honorine Ngou emphasizes that there are three principal elements around which Fang culture is centered—marriage, birth, and death—for the mere reason that these three realities are responsible for bringing together families, clans, and ethnic groups (16). It is no surprise then that women writers of Fang origin focus heavily on these subjects in their novels in general, with a special emphasis on how these realities impact women in particular.

FANG TRADITIONS IN SELECTED NOVELS BY JUSTINE MINTSA: *HISTOIRE D'AWU* AND *LARMES DE CENDRE*

Professor of English at Université Omar Bongo in Libreville, former president of the Union des Écrivains Gabonais, and the current Director of Culture in Gabon's Ministry of Culture and Arts,[10] Justine Mintsa is a *grande dame* of Gabonese literature and the first African woman writer to be published by Gallimard. Although Mintsa's novels illustrating elements of Fang culture written into French are routinely cited as celebrated examples of the African Francophone novel, her works have a special significance for the Fang diaspora, meaning that a Beti reader from Cameroon could conceivably have more insights when reading *Histoire d'Awu* than a Gabonese reader of non-Fang origin. This notion will be developed later in the analysis.

While Fang culture is a component in the works of many women writers from Gabon, Justine Mintsa's *Histoire d'Awu* is undoubtedly the quintessential example even though Mintsa's prose in other published works, *Un seul tournant Makôsu* (1994), *Premières lectures* (1997), and *Larmes de cendre* (2010), is also marked by Fang words and poetry clearly inspired by the *mvet* and other forms of oral literature. But Fang culture itself—not only language—is also an important aspect of Mintsa's writings; she seeks to challenge certain oppressive Fang customs at times, but often she educates her readers (Fang and non-Fang alike) about numerous facets of traditional culture that make us question the notion of "progress" in our contemporary world. The unsurpassed richness and intensity of *Histoire d'Awu* provide an obvious insight as to why Gallimard chose the text as one of the novels to launch their new series, Continents noirs, in 2000. In his book *Les registres de la modernité dans la littérature gabonaise*, Fortunat Obiang Essono sums up what *Histoire d'Awu* manages to achieve: "Mintsa transcribes raw life conveyed in her faraway native tongue into a more literary language" (137).[11]

One needs to look no further than Mintsa's title, *Histoire d'Awu*, to see her first attempt of "decolonizing" her novel. To the uninformed reader—which may even be an African reader who is an outsider to the Fang culture—"Awu" in the title refers solely to one of the protagonists in the novel. Awu, the diminutive of Awudabiran', is the second spouse taken by Obame Afane after his beloved first wife, Bella, cannot conceive a child after six years of marriage. Thus, the reader who does not understand the Fang language interprets the syntactic unit "Awu" as nothing more than a proper name. In this case, the title quite simply translates as "The Story of Awu." However, the Fang word *awu* means "death" and the literal translation of the character's full name, Awudabiran', is "death (it) destroys."[12] The reader must have knowledge of this linguistic information in order to seize nuances that allow him or her to interpret the title in two ways, either as "The Story of Awu" referring to the protagonist Awu, or rather "The Story of Death" with the character's full name throughout constantly reminding us about the foundation of the entire novel—scenarios revolving around death, both literally and figuratively.

The idea of death is indeed pervasive in *Histoire d'Awu* and there are four distinct references to this in the novel. For example, Obame's first wife, Bella, dies of a broken heart the day that twins are born to Obame and his new wife, Awu. In a different story line, Obame's twelve-year-old pregnant niece, Ada, is declared "dead" by her mother who is shamed by the adolescent's condition. There is Obame's own death in a bus accident toward the end of the novel. And finally, the clear threat of death hangs over Obame's brother if he dares to force sexual relations on Awu whom he has inherited as his own wife according to tradition after Obame's passing. All of these "deaths," which will be explained later in detail, have severe and often unexpected consequences on the surviving characters in the novel, proving in no uncertain terms that indeed, as the Fang say, "Awudabiran'" (death destroys).

What Mintsa does here in her use of a Fang phrase is ingenious in terms of the literary decolonization of the African Francophone novel. In "The African Writer as Translator," Kwaku Gyasi provides us with a more exact explanation: "In certain instances, comprehension is denied the monolingual reader who is then forced to recognize the importance of the other language in the narrative reconstruction of history and reality" (157). Mintsa's strategy is therefore what Gyasi would call an "experiment of blending African models with European [ones] while subverting or 'violating' them at the same time," by using techniques that "interrupt the narration in French and force the reader to reconstruct the text" (*The Francophone African Text* 119). Of course, readers who know nothing of the Fang language and rely solely on the French can most certainly understand the entire text and come away with a very profound reading, but the underlying layers of the novel provided by the references to Fang are no less than a hidden treasure for those readers who accept Mintsa's challenge to explore the text further.

Histoire d'Awu is separated into three enumerated parts, each with its own chapter divisions. The first part of the novel opens with Awu sewing, a scene that repeats itself throughout the text while drawing particular attention to the "point de chaînette" (chain stitch)—an obvious reference to life as a chain of events and in this case, death is the main link in the story and something that repeats itself. Following this three-paragraph introduction, a single sentence set off from the rest of the text abruptly informs the reader: "Awudabiran' était la deuxième femme de maître Obame Afane" (10; Awudabiran' was the second wife of the schoolteacher Obame Afane). Readers then learn in what almost appears to be a new introduction to the novel that Obame and his first wife, Bella, were very much in love but that they could not conceive a child after six years of marriage. Both realized and accepted that tradition would dictate that a man of Obame's stature would naturally take a second wife, since remaining without heirs was unthinkable as long as polygamy offered a possible solution. Other than the first image of Awu as seamstress, she is also later described by the narrator as "un terrain plus fertile" (10; a more fertile terrain), which plays into a Fang ideal of beauty and eroticism[13] tied to an expectation that women contribute children to the village (Essono 150). Mintsa writes: "Sa deuxième femme avait désormais fait de lui un membre incontestable de la société des hommes" (12; His second wife had made him an incontestable member of male society). This is in direct contrast with the description of Obame's first wife, Bella, who is referred to as "terrain aride" (11; arid terrain).

At no time do Bella and Awu consider one another as rivals; in fact both women are remarkably tolerant and even understanding toward each other. Bella knows that they are in this situation simply because she lacks "la qualité" (11; the quality)—that is, she is unable to produce children. All this rationalizing, however, does nothing to alleviate the sadness that the tradition has created for all three protagonists—Bella, Obame, and Awu. This is obviously a negative aspect of a custom (belonging not only to the Fang of Gabon) that does not allow individuals in a couple to choose each other in marriage, as cited by so many of Honorine Ngou's interviewees in her essay *Mariage et violence*. Bella dies the day Awu gives birth to twins and even years later, Awu still feels she is living with a co-wife since Obame's heart seems to have room for Bella alone. Upon reflecting on her own mother's experience with polygamy, Awu concludes the following about her own situation:

> Mais, en fin de compte, de sa mère qui avait son homme tout à elle une nuit sur deux et d'elle qui avait une moitié d'homme toutes les nuits, qui était la plus à plaindre? (13)
>
> But finally, between her mother who had her man all to herself every other night and she who had half of a man every night, who was to be pitied more?

The novel's second part focuses on the couple's niece, Ada, declared "dead" by her mother, Akut, when it is revealed that the twelve-year-old is pregnant. Akut's only purpose in life was assuring her daughter's success (32); thus in her mother's eyes, the pregnancy shatters all hope for Ada. Symbolically, Akut goes beyond disowning her daughter: "Tu ne viens plus dans ma maison. Pour moi, tu es morte" (31; You are no longer welcome in my house. For me, you are dead). Obame and Awu take Ada into their own home where Awu becomes a second mother to both Ada and the new baby.

The final part of the novel begins with the death of Obame who is killed in a bus accident at the entrance to the capital during his third and final trip to straighten out the documentation necessary in order to receive his teacher's retirement pension, an avenue Mintsa uses to criticize corruption and bureaucracy; if it were not for government inefficiency, there would have been no other reason for Obame to be in the vehicle leading him to his tragic end. The death of Obame is significant in that it shows, according to Arnold Nguimbi's aforementioned essay, the true sacrifice made by those who choose to serve people outside the highly centralized capital (139). Obame's full name is Sikolo Obame Afane, the word *sikolo* in Fang meaning "school" (Nguimbi 132), and thus Mintsa sends a powerful message in killing off Obame in her novel. Nguimbi points out that the giving of such a name is a sacrificial act on the part of Obame's father to show that there is a place for both Western-style education and traditional schooling in contemporary society (Nguimbi 133).[14] If Obame is indeed so intricately tied to the notion of change through new forms of education, his death can only call into question the future of his people and thus his loss is a severe blow to his community. However, Obame's death is to be interpreted as just one event in a cycle of deaths and rebirths in the novel. As tragic as Obame's death may seem, this "disturbance" allows for Awu's character to shine.

Once Obame's passing is announced, in fact, the focus quickly shifts to Fang rituals pertaining to widows to which Awu is subject. Awu is verbally and physically abused by her sisters-in-law as part of these rituals, her belongings are pilfered by guests attending the funeral, and after the mourning period, she discovers not so unexpectedly that she has been inherited by Obame's brother. In her study on Gabonese women, Rose Nguéma Ntsame explains that in terms of tradition, it is inconceivable for a Fang woman to become head of the family or a household and this belief has thus become the foundation for allowing wives to be inherited like property (244).

The writing of Fang culture into the novel is intriguing as well as innovative, for it is more than just an exercise in description for Mintsa—it is a mark of creativity and authenticity that also serves as a social commentary. Although the reader is often plunged into a scene from traditional Africa, he or she relates very easily to the characters who seem strikingly contemporary. Fortunat Obiang Essono confirms: "The trials and tribulations of Awudabiran' and her husband Obame Afane allow us see our own reflection in our desires, our values, and our norms as *modern* Black Africans" (133).[15]

FANG ORIGIN MYTHS, RITUALS, AND CONTEMPORARY LIFE

In the second chapter of the first part of the novel, Mintsa recounts the story of Obame Afane's birth next to the river and in many ways, this chapter serves to recreate some of the familiar aspects of numerous Fang origin myths and yet, "the narrator tells us about that which is universal, the birth of man, his beginning" (Essono 139).[16] It is common for such myths to be set in a location next to a body of water, usually a river, and Mintsa's version is no exception.

Oral literature of the Fang tells us that the founder of the first village was a woman named Ndabiare. With no one to assist her during labor, she gives birth to two children—as the story calls them both—one that is human and another which is an egg (Mba Abessole 9). Ndabiare has a vision that her human son will become the leader of his people. She takes both of the children into her arms and sets off to look for a place to raise them. She ends up walking a very long time until she reaches the edge of a large body of water where she decides to settle. She tosses the egg-child into the water and keeps her human son with her onshore. However, Ndabiare always keeps an eye toward the water to know what has become of her son, the egg (Mba Abessole 10). With this story as his reference, Mba Abessole gives insights as to how the woman was originally regarded within Fang culture. The Fang believe that woman is the carrier of all values in life. As spouse and mother, her specific role is to transmit to her child the story of his or her community (10). Mba Abessole mentions the woman's function as a spouse not as an indication that a wife exists to serve her husband but in the sense that marriage is not to be considered a simple union of two individuals but rather part of a broader construct whose main goal is to enlarge the community to ensure its prosperity. This idea in itself is what makes motherhood more empowering for African women while this notion is generally absent from Western feminist thought. Despite the fact that man is believed to be superior to women in Fang culture (Ngou, *Mariage et violence* 225), women come to their new villages upon marriage where it is not unusual for them to be given names reflecting the hope placed in them that they will help build the community: *ndâ ngoura* (literally, "the entire house"; Ngou 170), or *midzâ*, "the pillar of the village" (Ngou 231). Therefore, it is not uncommon for fathers to be absent from African origin myths, or if they are present, they are often relegated to a minor role.

In *Histoire d'Awu*, Mintsa rewrites the Fang origin myth into a more contemporary version without changing its core message or straying too far from symbols and beliefs revered by the Fang. Mintsa's own narrative describes the birth of Obame Afane, which coincides with the celebration of the building of the first school in the village. Thus, it is not merely by chance that Obame will grow up to be a respected teacher and a recognized leader in education, and in a way, his birth announces new values to be held by his people living in a changing, contemporary world. Through his values and moral standards, Obame is distinguished in his field in opposition to the schoolteachers at Ada's boarding school, for example, who are complicit in the sexual abuse of their students which is responsible, it is later revealed, for the pregnancy of Obame and Awu's pre-teen niece. Thus, in the same way that the aforementioned origin myth foresees Ndabiare's human son as a great leader of his people, the connection has already been made between the new school and Obame who will become the first in his village to introduce French-inspired education in complement with the traditional teachings of the Fang. At one point in the novel, Mintsa even writes that "maître Obame était le père universel" (22; schoolteacher Obame was the universal father).

But even the actual telling of Obame's birth bears much resemblance to the legend of Ndabiare. Like Ndabiare, Obame's mother, Oyane, is alone for the first stages of labor although she eventually crawls to seek the aid of her mother-in-law who tells Oyane to meet her at the riverbed. There, the mother-in-law finds three large and beautiful banana tree leaves for Oyane to lie on during the birth. Although there is no egg in this story, there are equivalent symbols of life much like the egg's purpose in the origin myth—the umbilical cord and the placenta which Mintsa refers to as the "Masse Nourricière" (25; Nourishing Mass) and the "Masse de Vie" (26; Mass of Life), respectively. Curiously, Mintsa concentrates more on these items within the story than on the child himself. Not only does the capitalization of these names given to the umbilical cord and the placenta suggest a sort of a personification of them, but Mintsa describes the mass as "palpitante" (throbbing) as if to say it too has life or relevant energy.

What Oyane's mother-in-law does with these next seems to offer an explanation as to why Ndabiare throws her egg-child into the river. Taking the same path back to the village as she followed to reach the river, the mother-in-law stops halfway to bury the umbilical cord and the placenta in a hole dug with the help of a magnificent machete that had just severed the cord linking Obame and his mother. The narrator recounts:

> La Masse de Vie fut en plein jour une dernière fois avant d'aller se loger dans de nouvelles entrailles: celles de la terre. Cette terre qu'elle allait aussi régénérer. . . . Si la Masse de Vie avait possédé la faculté d'entendre, elle aurait perçu à travers la prière de la grand-mère d'Obame Afane qu'une nouvelle mission lui était assignée: elle devait fertiliser et féconder la terre, qui devait produire pour permettre la vie des hommes et des femmes, appelés à leur tour à perpétuer la lignée. L'aïeule signait un pacte avec la terre: elles avaient toutes deux une mission commune, perpétuer la vie. Un instant plus tard, la Masse de Vie entrait dans sa nouvelle fonction avec la Terre qui se refermait sur elle. (26–27)

> The Mass of Life saw the light of day one last time before taking up residence in its new womb: that of the earth—this earth that it would also regenerate. . . . If the Mass of Life had possessed the ability to hear, it would have noted in the prayer of Obame Afane's grandmother that a new mission was being assigned to it: it was supposed to fertilize and impregnate the earth, it was supposed to produce in order to sustain the life of men and women who in turn were called upon to perpetuate the lineage. The grandmother signed a pact with the earth: both of them had a common mission, to perpetuate life. One moment later, the Mass of Life would enter into its new function with the earth that would close up around it.

Thus, the egg, water, earth, and umbilical cord and placenta all serve similar functions in the Fang origin myth and in Mintsa's retelling of it. The egg is swallowed up by the river just as the Mass of Life is absorbed into the earth, a uniting of symbols of life in both instances. Obame has connections to the symbols surrounding his birth all throughout his life. Obame often swims in the river next to which he was born, showing the unique relationship he has with this body of water, in what can only be described as a ritualistic manner reminiscent of his birth:

> Il se dirigea de nouveau vers la rivière et livra son corps aux fantaisies aquatiques. . . . Il s'allongeait, face au soleil, et nageait de dos au fil de l'eau. Il s'exprimait avec tant de liberté et d'indépendance qu'Awu était presque jalouse de cette rivière. (23)

> He carried himself once again toward the river and surrendered his body to aquatic whims. . . . He stretched himself out on his back, facing the sun, swimming against the current. He was expressing himself with such freedom and independence that Awu was almost jealous of this river.

The other prominent symbol for Obame, the machete used to cut his mother's umbilical cord at his birth, remains in his possession as a continuous source of strength for him. Even though the object technically separated him from his mother, it ironically united them at the same time through the machete's mirror-like qualities; his mother's image was reflected on one side of its shiny blade while the baby's image could be seen on the other as the umbilical cord was severed:

> Quand elle a coupé le cordon ombilical, une des faces de cette lame était de mon côté, et l'autre face, du côté de ma mère, m'unit aussi à elle. Elle représente toute l'ascendance, et moi la descendance. (80)

> When it cut the umbilical cord, one side of this blade was facing me, and the other side, my mother, uniting her with me as well. She represents an entire ancestry, and me, the lineage.

The narration of Obame's birth, striking in both actions and words, stands in stark contrast to that which adolescent mother, Ada, will later undergo at the provincial hospital in the company of a midwife. Instead of three large beautiful banana tree leaves on which to give birth, Mintsa notes that Ada lies on a "matelas recouvert d'une crasseuse toile plastifiée" (54; mattress covered by a filthy plastic-covered cloth). Although Ada's two aunts, Awu and Ntsame, are supporting her at the hospital, and Awu is by her side in the delivery room, their presence goes relatively unnoticed amid the relentless insults of the midwife who shouts at the adolescent mother with incredible hostility:

> Et ne viens pas faire la gamine avec moi. Tu n'as pas fait la gamine quand tu t'es fait engrosser. Tu vas donner la vie, tu vas être une mère. . . . Pousse, imbécile! Tu as suffisamment déshonoré tes parents comme ça en attrapant un gosse à ton âge! Au moins, sauve l'honneur en étant forte! Sors-nous cet enfant! Sinon je te gifle! (54)

> Don't come here acting like a child with me. You weren't acting like a child when you got yourself pregnant. You are going to give life, you will be a mother. . . . Push, imbecile! You have already dishonored your parents enough by having a kid at your age! At least save face by being strong! Send this child out to us! If not, I will smack you!

After the birth, the events remain unceremonious and even irreverent in comparison to how Mintsa narrates Obame's birth earlier. Instead of the polished machete-heirloom that severs the umbilical cord at Obame's birth, there is now nothing but an old razor blade for Ada (55), a blade so rusty that unlike the machete, no reflections of mother and baby could possibly be seen. The placenta is no longer a "Mass of Life" but is called quite simply a "masse de chair" (mass of flesh)—written in the text with no capital letters—handed over to Ada's aunts as medical waste on a bloodied steel tray (55). Awu and Ntsame need to immediately clean the delivery room for the next mother waiting in line, the floor tiles can only be as clean as the sickly pink stains left from previous successive births will allow. As Ada's aunt Ntsame stands outside the hospital perplexed as to what to do with the steel tray, an elderly woman approaches and says:

> Tu ne vas pas garder ce placenta jusqu'à ce que tu retournes dans ton village, tout de même! Cet enfant est né en ville. Et il faut que cette Masse de Vie fertilise la Ville. (59)
>
> You aren't going to keep this placenta until you return to the village, I hope! This child was born in the city. And this Mass of Life must fertilize the City.

This excerpt from the novel is one in which Mintsa laments the loss of the more beautiful Fang traditions and she attributes this loss to urbanization and Westernization which is at times falsely associated with modernity and progress. The fact that an elderly woman utters these words to Ntsame is of course intentional, for the woman's age represents wisdom as well as traditional culture. Her role is much like the one that Oyane's mother-in-law plays in the Fang origin myth. In the text, "Mass of Life" and "City" are capitalized in this citation, creating a new symbolism for "child" and "womb," respectively. It is thus the old woman who restores dignity to ancient Fang rituals that have been forgotten in the city by refusing to call the placenta a "mass of flesh." By saying that the Mass of Life must fertilize the City, Mintsa implies that there is still a place for certain Fang traditions and moral values in a contemporary urban world. In fact, this entire scenario mocks an illusory progress suggested through the harsh but realistic description of "modern Western-style medicine" in provincial hospitals in Gabon. There is something to be said for traditional births in the village when compared to the grossly overcrowded and unsanitary environment of the provincial hospital depicted in the novel. While the mere suggestion that a village birth is safer and more desired in Gabon than a provincial hospital birth may seem shocking to Western ears, this is precisely an example of a conclusion that Mintsa hopes to challenge by infusing traditional oral narratives into her novel. In her book *Recreating Words, Reshaping Worlds*, Aïssata Sidikou tells of the dangers African women writers face in regard to the reception of their novels, risks that Mintsa so skillfully tries to avoid through her approach to writing:

> But the image of African literature conveyed to the non-Western world is still highly distorted, first by the focus on male authors, and second by ignorance of the rich and diverse oral tradition. Even when a female breaks into this new

> literary scene, there is a danger of further distortion because of the profound difference between Western and African values. [Books by Mariama Bâ and Calixthe Beyala] have attracted considerable attention in the West, but there is much debate about the extent to which they convey—or distort—the values of women in Africa who live in both urban and rural contexts and who are not extensively exposed to Western values. (1–2)

Although not originally intended for publication, the verbal art of women, according to Sidikou, remains deeply rooted in people's minds because of its ability to reveal values that are far more representative of African women than one finds in written texts (2). Sidikou further concludes: "Some of this [verbal] art conveys themes of power that outsiders may find astonishing, especially since these narrators may live in societies that are patriarchal" (2). Thus, Mintsa's transmission of oral literature through a seemingly Western form of the novel is yet another means of "literary decolonization" which places African values at the forefront and questions certain aspects Westerners label as "progress" and this effectively empowers the African woman writer.

But of course, Mintsa is not implying that all Fang traditions should be preserved or that they are empowering, as she forcefully illustrates this in the final part of the novel which concentrates on Fang rituals pertaining to widows. In his book *Ngongo des initiés en hommage aux pleureuses du Gabon*, Gabonese *conteur* and scholar Mabik-ma-Kombil describes funeral rituals of several ethnic groups in Gabon, the Fang among them. Mabik-ma-Kombil depicts almost word for word what is recounted by Mintsa in the final chapters of *Histoire d'Awu*, such as the notorious treatment of the widow by her sisters-in-law (45). Following her husband's death, the Fang widow is ritually stripped of her clothing and shaved. She is to sleep on the ground for seven days, deprived of the right to raise her head, talk, eat, or wash unless she has earned permission (Mintsa, *Awu* 96). She is berated or even beaten publically by her sisters-in-law, and obligatorily accused of adultery during the final part of the ritual whether the allegation is true or not. Even in Mintsa's novel, Awu is forced to declare in public how many times she has cheated on her husband after which she is expected to pay a sum for each "offense." However, even a faithful wife such as Awu is not exempt from such punishment, as it is also considered dishonorable for the husband and community that the widow had not been more desirable to others (99).

At the beginning of the funeral ritual, Awu's sister-in-law Akut shouts at her:

> Tu es quoi maintenant? Un zéro, non? Pourquoi t'es pas morte avec ton mari? Hein? C'est pas pour rester à distribuer ton sexe et à jouir toute seule des biens de mon frère? Apportez le piment! Qu'on lui brûle un peu ce sexe qui nous a appartenu et qu'elle ne va pas tarder à faire posséder à gauche et à droite! C'est

> ça, l'amour? Tu ne sais pas qu'ailleurs les femmes qui aiment vraiment leur mari se laissent enterrer vivantes avec lui? (93–94)
>
> What are you now? Nothing, are you? Why didn't you die with your husband? Huh? It's not so you could stay and sleep around and enjoy our brother's possessions all by yourself? Bring the hot pepper! Let's burn this vagina a little, the one that belonged to us which she won't hesitate to offer to others left and right! Is that love? Besides, don't you know that a woman who really loves her husband lets herself be buried alive with him?

If we compare Mintsa's rendition of the ritual in the novel with words from an actual traditional one cited by Mabik-ma-Kombil in his sociological study, we see that the idea conveyed is virtually identical:

> Fais encore la maligne,
> Regarde encore les gens du coin de l'oeil.
> Voilà, il est parti n'est-ce pas?
> Tu veux garder tous les biens,
> Mais tu n'auras rien,
> Nous allons tout reprendre
> Tu le trompais avec d'autres hommes
> Montre-nous comment tu faisais. (45)
>
> Who is showing off now?
> Look around again out of the corner of your eye
> You see, he's gone, isn't he?
> You want to keep all his possessions,
> But you will have nothing,
> We are going to take everything
> You were cheating on him with other men
> Show us how you did it.

In the novel, Awu accepts all that is directed toward her without defiance, even spit in her face and hot pepper forced into her vagina (94). The only way to escape such torture and humiliation would be for Awu or someone else to make a symbolic offering—a coin or other valuable, but Awu rejects this since she is afraid it would send a message that her dead husband was not worth the sacrifice (94). Mabik-ma-Kombil cites two reasons as to why these funeral rituals are so severe. First, it is to remind each individual of his or her vulnerability as each will also one day have the same fate as the deceased. The second intention is to provide an outlet that allows others to air grievances so that the mourning period can remain free of bitterness or guilt (46). This perhaps explains why the harshest treatment comes from Akut, Ada's mother who Obame and Awu crossed by taking her pregnant daughter into their home after she had been outcast. So for Akut, the funeral is her chance for reparations and as Mintsa states in the novel: "En somme, subir ce rituel exorcisait le mal et apaisait l'esprit du conjoint disparu" (96; To sum it up, undergoing this ritual exorcised evil and appeased the spirit of the deceased spouse).

Among Awu's sisters-in-law, Ntsame is the most sympathetic as she attempts to stop the brutal treatment of Awu once and for all though she is unsuccessful. It is perhaps not so ironically the young Ada who finally is able to bring the abuse to an end by comparing the senselessness of her uncle's premature death with the harshness of the ritual toward someone with the innocence of Awu. Ada shouts at her mother, "Tu es en train de faire la même chose que l'injuste destin" (98; You are committing the exact same injustice as destiny has done). It is clear here that Mintsa entrusts the youth with changing such oppressive traditions.

LARMES DE CENDRE: COMPARING AWU AND BILOA

In her most recent novel, *Larmes de cendre* (2010), Justine Mintsa speaks out against the potential cruelty of the Fang ritual pertaining to widows just as she does in *Histoire d'Awu*. Mintsa describes the novel as being similar to *Histoire d'Awu* in that it captures a slice of reality in the north of Gabon. However, she emphasizes that she takes her protagonist Biloa much further when compared to how she chose to write Awu.[17] This is evident in the several unexpected twists that impact Biloa's life in *Larmes de cendre*, and in the unconventional manner in which the ritual for widows is carried out.

Unbeknownst to the reader, the first two pages of *Larmes de cendre* subtly reveal the conclusion of the story. These pages mark the reader so profoundly, however, that he or she immediately realizes upon reading the last page of the novel that it flows beautifully back to the beginning. Mintsa's displacement of the conclusion as an introduction to the novel is symbolic of a new beginning—and a new story—for the remaining characters. But initially, the reader knows nothing of nine-year-old Lili who calmly but resolutely vows to seek revenge on her mother's behalf, nor is the reader aware of what is provoking the actions of the father whom Lili is observing as he sets an object aflame in his garden (7–8). It is only understood that the novel's title emerges from this first scene.

After this brief introduction, the reader is introduced to a young physician and avid painter named Kan who is assigned to a provincial town given the fictitious name, Otôn. Once settled in, Kan solicits donations for medical supplies for his practice and one day, while picking up packages from customs at the airport, he crosses paths with a stunning woman dressed all in blue. From this point on, Kan refers to this character throughout as "La Bleue" (12) even though the reader learns much later her true name is Biloa. Kan subsequently cannot stop thinking about Biloa but as he knows nothing more about her at this point, he spends his free time almost obsessively painting portraits of her, highlighting all aspects of her beauty as he interprets them on canvas.

Although all of the characters in the novel initially seem very disconnected from one another, Mintsa soon skillfully links them together through her creative story line. In the following chapter, a brother and sister, Meduk and Cécile, appear at Kan's door seeking emergency medical treatment for their brother-in-law, Ondo. It turns out that Cécile and Kan have met before at a cocktail party for local professionals the night before. Ondo is obviously very sick, but Kan cannot pinpoint what is wrong with him exactly and suggests that he seek help at a better-equipped medical facility. Kan becomes curious about Cécile and has a premonition that she will reappear in his life in some capacity.

The next chapter begins with a "rituel de veuvage" (widowhood ritual) reminiscent of what Awu undergoes in *Histoire d'Awu*. The widow is none other than Biloa who submits to the harsh ritual much to the dismay of her in-laws but at the insistence of her own family (23). The Fang ritual that served as a reference in *Histoire d'Awu* reappears in *Larmes de cendre* as well, but in a much more brutal and devastating fashion. Although the ritual calls for severe treatment, considered a means of atonement for the wrongs of the couple and their families, Biloa's family knows no limits, arranging for her to be raped in secret as she is led away supposedly to be able to relieve herself (24). The disturbing scene likens Biloa to a ewe being attacked by an unleashed ram:

> Seulement cette fois-ci, elle sentit à mi-chemin qu'on lui faisait changer de direction. Ensuite, tout se passa très vite. Elle entendit une porte s'ouvrir. Elle fut presque poussée à l'intérieur . . . deux paires de bras la maintinrent fermement dans la position courbée tandis que deux mains viriles dénudaient fiévreusement son postérieur . . . on lui enfonça un chiffon dans la bouche pour l'empêcher de crier. Et la brebis, enserrée dans l'étau, subit, sans recours, les assauts séismiques d'un bélier déchaîné. (23–24)

> Only this time, she felt midway that they were making her change direction. Next, everything happened so fast. She heard a door open. She was almost pushed inside . . . two pairs of arms held her firmly in a hunched-over position while two male hands feverishly exposed her buttocks . . . someone shoved a rag in her mouth to prevent her from screaming. And the ewe, held tight in the vice, underwent with no recourse, an unleashed ram's seismic attacks. (24)

A violated Biloa sinks into a state of madness shortly thereafter, imitating the actions and sounds of the helpless ewe under attack, ultimately revealing to the family what had happened to her (29). In his essay on *Larmes de cendre*, Didier Odounga describes the rape as a ritual of its own, devised by

Cécile; it is Biloa alone subjected to an initiation leading her to an "emotional, spiritual, and psychological death" (Odounga 54).

The following chapter shifts once again to Kan who has by chance run into Cécile at a reception. During their conversation, she informs him of her brother-in-law's death while he speaks casually to her of his plans to travel to Benin to discover the country and origins of his father, a subject about which his father had always remained curiously silent (31).

Six months pass, and Kan decides to visit his parents in the capital where he learns that his father, a lawyer, is defending a client who had been raped during a ritual called "akengha" (33). This launches a commentary about the destruction and harm caused by certain traditions in contemporary society: "Quand une coutume deviant génocidaire, il faut quelqu'un pour dire 'stop'" (34; When a custom becomes genocidal, it needs to stop). Kan leaves his parents and returns to his work in Otôn, not knowing the exact details of the case. However, he is more determined than ever to realize his trip to Benin to know if such customs exist there as well. He runs into Cécile again and she accepts his rather spontaneous proposal to accompany him on his travels.

At the airport in Cotonou, the two are greeted by Kan's cousin, Gou, who brings them to the palace where Kan learns his grandfather is a king. However, when the three enter the courtyard of the family's residence, Cécile is knocked to the ground by a mysterious force emanating from the "arbre tentaculaire" (sprawling tree) there (42). Kan is informed that Cécile is no longer welcome at the family home for it is obvious that she is harboring evil. At first, Kan protests, but Cécile is more than happy to continue her stay at a nearby hotel. From this point on, Kan and Cécile go their separate ways, except for an occasional breakfast together at the hotel. Kan connects with his family about whom he knew so little, eventually learning that all the men in his family line are mysteriously protected by this same tree. Therefore, Cécile's succumbing to its forces becomes proof of her intention and/or willingness to do harm to Kan (67).

Upon returning from Benin, Kan visits his parents and learns that the client his father is defending is none other than La Bleue/Biloa and one of the accused is her powerful sister, Cécile (73). A couple of months later, La Bleue, still in a state of profound madness, is brought by her sister-in-law for a consultation with Kan. At this point, Biloa can no longer speak (83) and she is a "corps sans âme" (body without a soul) resulting from "an absolute hatred of her body that she rejects as something that is outside herself" (Odounga 54). Kan proscribes Biloa a treatment that includes art therapy, advising her to draw the images that haunt her. Eventually, Biloa's condition improves, especially after a time composing a magnificent flower garden in Kan's courtyard, another component of her therapy (93).

Kan and Biloa fall in love and eventually marry after a few years, but Biloa refuses a customary marriage in light of what happened to her in the name of "tradition." This causes all kinds of complications for both sides of the family and even for Kan who admits missing the opportunity to take advantage of some of the rich culinary and symbolic traditions concerning marriage:

> Cette position de La Bleue me frustrait un peu, car le mariage coutumier est pour tout bon Africain l'occasion de s'affirmer socialement à travers les nouvelles alliances; l'occasion de se réjouir sur les airs et les danses du terroir; l'occasion d'apprécier des morceaux d'éloquence traditionnelle; de s'imprégner des règles de bienséance entre alliés et, pourquoi pas, de faire valoir notre art culinaire, ainsi que nos costumes traditionnels. (100)

> La Bleue's position frustrated me a bit because traditional marriage is for any true African the occasion to affirm oneself socially through the establishment of new unions; the occasion to delight in local song and dance; the occasion to appreciate traditional bits of eloquently expressed wisdom; to be steeped in family rules of etiquette, and why not, to highlight our culinary art as well as our traditional clothing.

Biloa's family refuses to participate in the civil marriage and essentially abandons her thereafter. Kan's parents, especially his mother, never quite accept Biloa because of her tainted past and Biloa is overwhelmed by feelings of guilt when she realizes that even the relationship between her husband's parents has suffered because of her (109). In addition to all this, Biloa still has to contend with the consequences of her *akagha*[18] placed on the daughters of the family by their aunt, Biloa's mother's childless sister-in-law. According to Odounga, the *akagha* is linked to the Fang legend of the Evu, a being that embodies evil and who lives in the forest until a woman brings him back with her to her village—thus the belief is, according to Odounga, that it is a woman who first introduced death into the community (53).

The *akagha* dictated that the girls in the family would be powerful, wealthy, and of high social standing, but in turn, they could never marry or have children without risking death (21). Cécile willingly accepted her *akagha*, and became the most powerful, even replacing her father in importance and authority in the family. Biloa was the only sister to openly defy the *akagha* by marrying Ondo, and later, Kan. Biloa is troubled by all of these issues to the point of suffering debilitating feelings of sadness. In an attempt to improve the couple's morale and to show their devotion to each other, Kan convinces Biloa that they should have a child together (118), even though it will defy once again the restrictions established by the *akagha*.

Cécile is never convicted in court for lack of solid evidence proving that she played a role in organizing the rape, and not unexpectedly, there is a hatred that lingers between the two sisters. Biloa dies of a mysterious allergic reaction hours after giving birth to her daughter, leading family members to debate if her death was a murder or a suicide (129), but the reader senses it is linked to the *akagha*. Thus, Odounga's aforementioned interpretation of the *akagha* can readily be applied here to the character of Cécile in the novel. Cécile brings death to her family and to Biloa in particular, literally and figuratively. In the end, Biloa's rebellion is no match for the power of the *akagha* and tradition. Because of the absence of a dowry and a formal ceremony, Biloa's family use this as an excuse to claim her body, and prevent her husband from knowing any details about her burial. Traditional law furthermore supports this action by Biloa's family: "Et une femme qui n'est pas dotée n'est pas une femme mariée" (134; And a woman for whom there is no dowry is not a married woman).[19]

Biloa's family proposes to release the body to Kan upon payment of a ransom of sorts, but Kan ultimately refuses, reasoning that in doing so, he would be surrendering to the evil of the very rituals that Biloa despised so much. He resigns himself to a fact: "Cette tradition avait fini par nous rattraper" (137; This tradition has finally caught up with us).

The novel ends with Kan's father opening up to him about his reasons for leaving Benin, a story similar to his son's in that he too was threatened by evil forces that he did not want to see affecting Kan's life (140). Cécile eventually loses her lucrative job which had ultimately given her power in the family, and she ends up in a psychiatric hospital. On the final page, Kan burns the khaki-colored envelope containing the disturbing drawings his wife completed at the start of her treatment with him over a decade before (143).

In *Histoire d'Awu*, the ritual for widows is an important element of the novel, but it is by no means the sole focus; the story is very much about the rich lives of both Awu and Obame and their growing into a relationship with one another in a changing society. The novel does not actually truly become Awu's story alone until after Obame's death and the widow's ritual marks that transition. In *Larmes de cendre*, however, this ritual is the point around which every aspect of the novel revolves and every character is plagued by it in some manner. In both *Histoire d'Awu* and *Larmes de cendre*, however, Mintsa emphasizes that tradition has become a tool of manipulation, used for purposes that society perhaps never intended. "On ne fait pas appel à la coutume que quand on y trouve son intérêt, sinon on marche dessus!" (*Larmes* 120; People only bring up tradition when it serves their interests, if not, they walk all over it!). Gabonese literary critic Béatrice Bikene Bekale calls this an example of the "falsification of traditions" (92). Mintsa also calls this manipulation a form of "terrorism" (99), and this was the very message that Angèle Rawiri conveyed in *Elonga* in her explanation of how sorcery impacts development and rids the country of its most productive citizens. Despite their claims of loyalty to "African-ness," Biloa's family in the end does not even hold or participate in a widower's ritual for her husband, according to the custom (133).

Thus, Mintsa presents a new analysis of tradition and how it plays out in contemporary society; often it is a criticism of people and not of tradition itself. As Mintsa reminds us in *Histoire d'Awu*, "La coutume, c'est les gens . . . " (Awu 106, ellipsis in original; The custom is people . . .). In the Fang ritual, it is usually a widow's in-laws that control her fate. But in this case, it is ironically Biloa's in-laws who wish to protect her and save her from the wrath of the full ritual: "Beyeme et sa femme Mayenamis avaient été fermes: ils ne voulaient pas qu'on fît subir à la veuve de leur fils, le rituel dans sa totalité" (20; Beyeme and his wife Mayenamis had been firm: they did not want the widow of their son to be subjected to the ritual in its entirety). Biloa's own family is actually against the wishes of her in-laws to spare her and cite as their reason that they respect the tradition because it is part of a rich heritage, thereby suggesting that those who do not follow it are somehow less African:

> Nous sommes des Africains. Nous sommes de vrais Noirs. Eux, ils veulent jouer aux Blancs. Ils rejettent leur culture, et ça, les Ancêtres le font payer très cher. (22)

> We are Africans. We are true Blacks. As for them, they want to act like Whites. They reject their culture and for that, the Ancestors will make them pay dearly.

The Fang ritual pertaining to widows is meant to be one of purification and atonement, but it is also considered a way of casting out evil spirits and of sheltering a widow from psychological turmoil after the mourning period (Ngou, *Mariage et violence* 236). However, underlying factors explaining Biloa's family's thinking are revealed as the novel progresses and thus, the reader is soon suspicious of the family's declaration of "African-ness." With the exception of Biloa, most of the family members spanning two generations are jealous and weak or else those who are strong are incapable of love, compassion, or empathy and prefer to operate instead using power struggles, manipulation, and fear. This is the impact of the *akagha* on the family.

Publically, the family adheres to a belief that undergoing the full ritual is Biloa's ultimate proof of her commitment toward her late husband and thus the only way of dissuading claims that she did not love her husband enough (23). But the ritual is an act of revenge by her own family for her defiance of the *akagha*. Pretending that they are concerned for Biloa and Biloa alone, her family convinces her to go through with a version of the ritual—undisclosed to Biloa—that they offer to stage for her. This "protection" is a manipulation that will serve their own interests since they believe Biloa's defiance might in some way jeopardize their own promise for acquiring wealth and power, and thus they consider the full ritual as reparations for this defiance:

> Les parents de Biloa voulaient réparer l'erreur de cette dernière en lui donnant une nouvelle chance de refaire sa vie, dans le sens qui les arrangeait. Le rituel de veuvage était une occasion inespérée. (22)
>
> Biloa's family wanted to fix her error by giving her a new chance to start her life anew, in a way that they found suitable. The widowhood ritual was their only chance.

As the Fang *rituel de veuvage* dictates, Biloa's head was shaved, and she was dressed in a worn *pagne* and placed onto the ground with female family members overseeing her (20). But her in-laws wished the ritual to go no further than the point where Biloa is installed on the ground, with the rest of the gestures to remain symbolic: "Les instructions étaient formelles: on ne devait ni l'insulter, ni porter la main sur elle" (20; The instructions were clear: no one was supposed to insult her or lay a hand on her). Her sisters-in-law even bring Biloa a blanket, an act of kindness that outrages her immediate family, causing them to react as such: "Vraiment, ils n'aiment pas notre fille! Ils font tout pour qu'elle ne souffre pas!" (21; They really don't like our daughter! They are doing everything possible for her not to suffer!).

Although the *rituel de veuvage* is known to be brutal, the "acte clé" (key act), as Biloa's sister calls it (22), surpasses anything imaginable that would typically stem from the traditional ritual as we are speaking of actual rape here; the scene proves that Biloa's family knows no limits in citing "tradition" not only as an excuse to manipulate a situation in their favor, but also to morally and physically ruin others to gain more power. Throughout *Larmes de cendre*, Mintsa criticizes those who misrepresent and twist tradition in this manner, with its victims amounting to "hostages" (127).

In *Histoire d'Awu*, Awu's destiny is not quite as tragic as that of Biloa and in fact, we can say that Awu is not entirely helpless in affecting change in her society. At the same time, she is cautious about assuming certain roles and positions not only because they may hurt Obame's legacy, but also because she is realistic about what she can accomplish as one woman. When Awu's brother-in-law, Nguema, comes to the very bedroom she had shared with her husband, he reminds her quite frankly: "Tu es une chose et les choses ne possèdent pas" (104; You are a thing and things can't be owners). Awu admits: "La chose que je suis ne peut rien contre toute une communauté, contre toute une tradition" (105; The thing that I am can do nothing against an entire community, against all of tradition). Privately, however, she has begun to refuse certain traditions in trying to reconcile two different worlds. For the sake of appearance and to protect her children, Awu will acknowledge publically that she is traditionally bound to her brother-in-law, but she informs him behind closed doors that none of the money she earns from sewing will go to him or to his family (107) and that most importantly, he should not expect to have sexual relations with her, threatening him with death by the very machete used at Obame's birth to separate him from his mother. The brother-in-law inquires in disbelief, "Et la coutume?" (106; And what about the custom?). Once again, we are reminded that "the custom is people" (106).

As her brother-in-law continues to insist, Awu makes one final analogy to convince him of her determination. She illustrates her point through the red ink of her husband Obame the schoolteacher's grade book, which stains her hands like the blood that will potentially spill through the force of her own "corrections," as she calls them. Awu claims:

> Ecoute, à partir de cet instant, ces deux mains que tu vois vont se mettre à corriger beaucoup de choses dans ma vie, aussi vrai que je m'appelle Awudabiran'. (106)

> Listen, from this moment on, these two hands that you see are going to start correcting a lot of things in my life as sure as I am called Awudabiran'.

Of course, the reference to the true meaning of her name, "death destroys" is apparent here. The first "correction" being the refusal of financial help for her brother-in-law's family, the second correction, however, refers directly to a warning:

> Et pour la deuxième correction, la tradition n'arrêtera pas ma main le jour où tu poseras ta tête sur mon oreiller, regarde de quelle couleur sera ta semence. Regarde bien, lorsqu'elle jaillira de ton corps, tu auras déjà rejoint Obame Afane, je te le promets! (107–108)

> And for the second correction, tradition will not stop my hand the day you rest your head on my pillow—look what color your semen will be. Take a good look, because when it gushes forth from your body, you will have already joined Obame Afane, this I promise you!

The suggestion here that Awu is also an educator is intriguing. Although it offers an additional connection to her deceased husband—making her a warrior of sorts—Mintsa is also distinguishing between formal and traditional education and the need to raise children with both. While Mintsa implied early on that Obame Afane was a contemporary schoolteacher who had not forgotten his roots, this new focus on Awu as educator reminds us of a variation of an African proverb common to many oral traditions that Nigerian writer Buchi Emecheta summarizes in her essay "Feminism with a Small 'f'": "It is true that if one educates a woman, one educates a community, whereas if one educates a man, one educates a man" (175).

The term "correction" is also not used in an incidental manner. Aside from its reference to a correction made by an educator, the term is used in the novel to convey a moment where Awu appropriates power from a man who in turn had believed himself endowed with such authority because of tradition. It is a story reminiscent of the brave fighters of the *mvet*; Awu is now one of these warriors in Minsta's contemporary *mvet*, and the weapons that will serve her are none other than the symbolic red-ink pen and most importantly, the machete hidden in the secret compartment of her bed, placed there, unbeknownst to Nguema, by her husband well before his death (80–81). The machete is, of course, the same one used to separate Obame from his mother at birth. Both of these weapons have been passed along to Awu; while they will not ensure her immortality, they will certainly empower and protect her.

This authority that Awu manages to conquer in her own way is that which allows a man to believe he can "correct" his wife as if she were a child, but in this case with a "sometimes inexplicable physical violence" as Pascal Mulangu Binene explains (29).[20] As Honorine Ngou states in *Mariage et violence*: "Submission, respect, and fidelity were thus the magic words in women's lives of traditional Fang society" (216).[21] Of course, Awu exhibited all of these characteristics throughout her marriage to Obame and most notably during the entire course of the *rituel de veuvage*. However, Awu demands now that her brother-in-law submit to her will, and threatens the utmost in physical violence as her mode of correction if he chooses not to respect this. Even if only within the confines of the bedroom she and her husband Obame once shared, Awu has effectively overturned an oppressive power structure. The machete symbolizes to Nguema the threat of death hanging over him. As Pascal Binéné points out, "Power is effective only if one can decide the life and death of individuals, if one's desires can be carried out in the reality without obstacle. This is why power is frightening" (51).[22] This is exactly what Nguema realizes, forcing his submission:

> Awu la Docile pour tout le village. Mais pour lui, c'était Awu la Furie, qui au fil des nuits, se métamorphosait en Awu la Diablesse dans ses rêves. (108)
>
> She was known in the entire village as Awu the Docile One. But for him, it was Awu the Fury, which after several nights morphed into Awu the She-Devil in his dreams.

In the final pages of *Histoire d'Awu*, readers are shown one last time the true meaning of the name, Awudabiran', or "death destroys." In spite of the initial impressions conveyed in the title, Mintsa soon makes it clear that Awu as protagonist is not to be considered a negative force in the novel, but rather one with power that is uncorrupted. Through scenarios surrounding death and Awu's subsequent handling of them, the reader becomes aware of how death can lead to reflection and healing for an individual or a community and these outcomes are certainly some of the more positive aspects conveyed in such rituals and customs found in Gabon and elsewhere on the continent. As Africanist Jeanne Dingomé writes: "In ritual cosmology, even death is not a final stage, but an initiatory journey and a higher state of consciousness that everyone must attain" (15).

Gabonese women authors like Mintsa are not alone in rewriting authentic funeral rituals into their works. Indeed, Cameroonian author Werewere Liking takes on a similar approach in her play *The Power of Um*, a contemporary version of a Bassa funeral ritual. Like Mintsa's Awu, Liking's protagonist, Ngond Libii, rebels against the harsh treatment imposed upon widows in her society. In the Bassa context, tradition dictates that widows be silent with their ears plugged after the death of a husband. However, it is the normally voiceless and supposedly ritually silenced Ngond Libii who brings mourners to the realization of their faults that have led in part to the death of their leader and to the symbolic death of their rich culture. Similarly to what Liking does with Bassa culture, Mintsa questions Fang tradition as much as she praises it, criticizing certain aspects of both urban and rural lifestyles, showing both African and Western values each having their merits and flaws. This is one of the essential contributions of African women's writing since Western feminist studies tend to emphasize erroneously, according to Oyèrónké Oyěwùmí, "how tradition victimizes women" (1997, xiv). Mintsa expresses her utopian vision of tradition through Biloa's words in *Larmes de cendre*, a vision without which neither man nor woman can truly be free:

> Pour moi la chance, c'est d'abord de n'être pas d'ici, c'est de vivre dans un pays où la tradition n'est pas une arme d'intimidation qui oblige les gens respectueux de leur culture à servir les intérêts des gens sans scrupules, calculateurs de bas étage. Pour moi, le premier visage de la chance, c'est la liberté avec le respect de l'autre. Ici, qui est libre? Mon cas mis à part, qui est vraiment libre? Dis-moi. Les femmes? Non. Les hommes? Non. (114)

> First of all, I wouldn't call it luck to be here; I would be lucky if I lived in a country where tradition is not a weapon of intimidation that obliges people who are respectful of their culture to serve the interests of the unscrupulous, calculating people of the lowest kind. For me, the true face of luck, it is freedom with respect for the other. Who among us is free? My case aside, who is truly free? Tell me. Women? No. Men? No.

As is the case with many works by Gabonese women writers, the names of countries, cities, and villages in Mintsa's novels are fictitious even though they, along with many of the traditions, are readily identifiable. However, Mintsa's intent is to direct her question not only to her fellow Gabonese, but rather this philosophical inquiry is relevant universally and is one of the many ways which Gabonese literature speaks to the masses. Still, Mintsa stated in a personal interview that she is sometimes criticized for writing about traditional Africa, implying that others believe there are more contemporary issues to address in literature. To this, Mintsa confidently retorts, "But who will write about Gabon if I don't, if we don't?"[23] Undeniably, however, Mintsa addresses modernity in her texts that seem very much about tradition. As Fortunat Obiang Essono explains: "Modernity in the work of Justine Mintsa comes through in the expression of concern and disillusionment over the post-colonial world, prisoner of its own contradictions between progress and decline, novelty and archaism (163)."[24]

In *Les orthographes de l'oralité*, Bellarmin Moutsinga states: "The fact that Gabonese literature is directly inspired by oral tradition shows that the author's own people are the primary audience." Speaking about texts by the Fang diaspora writer, Moutsinga further claims, "It is first and foremost the Fang people who will understand the best, and before anyone else" (65).[25] Moutsinga is referring here specifically to images, symbols, and systems commonly known to anyone immersed in the Fang culture. Two more writers of Fang origin, Sylvie Ntsame and Honorine Ngou, will be the focus of the following chapters as we further explore this question of addressing a Fang audience without alienating other readers, exploring the struggle between what is modern versus what is traditional and the reworking of oral traditions and rituals of the Fang in the Gabonese novel.

NOTES

1. I chose not to include Bessora as a Gabonese writer per se and thus a chapter is not dedicated to her works in this study. Born in Brussels to a Swiss mother and a Gabonese father, Bessora is considered by many as a European writer and my research has shown that she has much fewer ties to Gabon than other diaspora writers such as Alice Endamne who lives in the United States and Nadia Origo who resides in France. Like Mintsa, Bessora publishes with Gallimard and has produced more novels than Mintsa overall so if she is to be considered as a Gabonese novelist by some, she is certainly one of the most prolific and acclaimed.

2. Westerners did not have any contact with the Fang until the early nineteenth century and although some Fang believe that Afiri Kara was a descendant of Noah (Fouda 23), the exact origin of the Fang people is still debated by scientists and researchers. There is more to follow on this subject in this same chapter.

3. The quote from the French reads: "berceuses, comptines, jeux, contes et fables, proverbes, énigmes, formulettes, devises, généalogies, récits mythiques, chants, épopées." It should be noted that these are only to be considered relative equivalents in French since for some of these oralities, it is particularly difficult to apply a French term to the African context since they denote terms of genre adopted from French which does not always capture the cultural nuances of these oralities created and practiced in Francophone Africa.

4. The term *mvet*, in addition to the epic poem itself, also refers to the instrument and the musician/*conteur* who performs the *mvet*. I have used the common spelling "mvet" throughout this text but it is not uncommon for the term to be written as "m'vet" and "mvett" as well.

5. Tsira Ndong Ndoutoume was actually a disciple of Zwe Nguema who published *Un Mvet par Zwe Nguema* with Armand Colin in Paris in 1972 even though the text and the recording were actually prepared in 1960.

6. In the Fondation Mebege's video entitled *Quelques maîtres—Mvett* (2010), a female, Ayingone Ondo, is pictured among the masters. www.youtube.com/watch?v=HSe86jlabvo.

7. In Essindi Mindja's 2009 interpretation, for example, the sorcerer decries, "Femmes, eloignez-vous! Y a-t-il encore des femmes aux environs?" (15; Women, go away! Are there still any women around?).

8. The original French citation reads, "Le roman gabonais procède de la tradition orale et la perpétue, mais pouvons-nous dire que le discours archaïque concernant la femme est le même? N'a-t-il pas évolué? Le problème actuellement n'est plus de dénoncer l'hégémonie masculine, mais de faire entendre sa voix sur tous les plans."

9. Nguimbi's quote in French reads: "L'oraison faite par le père d'Obame Afane est présentée par le narrateur comme une version actualisée du mythe fondateur de son clan. Issu d'une lignée de guerriers et de prêtres (référence faite au Mvett), Obame Afane réactualise avec 'l'arme de son temps,' la légende ou l'épopée Fang: le mvett. Telle Oyono Ada, l'esprit d'Obame Afane doit constituer la sève qui coule dans les veines de tous ceux qui appartiennent à la culture Fang."

10. Mintsa's official title is Directrice de la Culture au Ministère de la Culture et des Arts.

11. Essono's original citation in French reads: "Mintsa transcrit la vie brute de sa lointaine langue d'origine dans un langage plus littéraire."

12. In "*Histoire d'Awu* de Justine Mintsa," Ovono Mendame translates the full name Awudabiran' as "la mort dérange" (death disturbs) or "la mort nuit" (death destroys). Taking the name apart syntactically with the help of Akomo-Zoghe's *L'art de conjuguer en fang*, however, confirms the translation is closer to "death, it destroys."

13. Awu's svelte figure is actually looked down upon in her village and not considered beautiful. She considers this to be one possible reason why her husband may not find her attractive despite her ability to provide him children. "Elle savait bien qu'à cause de cette taille fine en dépit de plusieurs maternités, elle n'était pas un canon de beauté pour le village" (16; She knew well that because of this slim waistline despite several pregnancies, the village did not consider her beautiful).

14. Nguimbi states in French: "Il y a une place pour les deux entités: l'école et la tradition. Sans se renier, le père d'Obame Afane a choisi Sikolo tel un geste sacrificiel. Il donne en effet, à l'école, son fils censé devenir prêtre comme lui, dans une société où les valeurs se transmettent de génération en génération, de la même manière, c'est-à-dire de père en fils" (There is a place for the two entities: school and tradition. Without betraying his own ideals, Obame Afane's father chose Sikolo as a sacrificial act. He literally gives his son who had been destined to become a priest like himself, to the school, this in a society where values are transmitted from generation to generation in the same way. That is, from father to son).

15. The original French quote reads: "Les vicissitudes d'Awudabiran' et de son mari Obame Afane nous permettent de nous mirer dans nos désirs, nos valeurs et nos normes de négro-africains *modernes*." The quote is cited from Volume 2 of *Les registres de la modernité dans la littérature gabonaise*.

16. Esssono's original citation in French reads: "Le narrateur nous conte l'universelle naissance d'un homme, son commencement."

17. Personal interview with Justine Mintsa, March 8, 2011.

18. According to Akomo-Zoghe's book *Parlons Fang*, the French equivalent for the word *akagha* is *ordalie*. Dictionaries define *ordalie* as "a judgment handed down by god(s)" and the French term was mostly used in the Middle Ages.

19. Mintsa shows here that traditional law often overrides judicial law. Honorine Ngou points out in *Mariage et violence* that dowry has been officially declared illegal in Gabon since 1963 (222). However exchange of dowry still occurs almost without exception today in both urban and rural areas, and not just among the Fang. Sometimes a dowry is offered in a more symbolic manner, but in rural areas, the collection of a dowry may cause tremendous financial hardship for a family (Ngou 200).

20. The French citation reads, "C'est fort de ce pouvoir qu'un homme peut se permettre de 'corriger' sa femme, comme on le fait avec les enfants, par une violence physique parfois inexplicable."

21. The original French citation reads, “Soumission, respect, fidélité étaient donc les maîtres-mots dans la vie des femmes de la société traditionnelle Fang.”

22. The original French citation reads, “Le pouvoir n’est effectif que si l’on peut décider de la vie et de la mort des individus, si ses désirs peuvent s’inscrire sans obstacle dans la réalité. C’est pourquoi le pouvoir est effrayant.”

23. Personal interview, March 8, 2011, in Libreville.

24. Essono’s original quote in French is as follows: “La modernité dans l’œuvre de Justine Mintsa s’exprime à travers l’inquiétude et le désenchantement devant un monde post-colonial, prisonnier de ses contradictions entre progrès et régression, nouveauté et archaïsme.”

25. The original quotations in French read: “Le fait que la littérature gabonaise s’inspire directement de la tradition orale montre que le premier public sollicité par les écrivains est leur peuple” and “C’est d’abord le peuple des Fang qui saisira le mieux, et avant tout autre” (65).

Chapter Three

Fang Culture, *Bwitifang* Spirituality, and the *Mvet* in the Novels of Sylvie Ntsame

Former president of the Union des Écrivains Gabonais[1] and founder of one of the first female-owned publishing houses on the African continent, Éditions Ntsame in Libreville,[2] Sylvie Ntsame is undoubtedly one of the most ambitious and active promoters of Gabonese literature today. A major presence in African literature, Ntsame has published four well-received novels and a collection of short stories. Ntsame's works *La Fille du Komo* (2004), *Malédiction* (2005), *Mon amante, la femme de mon père* (2007), *Femme libérée, femme battue* (2010), and *Le soir autour du feu* (2010) teach us about oralities, customs, and spiritual beliefs while at the same time providing a window on contemporary society in Gabon. Much like we observe in Justine Mintsa's *Histoire d'Awu* in which the Fang language is given a privileged and unique position thereby adding symbolism and depth to the novel, Ntsame's usage of the Fang language is as equally pervasive if not more so and adds additional layers of meaning to the reading to most of her works. In *Mon amante, la femme de mon père*—the only one of Ntsame's works to take place entirely in the Fang village[3]—one finds numerous pages of dialogue written in Fang and presumably followed by an exact translation in French such as this example demonstrates: "Minkueh ma ke awu! Je pars demain à un décès, lance-t-elle à leur endroit" (74).

However, breaking down the Fang sentence syntactically shows that what follows in French is not an exact translation. In Fang, "ma" is the personal pronoun "I," "ke" is the verb "partir," and "awu," as we learned from Mintsa's *Histoire d'Awu*, signals death. However, the term "minkueh" is a form of address and could not be confused in any way with "demain" as a reader could be led to believe by reading the French sentence only. "Tomorrow" translates into Fang as "okiri," a word that does not appear in the sentence at all. Had "okiri" been included, it would have been placed last in the statement. Ironically, a reader who does not know the Fang language may even end up annoyed at reading throughout the novel what appears to be the repetitiveness of the same sentences, first in Fang and then in French. And yet, a closer analysis reveals that Ntsame is preciously hanging on to nuances in Fang which will escape the non-Fang reader who is nonetheless provided with enough linguistic information in French to comprehend the dialog and the novel. Ntsame intentionally approaches writing in this manner as a means of decolonizing the African text and redefining the Francophone novel.

In his essay on Ntsame's works included in the collection entitled *Littératures francophones et comparatisme*, Rodrigue Ndong ultimately agrees with this assertion, claiming that Ntsame's ideal reader is one who knows both French and Fang and who can thus authenticate or invalidate Ntsame's translation and/or paraphrasing (96). In the same essay, Ndong cites at least three other examples in the novel *Malédiction* where only the Fang reader can truly be in the know, forcing others to look for additional meaning beyond the text. In the sentence, "Souhaitons seulement que notre *mone* Nguema soit comme Ondo" (Ntsame 58; Let's just hope that our *mone* Nguema is like Ondo), Ndong rightfully points out that "mone," or the Fang word for "child/son," here perhaps can be grasped from context (Ndong 95). However, in two other instances, the reader cannot rely so easily on such clues. Ntsame refers to a village named Bote-ba-yene-mame (50) and as the name is more complicated than most that appear in the novel, the reader wonders if it is significant. Ndong remarks that a hint of what the name means appears eight pages later (Ndong 95) where the reader understands the name is loosely translated as "people here see things clearly." Finally, the most intricate example refers to one of the protagonists, Sandrine, who is described as "une vraie minga ntahane" (a true *minga ntahane*) with no further explanation (Ntsame 104).[4] Since the description of Sandrine is quite positive, the reader gathers that the Fang expression probably is flattering as well. But even Ndong admits that only a speaker of Fang could give a truly reliable translation (Ndong 95). According to Ndong, the expression literally means "white woman," and in this context, the use of the term conveys that Sandrine feels her marriage to Joël has earned her a higher status to be respected and envied by the community. Because of his success, Joël himself is referred to as "un vrai blanc" (104; a true white man).

There are significant examples of the linguistic decolonization of the Francophone African novel in Ntsame's other works as well. In *La fille du Komo*, a three-page "récit" or narrative interrupts the text without much explanation from the author (100–102) and serves as a clear illustration of the French language being forced to the position of "minor" language, as linguist Kwaku Gyasi remarks ("The African Writer as Translator" 156). The narrative is presented as Georges looks back on the mysteries of his initiation journey in Gabon and the only background information that the reader receives about the narrative is that Georges had recalled reading the passage at his godfather's house (100). Unlike other instances where Ntsame alternates Fang and French words with similar meaning, the narrative is presented in such a manner that the non-Fang reader is completely lost. Among the three pages of rhythmic French text are at least two dozen Fang words whose meaning cannot be determined from context alone. The reader literally is forced to "reconstruct the text" (Gyasi, *The Francophone African Text* 119). Upon researching the Fang words, it becomes clearer that the narrative serves as a call to a community by the *oga* (chief) and lauds various rituals—for example, the *élombo* and the *ndjobi*, a women's healing ritual and a male initiation ritual, respectively (100). Further research on the passage shows that Ntsame then shifts to references to natural materials used in rituals—*iboga* (the emblematic plant of Gabon to be explained later), *mpemba* or kaolin, and *tsingo* or a powder made from redwood (100)—materials either to be ingested (*iboga*) or painted onto skin (*mpemba* and *tsingo*) during the course of various rituals. Finally, there is mention of very specific instruments unrecognizable to most Western readers but which are of utmost importance traditionally:

> Les candidats craintifs passent cet examen
> Exigeant d'eux, souvent, un effort surhumain,
> Au son de l'obaka,
> Au son de la sanza,
> Des ngomas et ngombis (101)[5]
>
> The fearful initiates submit to this test
> That often requires from them a superhuman effort
> To the sound of the *obaka*
> To the sound of the *sanza*,
> And *ngomas* and *ngombis*[6]

Intriguingly, some of the rituals to which Ntsame refers are not Fang. The *élombo* belongs to the Myènè and the *ndjobi* to the Mbéti among other ethnic groups in Gabon. However, those rituals mentioned have clear equivalents in Fang tradition and it may be that Ntsame's purpose is to highlight Gabon's diversity in this narrative and to show solidarity with other ethnic groups, praising all indigenous sacred spaces in an effort to be inclusive. The reader is often reminded throughout *La fille du Komo* of Gabon's multiculturalism since some of Roberte's Fang family members have intermarried with Gabonese of Punu descent. Through all of these references to diversity, Ntsame is affirming her stance that she should not be considered merely a Fang writer, but also a Gabonese one who is contributing to a national literature.

By using elements of African languages in literary texts, writers like Ntsame have called the very term "Francophone" into question. Like Mintsa and other well-known Gabonese authors, Ntsame can be considered both a Francophone and Fang diaspora writer. Using African and African American studies scholar Janis Mayes' definition of "Francophone" as a reference, we can say that "Francophone" in the context of what is happening in Mintsa and Ntsame's novels may be understood more accurately as a space "where French in heard" (xxxiii).

As Arnold Nguimbi rightfully points out, Justine Mintsa successfully integrates the *mvet* into her novel *Histoire d'Awu,* although she never names this renowned form of epic poetry directly in the text. Starting with her first novel, *La fille du Komo*, however, Sylvie Ntsame often mentions the *mvet* in her works and this alone distinguishes her from other Fang writers.

Despite its illustrious status as one of the most acclaimed forms of African oral literature, the traditional *mvet* is to be considered an art form in jeopardy. In his 1974 essay, "Introduction to a Fang Oral Art Genre: Gabon and Cameroon Mvet," Pierre Alexandre had predicted that the two highest levels of the *mvet*—the *mvet engubi* and the *mvet ekang* would disappear by the end of the century, leaving only the least sophisticated level, the *mvet bibón*, since it requires no formal initiation, physical challenges, or significant finances in order to gain the right to perform it (3). In addition to the aforementioned constraints threatening the very existence of the *mvet*, Alexandre identified other obstacles that would ultimately lead to the disappearance of the *mvet*—the fact that *mvet* masters are not being replaced, that the youth are finding the art form less attractive due to increasing Western acculturation, and finally the infiltration of Christianity into the region is significant, meaning that the teachings of Western religions run "contrary to the mystical and magical aspects of the *mvet*" (3). In her book *Mvett Ekang: Forme et sens*, Angèle Christine Ondo confirms that with the death of Tsira Ndong Ndoutoume in 2005, the Fang ethnic group indeed has already lost the last of its great masters (18).

Why then is it important for women writers in particular to preserve the *mvet* especially considering they have traditionally been excluded from it? Honorine Ngou claims that even today, the *mvet* remains the only *épopée* or epic poem that retraces the existence of the Ntumu people (that is, men and women) of the Woleu-Ntem (*50 contes éducatifs fang* 193).[7] While Ngou condemns customs and practices that are oppressive, she warns that abandoning all traditional rituals, practices, and philosophies comes at a price: "la perte de la mémoire des peuples négro-africains" (193; the loss of memory of Black African peoples). In terms of preserving collective memory, women have just as much at stake as men and they arguably play an essential, if not the main role in keeping valuable traditions alive. In Gabon, women writers overwhelmingly contribute to the construction of a national identity through literature of which the *mvet*, like other *épopées*, is an integral part. In his article "Le conte oral traditionnel," Pierre Monsard reminds us that there is a definite relationship between the African storyteller and the public in that the public becomes a veritable "co-author" of the *mvet* (59). With this in mind, the contemporary woman writer of Gabon has a particular interest in becoming such a "co-author," especially if this serves to save art form that might otherwise be lost.

It has already been stated that the *mvet* is an art form that has traditionally excluded female performers. What is interesting to note, however, is that there is a complementary women-centered tradition, the *mengane*, virtually unknown to those outside the culture. Even among the Fang, the *mengane* is a considerably less prestigious an art form than the *mvet.*[8] This repertoire of stories and dances performed exclusively by women is a manifestation of female empowerment, much like the *mvet* and its telling of heroic battles that exhibit the strength, courage, and solidarity of its male warriors. As anthropologist Bernardin Minko Mve claims: "For the Fang, the *mengane* is to women what the *mvet* is to men" (119). Thus, as the Fang culture has a particular influence on the Francophone novel of Gabon, it is only logical that writers find ways of infusing the poetic language and musicality of the *mvet* and the *mengane* both linguistically and metaphorically into contemporary Gabonese writing as evidence of yet another form of literary decolonization.

In addition to the usage of Fang expressions and terms, Ntsame reveals an impressive amount of information about Gabonese and Fang culture in the second half of her first novel, *La fille du Komo*, and these details are well integrated into the story line that focuses upon Georges and Roberte, French and Gabonese, respectively, who meet at a hypermarket in the Paris suburbs where Roberte works. Georges comes to appreciate many aspects of Fang culture, especially those he believes Westerners lack, namely solidarity and mutual support (104). But this realization does not come easily at first; many times throughout the first part, Georges implies that African societies are backward (42, 54). Roberte, his fiancée who has come to France from Gabon to pursue university studies, has seemingly effortlessly assimilated into French society without losing sight of values and traditions that she upholds from her Gabonese upbringing.

When Georges travels to Gabon and meets Roberte's relatives for the first time, he is impressed by the structure of the African family and its ability and obligation to be responsible for all of its members (104). He also appreciates the mutual respect that exists between a married man and his in-laws in Fang culture. This explains why Roberte's parents naturally treat Georges as if he were their own son. As Roberte's husband, Georges enjoys a certain status in her family; he even is entitled to a say in family affairs. In turn, Georges defers to his mother-in-law and father-in-law in particular and shares a similar sense of responsibility for the well-being of other members of the family (104).

While Ntsame does point out positive aspects of Fang tradition in her novels, she also finds purpose and relevance in criticizing customs that need to change or that no longer have any place in a contemporary society. This is evidenced in *La fille du Komo* as well as in Ntsame's next two novels. Her second work, *Malédiction*, for example, illustrates the devastating consequences surrounding an accepted (albeit increasingly more rare) Fang custom whereby a father can choose a wife for his son and have the couple traditionally married[9] without the consent of either party involved.[10] Furthermore, the couple has no right to reject the union at any time before or after they are officially wed. *Malédiction* tells the story of Joël, a young, successful, and urbanized man who is appalled that his rather abusive father has married him traditionally without his consent to a village woman, Sandrine (23). Joël—who already has a fiancée he has chosen out of love—categorically rejects his new wife, even going back to his native village to embarrass publically not only his father (53) but also Sandrine (52) who bears no responsibility for the situation and who is in fact a victim of the tradition just as he is. Sandrine subsequently commits suicide and Joël is soon haunted by hallucinations of his dead wife seeking revenge for the humiliation she had suffered because of him. Predictably, Joël starts to incur several losses in his life including a girlfriend (67), his mother (69), his boss (76), and eventually his wife and child (93). Joël blames this on a curse placed upon him for having refused the marriage arranged by his father (68). Although he moves to France to try to start a new life and to escape the curse, he once again finds himself dealing with the same situation when the life of his new wife and baby are threatened under mysterious circumstances. In a last attempt to save their lives, he implores Sandrine's spirit to spare them, admitting his guilt in mistreating her:

> Il se revoit au village, lorsqu'il a jeté la femme que son père avait epousée pour lui. Avec dédain, il l'avait projetée, insultée. Cette jeune fille qui comme lui tombait sous le coup de la tradition. . . . Joël supplie Sandrine de bien vouloir lui pardonner. Lui dit que, selon la tradition, il est son époux. (123)

> He sees himself back in the village the day when he rejected the woman to whom his father had married him off. With disdain, he drove her away and insulted her. This young woman, who like himself, fell under the burden of tradition. . . . Joël begged Sandrine to forgive him. He told her that, according to tradition, he was indeed her husband.

In Ntsame's third novel, *Mon amante, la femme de mon père*, polygamy and patriarchy in Fang society are scrutinized. The patriarch of the family in the novel, Mendang, has taken three wives but his honor is jeopardized when his son, Nzé-Mendang (whose mother is his father's first wife), falls in love with his father's young third wife, Ngonetang. Nzé-Mendang and Ngonetang have three children together before Mendang takes measures to finally separate them. Nzé-Mendang ends up leaving the family village of Nko'o for Nkoum-Ekieng (also known as Oyem, the regional capital of the Fang in Gabon) in search of work that will allow him to take care of his lover financially. However, while in Nkoum-Ekieng, Nzé-Mendang meets Ada and slowly starts to build a life with her even though his heart is torn between her and Ngonetang for a long time (87). Meanwhile, Ngonetang is forced to live indefinitely in a nearby village with a traditional healer and his wife with the aim of "curing" her of her love and desire for Nzé-Mendang (106). Ngonetang and Nzé-Mendang are portrayed as victims throughout most of the novel as they are the only characters whose relationship is consistently driven by love and not power, honor, and tradition. Consequently, as Mba-Zué points out, this "modern" relationship is dramatically different than what is deemed acceptable or permissible in village life since time immemorial (*L'œuvre de Sylvie Ntsame* 196–197).

Ntsame interestingly presents Ngonetang, however, as the protagonist incurring the most losses by the end of the novel for the sole reason that she is female and she is therefore unable to control her own destiny unlike Nzé-Mendang who nonetheless is guaranteed a permanent place in the Fang construct of family. Ngonetang eventually returns to Nko'o, escorted by the traditional healer, but she harbors seething anger and resentment toward her husband, Mendang, for all he has put her through (123). Although she resigns herself to the fact that she has no control over her life, and her relationship with Mendang does improve somewhat over time—they even have a child together (152)—she is never able to completely shake off her love for Nzé-Mendang whereas the latter manages to put his love for her aside (179).

The novel ends ironically with a joyful and triumphant reconciliation between Nzé-Mendang and his father in Nko'o, a reunion facilitated by Eseng, Nzé-Mendang's mother. However, Ngonetang is physically and emotionally excluded and there is a last image of her trembling and defeated (179). In his essay entitled "L'inceste dans l'espace romanesque de *Mon amante, la femme de mon père* de Sylvie Ntsame," Faustin Mezui M'Okane points out that it is the father's wisdom coupled with maternal love that ultimately brings peace to the family and the community (142). However, Ngonetang never finds any real closure or lasting comfort and it is obvious that she is excluded here from the definition of "family."

There are thus two instances where Ntsame emphasizes the misogyny that ultimately determines the lower status of women in Fang traditional society. First of all, when Ngonetang gives birth to Mendang's son after her return to Nko'o, villagers congratulate Mendang not for the birth itself, but for having had the power and tenacity to gain control over his rebellious and disobedient wife once again, with the crowning achievement being that the resulting child is indeed male and not female (159). Secondly, although woman plays an essential role in creating life and perpetuating the family lineage, she herself is a mere "pièce rapportée" (family member by marriage alone) as Nicolas Mba-Zué explains, and she could never be important enough to threaten the bond between father and son (*L'œuvre de Sylvie Ntsame* 60–61).

The reader of Ntsame's first three novels in particular thus sees the various customs with which the author takes exception, and most of these manifest themselves within the context of the village. Returning to Ntsame's first novel, *La fille du Komo*, however, one sees how often these customs surprisingly have been preserved in urban life as well. One such custom in particular is the practice whereby a widower must have sexual relations at the end of the mourning period with the purpose of "cleansing" away the misfortune of his spouse's death. The female partner—who in reality is a victim—must be unknown to the widower prior and she is someone he should not encounter again after the experience. Thus her body is used only as the "dépotoir à un mauvais sort" (107; depository for ridding a curse). In the novel, this is witnessed by Georges and Roberte at a Libreville dance club, leading the couple eventually to the conclusion that the widower and his prey are indeed both victims of this custom (108). Ntsame uses the scene from the Libreville dance club in *La fille du Komo* to comment on the necessity to eliminate traditions such as this one that may contribute to the spread of HIV/AIDS in African society, especially because this particular cultural practice forbids the use of condoms: "Avec le préservatif, il ne pourra pas transmettre la poisse" (106; By using a condom, he won't be able to hand off his misfortune). Georges points out this is completely illogical; if the widower exchanges one misfortune (the loss of his wife) for another (contracting HIV/AIDS), the practice serves absolutely no purpose (108).

From highlighting the richness of the Fang marriage ceremony (161–169) to questioning, like Justine Mintsa, the "inheritance" of a wife by the brother of a deceased man (145–147), Ntsame provides readers with plenty of opportunities for discussion about the culture and customs of the Fang and these points undoubtedly add richness to *La fille du Komo* and her other novels. But perhaps Ntsame contributes in the most unique way to African literature in the manner in which she shares aspects concerning Bwiti spirituality (a widely practiced indigenous religion in Gabon and especially in the Fang region) and the epic poetry known as the *mvet*.

NTSAME'S *LA FILLE DU KOMO* AND *BWITIFANG* SPIRITUALITY

Ntsame's novel, *La fille du Komo,* is separated into two parts. The first is set in the Paris region and more specifically in the suburb of Mantes-la-Jolie.

This first part culminates with Roberte leaving for Gabon to pay her family an overdue visit. As the couple has lived together for a long time, Roberte promises Georges that she will give him upon her return to France an answer to his marriage proposal about which she has some apprehension. The second part thus takes the reader to Libreville where Roberte reunites with her parents at first, but as Roberte becomes seriously ill soon thereafter, the action shifts to Metec-M'avié,[11] the village of a Bwiti traditional healer where she is taken to be cured of serious symptoms believed to be related to a "fusil nocturne" (76; night rifle). In his book, *Qu'est-ce que le Bwiti?* (2014), Landri Ekomie Obame defines the *fusil nocturne* as a disease or condition that is the consequence of an ill-intentioned person who has placed a curse upon another individual. Obame claims that these illnesses that often baffle modern medicine are nonetheless a social reality profoundly affecting the collective psyche of the Fang, if not of Africans in general (78). Another Fang author, Honorine Ngou, speaks about the *fusil nocturne* (134) as well in her novel *Féminin interdit*, to be discussed in a later chapter.

As Roberte is unable to send news to Georges in France or even contact him at all from the rather remote village, he begins to worry about her to the point of obsession; at first, he does not even consider the possibility that she is gravely ill, but rather he believes she has decided not to marry him and therefore doubts she will ever return. Yet he questions why she would leave all her possessions behind in France without coming to collect them. As he cannot accept this abandonment especially with no explanation, Georges leaves for Gabon with relatively little information to track down Roberte as he is determined to profess his love for her. Upon his arrival in Libreville, he locates Roberte's sister at work and it is in this manner that he learns of Roberte's illness and her inability to communicate with him. Not only does he travel to the village to be with her, but he undergoes certain initiations not only to ensure her health but also their marriage and future together. The second part ends with the couple's return to Paris after their traditional marriage in Gabon. Roberte eventually gives birth to twins prematurely but their son does not survive. After battling several months of depression over this loss, Roberte finally bonds with her infant daughter and the novel ends on a hopeful note that the new family will be able to move forward.

The novel is set in 1990. As Georges is French and white and Roberte African and black, there are ample commentaries concerning interracial dating and marriage made by various characters in the novel. Although the observations reflect the time period indicated, the situation is not viewed so drastically differently from what we encounter today. As the two protagonists come from the capital of their respective countries, interracial relationships are common at best and tolerated at the very least, but this does not prevent underlying prejudice from revealing itself at times; this is especially true in the case of Georges' mother.

Roberte hesitates to marry Georges, however, not because of societal taboos or the perception of others but rather she needs to be assured that Georges will respect the African construct of family that is so very different from his French upbringing. In the end, the marriage takes place, but Georges is never portrayed as a conqueror. In fact, any instance of aggressive behavior on his part typically ends in failure. He is thus seen as a sort of antithesis of the colonizer. Despite his initial criticism of African values and tradition that he believes to be at odds with certain Western values like individualism, Georges eventually demonstrates a deep understanding and even develops a genuine appreciation of Roberte's culture, to the point of declaring: "Il n'y a pas de peuple primitif. Chaque peuple développe par la richesse de sa culture, ce qui ne lui interdit pas de s'ouvrir aux autres (110; There is no such thing as primitive peoples. Thanks to the richness of its culture, each group evolves without closing the doors to others).

Roberte would not be able to accept Georges' marriage proposal without such reassurance. Nicolas Mba-Zué points out that becoming a husband and father in an African context are skills Georges must not only acquire but apply successfully and he does so in both instances (*L'œuvre de Sylvie Ntsame* 111). George's immersion into the Fang culture of the village is the only manner in which he can truly comprehend the richness of Fang traditions and this is what allows him in a way to become Gabonese (Mba-Zué, *L'œuvre de Sylvie Ntsame* 133).

Although the couple speaks French and the reader comes to expect Roberte's occasional interjections in Fang throughout the novel, one is nonetheless surprised when Georges begins using the Fang language as well in an authentic way, going well beyond communicating in the language just to impress his wife or in-laws (171). It is therefore symbolic of Georges' assimilation into African culture. Georges tells his soon-to-be in-laws: "Votre culture est désormais la mienne" (95; From this point on, your culture is my own). Thus, the couple's relationship survives and even thrives not because of Roberte's ability to assimilate to French society—she has already proven this prior to the couple's first meeting and continues to be self-sufficient, keeping her job at the hypermarket despite Georges constantly reminding her he has more than enough money to take care of both of them. Georges' willingness and efforts to be integrated into African life and family thus becomes the determining factor in the relationship.

The *Mbandja* or the Bwiti temple becomes an important focus in the second part of the novel for several reasons—it is here that Roberte is taken to be healed, but it is also the place where the couple is reunited in Gabon and it is also the space where Roberte but also Georges will undergo the iboga secret ceremony to be officially initiated. In his aforementioned book, Landri Obame describes the Bwiti religion as a form of spirituality found in Gabon and parts of Cameroon that entails a profound and direct experience between initiate and the divine (13).[12] Ceremonies often involve local medicinal plants, more specifically the iboga or a type of wood considered sacred throughout Gabon. In the novel, it is indeed iboga that both Georges and Roberte must ingest in order to be put into a trance allowing them to be transported to the spiritual world. As a white man, Georges must obtain permission from the *guérisseur* or the traditional healer to take part in the ritual.[13] This detail is indeed important since the possibility of the couple remaining together ultimately relies on how well Georges can assimilate into African culture. According to Obame, Bwiti is one of the few religions that has been able to resist colonization and transcend ethnic barriers and borders (14). Obame specifically mentions that *Bwitifang* is to be distinguished from other Bwiti practices since the Fang version remained relatively unchanged in regard to its beliefs and ancestral heritage in spite of the persecution of the Fang by Catholic missionaries in the region during colonial times (75). As a Frenchman, Georges is concerned about not being allowed to participate in the ritual and he is certainly at the mercy of the *guérisseur* and Roberte's family; he has no power to conquer or coerce (95). This scene is a powerful reminder of how the former interaction between the omnipotent colonizer and the colonized no longer has a place. Obame reminds us in his book "One must recognize that there was a period where Bwiti was perceived by the white capitalist and colonizer to be the black man's cultural, religious, and economic tool of emancipation. It therefore became a major obstacle to colonial and neocolonial enterprise" (161–162).[14]

Upon learning that he can indeed undergo the ritual, Georges enthusiastically embraces Roberte in front of the elders and gasps subsequently abound; he is meant to feel humiliated for his open display of affection in public, a taboo in Roberte's society. He immediately stops and apologizes for being ignorant of the cultural norms and avows to learn and abide by what is acceptable and respectful within the culture (Ntsame 95–96).

The iboga ritual itself—also known as the *mbiri*—is described in great detail in *La fille du Komo* (98–99). The reader is thus introduced to a world which few outsiders find accessible;[15] here one is able to visualize not only the elements of clothing, makeup, music, and dance essential to the ritual, but one also comes to understand the use of fire and other symbols along with the behaviors and reactions of both the initiates and the spectators. One particularly indelible image is that of the initiator or the *Nima*:

> Le guérisseur, appelé *Nima*, est plus que vénéré. On le dit investi de pouvoirs lui permettant de contrôler le monde visible et invisible. Il a la confiance totale de ses malades. Ventripotent, avec des seins qui tombent sur son ventre comme ceux d'une femme qui allaite, un pagne noué autour de sa grosse taille. Impressionnant avec sa barbe de chèvre grisonnante, il passe d'un malade à un autre. Il tient un paquet de feuilles dans une main, de l'autre il sort une boule d'iboga qu'il dépose dans la bouche de chaque initié. (99)

> The healer, called *Nima*, is more than venerated. One would say he is invested with powers enabling him to control the visible and invisible realm. He has the complete confidence of his patients. He has a potbelly and breasts that fall onto his stomach like those of a breastfeeding woman; a *pagne* is tied around his large waist. Larger than life with his graying beard, he goes from one ailing individual to the next. He is holding a packet of leaves in one hand and with the other, he takes out a ball of iboga that he places in the mouth of each initiate.

Although Ntsame provides meticulous details about the ritual leading up to the "departure" of the initiate, the actual journey to and the return from the *si eboga* (or rather, the spiritual realm that is to be visited by the initiate) is not described at all. The only observation that is mentioned is the haunting and worrisome message that Georges receives during his journey—the first time Roberte gives birth promises to be very bloody: "Roberte enfanterait la premiere fois dans du sang" (100). Indeed, Roberte does lose one of her twins during a difficult labor and birth. But the message itself is an important detail that the unknowing reader may overlook. Obame explains that in Bwiti tradition, it is believed that an initiate is to transmit a certain message from the spiritual world to a given individual (105). The initiation is therefore invaluable to those who believe that it is the only means by which such a message can be transmitted.

THE *MVET* IN *LA FILLE DU KOMO*

There may be no other contemporary writer—male or female—who integrates the *mvet* into the contemporary novel the way that Ntsame does in *La fille du Komo,* resulting in a greater understanding of the celebrated epic poetry. The *mvet* is arguably more than a poem; it represents the philosophy and conscience of the Fang people and is considered a uniting force of the diaspora. It is an invitation to contemplate the meaning of life. Although it may appear that the *mvet* master—the initiated storyteller—is performing the same story repeatedly, every performance is different in that spectators are also participants and thus each interpretation brings new meaning and reflection for all involved. In his preface for Angèle Christine Ondo's study entitled *Mvett Ekang*, Bonaventure Mve Ondo likens the importance of the *mvet* to the significance Homer's works hold in Greek thought. Mve Ondo considers both Homer and the *mvet* masters as "instituteurs de l'humanité" (8; teachers of humanity).

Those unfamiliar with the art form might mistakenly consider the *mvet* to be no more than a legend, folktale, or story of two warring clans, but as Mve Ondo explains, the *mvet* transcends both geography and time and is relevant to real life as it draws its inspiration from history, religion, and philosophy. "Being does not mean being alone, it is being part of a world, a family, a clan . . . it means recognizing that we are part of a chain that includes those who have passed on as well as those who are still with us" (*Mvett Ekang* 8–9). The *mvet*'s universal appeal lies in the fact that it potentially speaks to every individual who at one time or another searches for the meaning of life.

The *mvet* happens to be a genre of epic poetry that has traditionally excluded women. As the *mvet* tells the story of warring clans who are in a fierce battle to gain immortality, there are undoubtedly female characters in the *mvet* and it is thus not in this way that women are excluded. However, as the *mvet* is an example of oral tradition and therefore, performed and generally not read, women have been denied access to the *mvet* by being prohibited from being initiated into the art form and like all non-initiates, male or female, they are not allowed to interpret or perform it. In fact, the spaces where the *mvet* is traditionally performed are not typically women-centered to begin with; to cite a few examples, the *mvet* is often part of the *nku'u awu* or *retrait de deuil* in French—the activities that formally end a period of mourning—and this ritual occurs in the *corps de garde*, the general meeting place at the entry of a Fang village designated for men. The *corps de garde* regularly appears in the novel of a Fang author, which is understandable in light of the essential role it plays in daily life. Nicolas Mba-Zué describes it as the space *par excellence* where all matters large or small are decided (*L'oeuvre de Sylvie Ntsame* 99). It is precisely in the *corps de garde* that a master or *conteur* typically interprets the *mvet* while women are away in the fields working.

Demonstrating the considerable impact that the *mvet* has had on rural Fang culture, Ntsame peppers *La fille du Komo* with references to it, especially in the second half of the novel. For an art that has traditionally excluded women, it is both ironic and bold that Ntsame, as a female author, has chosen to retell elements of the *mvet*, and furthermore, she does it most often through the eyes of her female protagonist, Roberte.

It is Ntsame's first mention of the *mvet*, however, that is the most significant reference in the novel for the general information it reveals to the reader, African or not. This reference pertains to Georges' successful initiation that affords him full acceptance into Roberte's society, a recognition that is made public by Roberte's father in the form of a toast:

> Cet homme n'est autre que notre vaillant Georges, qui, de son propre gré, s'est initié à l'iboga, notre patrimoine national. Il a pris le risque de vouloir partager notre rite secret, de s'imprégner ainsi d'un élément essentielle de notre culture et de notre vision des choses, d'accepter nos croyances: celle de l'existence des esprits après la mort, celle de leur influence sur notre vie sur terre. Il est désormais gabonais par cet acte. Je vous invite à lever solennellement vos

> verres à notre fils, Georges Tonnelier, qui a su nous démontrer la force de l'amour, et que nous baptisons du nom d'Engouang Ondo. (109–110)

> This man is none other than our brave Georges who willingly accepted to undergo the iboga initiation, a part of our national heritage. He took a risk in wanting to share in our secret rite, immersing himself in this essential element of our culture and our vision of things, accepting our beliefs of the existence of spirits after death and their influence on our lives on earth. Through this act, he is Gabonese from here on out. I invite you to solemnly raise your glasses to our son and brother, Georges Tonnelier, who knew how to demonstrate the power of love and whom we baptize with the name Engouang Ondo.

The name chosen for Georges is in no way meaningless. Engouang Ondo is a name taken directly from the most celebrated and most sophisticated form of the epic poem of the Fang—the *mvet* Ekang. In fact, Engouang Ondo is a character that appears in all levels of interpretation of the *mvet* for the obvious reason that he, as the leader of the Ekang, is arguably one of its most important figures who hold the secret of immortality.

As Ntsame noted in a footnote in *La fille du Komo* (110), Engouang Ondo is the head of the army and security for Engong. His nemesis is Oteng Ndoumou Obame with whom he rages battles for the hand of the beautiful Eyenga Nkabe. By giving Georges this Fang name, Ntsame shows the significance of Georges' journey to win the heart of Roberte, equating it with the trials and triumphs of one of the *mvet*'s most important figures. In doing so, Ntsame shows here the universality of the *mvet*'s message that transcends time, history, culture, and of course, gender.

For the rest of the second half of the novel, the reader learns more about the *mvet* through Roberte's explanations to Georges and the reader is made aware of the precarity of the art form. While on a road trip away from the capital, the couple stops in the village of Ebiwas where Roberte recalls the *mvet* storyteller, Nzigue Nzoghe, who was often invited there to perform in years past. Roberte's memories of his performances show how the *mvet* becomes a collaborative endeavor; the *mvet* storyteller is the essential leader, of course, but the participation of the community is also crucial, as shown in the manner in which villagers keep rhythm with Nzigue Nzoghe through the use of small bamboo instruments. There are also specific refrains that the audience sings in unison and it is their duty to encourage but also to revere the *mvet* player.

Roberte mentions that Nzigue Nzoghe had moved to city and yet still came regularly to Ebiwas to perform the *mvet*: "[Nzighe Nzoghe] pérenisait sa culture, bien qu'il se soit installé en ville" (134; He promoted his culture even though he had moved to the city). This statement serves as a clear admonishment for the Fang who may have forgotten such traditions that seem to no longer have a place in an urban environment. Georges ironically asks, "Crois-tu qu'il en existe encore?" (134; Do you think any of [the *mvet* masters] still exist?). It is evident that Ntsame believes that all who belong to the Fang diaspora are responsible for the survival of this art form and thus must be held accountable if it one day ceases to exist.

Later in the novel, Ntsame explains the role of the *mvet* in the *retrait de deuil*, known as the "*nku'u awu*" in Fang. In addition to marking the end of the official mourning period, the ritual is believed to liberate both survivors and the spirit of the deceased (139).[16] Ntsame uses this opportunity not only to introduce the ritual but also to make readers aware yet again of the exclusion of women from the traditional *mvet*—an exclusion she is ultimately defying herself through her literary work as she assumes responsibility for saving the endangered art form:

> Lors du retrait de deuil d'une femme, il n'y a pas de conteur de Mvett. Les contes du Mvett sont l'apanage exclusif des hommes. Dans les villages, le Mvett n'est pas exclusivement réservé au retrait de deuil. Les hommes l'écoutent également lorsqu'ils ont un moment de libre. Assis au corps de garde, ils suivent majestueusement le conteur de Mvett, pendant qu'ils attendent leurs femmes parties aux champs. Le conteur accompagne le récit d'un instrument dont il joue avec ses mains et qui se nomme aussi le Mvett. L'assistance suit attentivement le récit, ne voulant en rater aucune parole, tenant dans les mains les deux baguettes de bambou de chine que l'on frappe au rythme du chant du Mvett. (140)

> When a woman dies, there is no *mvet* performer for the *retrait de deuil.* The stories from the *mvet* are a privilege reserved exclusively for men. In the village, the *mvet* is not only for the purpose of the *retrait de deuil.* Men can also listen to it in their free time. Sitting in the *corps de garde*, they magnificently follow along with the *mvet* storyteller while they wait for their wives to come back from the fields. The story is accompanied by an instrument that the storyteller plays with his hands and this instrument is also called the *mvet.* The audience follows the story attentively, not wanting to miss one single word of it, all while holding in their hands two sticks of bamboo wood, keeping to the rhythm of the music of the *mvet.*

Ntsame educates her readers on aspects of this art form and alludes to others, reminding them the *mvet* is just one of several performances during the *retrait de deuil.* The women meanwhile are participating in various other dances performed for the same occasion even though admittedly these creations are not as highly esteemed within the culture. Ntsame says nothing more about these dances, in fact, except that they exist. This is not done to dismiss them, however, but rather Ntsame's goal here is to bring women into the *mvet*; if she is successful, this ultimately becomes a much more significant *coup.*

NTSAME'S RECENT WORKS

Fang tradition and heritage are at the very core of Sylvie Ntsame's first three novels, with *La fille du Komo* arguably being Ntsame's most significant contribution to Fang diaspora writing and Gabonese literature. Ntsame's most recent works, *Le soir autour du feu* and *Femme liberée battue*, follow a very different trajectory. Although seemingly a collection of traditional stories inspired by oral traditions, *Le soir autour du feu*, as Ntsame explains in the preface, was a project to generate funds to support the Association Sourire à l'Enfance Démunie, an organization created by Ntsame and others in 2001 to support economically disadvantaged children in the country (6). As Ntsame and her peers aim to aid all Gabonese children regardless of ethnicity, the collection of tales reflects this spirit of solidarity and unity supported by the organization and thus, Fang tradition is not predominant in *Le soir autour du feu*. In fact, the work exhibits a more creative writing style and is more or less a hybrid collection of sorts, featuring the rewriting of certain elements of traditional stories commonly found in many African ethnic groups, this time fused with more contemporary cultural realities. Like most African tales, every story in Ntsame's collection has a moral or clear message and it is common to see both animals and humans as protagonists. Ntsame presents eight stories; the one entitled "Okeng" (the word for knife in the Fang language, but here it refers to the name of the young female protagonist and heroine) obviously uses Fang names throughout—Okeng, Nguéma, etc. (27–36), but after consulting known anthologies of Gabonese tales (*Contes gabonais* 1967; *Contes du Gabon* 1991; *50 contes éducatifs fang* 2013), it appears that the story itself is Ntsame's own creation.

Interestingly, by comparing Ntsame's stories with those in Raponda-Walker's *Contes gabonais* (1967), arguably the most celebrated anthology of Gabonese tales, one finds that Ntsame's "L'éléphant et le crapaud" (37–39; The elephant and the toad) is a relatively unaltered version of the Ngowé tale, "L'éléphant et la grenouille" (405–407; The elephant and the frog). Ntsame's "Le jeune homme qui savait tout" (17–18; The young man who knew everything), however, is a reworked version of the classic Fang tale found in Raponda-Walker's work, "L'arbre aux fruits rouges" (232; The tree bearing red fruits), with the most glaring difference being that the family of chimpanzees and gorillas has been replaced by humans in Ntsame's rendition.

Ntsame's most recent novel, *Femme libérée battue*, also strays significantly from the pattern of her first three works. Like *La fille du Komo* and *Malédiction*, the novel *Femme libérée battue* unfolds in both Gabon and France. However, the similarities end there. In *Femme libérée battue*, the reader is taken far away from the traditional Gabonese village and plunged into urban turmoil and poverty in Libreville. The novel is Ntsame's reaction to regularly witnessing—like all those who live in Libreville have—the all too familiar sight of prostitutes waiting for potential customers along a particular stretch of the capital's seafront. Like most who pass by, Ntsame has never entered into the personal world of any of the women she has observed, but her novel seeks to recreate the possible situations and conditions she imagines that such young women face not only in Gabon but in many Sub-Saharan African cities today. Ntsame thus speaks for the voiceless who have had few other choices but prostitution or who have been actually forced into it for economic reasons or simply for survival. Feeling the profound need to present many aspects of this issue, Ntsame developed her fictitious protagonists Hortense, Sita, and Africa in this light.

Her main protagonist, Africa, decides she will try online dating with the aim of meeting a Frenchman who can become her ticket out of poverty and prostitution. She eventually leaves behind her life in Libreville to join Edouard, her online dating partner, in France, but it is not long before she is enslaved, sexually abused, and subjected to numerous other horrors.

In a 2011 interview, Ntsame admitted that the finished product is not exactly the book she had intended to write.[17] Indeed, *Femme libérée battue* is filled with gratuitous violence and disturbing scenes of sexual assault and torture (104) culminating with a terrifying gang rape carried out by Edouard and eight of his friends (106–107). It is also perhaps too obvious that Ntsame chose to name her protagonist Africa to make the connection between Africa and Edouard's violent relationship and the raping of the African continent by European colonial powers. Nonetheless, the novel is successful in shedding light on the problem of prostitution in Sub-Saharan Africa and the distressing fact that some African women consider marrying a rich white male as the only solution for overcoming poverty. Despite the perceived shortcomings of this most recent novel, however, it undoubtedly succeeds in giving a voice to three women who would be otherwise unheard in their society and it speaks volumes about choices available for economically disadvantaged African women living in urban environments today.

In his essay on Ntsame's works, Faustin Mezui M'Okane rightfully suggests that Ntsame is to be counted among Gabon's most important writers for her ability to valorize African heritage and ancestry (147). The material in this chapter is a case in point. Although all of her works are notable, *La fille du Komo* will remain perhaps one of her greatest works as it offers a woman writer's bold introduction of the *mvet* into contemporary literature. With an obvious barrier already broken, it will now be curious to see what other Gabonese authors and/or Fang diaspora writers—male or female—might also do with such a challenge in their own writing in the future as we will surely continue to see creative ways of preserving the *mvet* and other oral traditions in contemporary literature.

Concentrating on both her recently established publishing house as well as her non-profit organization for children, Ntsame has not published a creative work since 2010. However, this should not necessarily serve as an indication that Ntsame has ended her writing career for good and in fact, one fully expects to see more from this writer in the future.

NOTES

1. Ntsame was president from 2006 to 2012.

2. Chantal Magalie Mbazoo-Kassa actually founded La Maison Gabonaise du Livre in 2003, a few years before Les Éditions Ntsame (founded in 2010), but the latter is the first publishing house where all aspects of publication are done on site (printing, distribution, etc.). The website of Les Éditions Ntsame can be consulted at leseditionsntsame.com. Ntsame also has a Facebook page for the publishing house: www.facebook.com/LesEditionsNtsame. The press can also be followed on Twitter at twitter.com/editionsntsame.

3. Ntsame's other works are recognized for their depictions of not only a clash of cultures but also a reconciliation of them and thus her stories take place in both Gabon and France. In *L'oeuvre de Sylvie Ntsame*, Mba-Zué points out that Ntsame distinguishes herself from other African female authors in the manner in which she "constructs a universe where Africa and the West co-exist" (11; construit un univers où se côtoient l'Afrique et l'Occident).

4. The Fang expression appears in several forms actually. Although it is written "minga ntahane" in *Malédiction*, an email conversation with Rodrigue Ndong in January 2016 revealed that it should be written "minegan ntagane." This is also consistent to information found in Cyriaque Akomo-Zoghe's book, *Parlons Fang* (2005). However, there is yet another version given in *Littératures francophones et comparatisme* in which the expression appears as "minega ntagane" (95). Akomo-Zoghe's book explains this possible confusion as the result of the Fang language being a transliteration from a phonetic base (16–17).

5. All citations quoted with permission. *LA FILLE DU KOMO*, Sylvie Ntsame, © Editions L'Harmattan, 2004.

6. The *obaka* is wooden rod used as a percussion instrument, the *sanza* is small finger-piano–like instrument with metal keys, a *ngoma* is a drum, and a *ngombi* is similar to a harp.

7. Woleu-Ntem is the northernmost of Gabon's nine provinces and is the heart of the Fang region with Oyem as its regional capital. The Fang-Ntumu people are settled along Gabon's border with Cameroon and on Gabon's eastern border with Equatorial Guinea.

8. In his article "Qu'est-ce que le Mvet?," Bonaventure Mve Ondo is surprisingly and unnecessarily condescending in his remark about the *mengane*. As a literary specialist, he could have helped to valorize it instead. He claims: "En effet, le récit du *Mvet* n'a rien à voir avec les simples contes (Mengane)" (61; Actually, the story of the *Mvet* has nothing to do with simple tales [Mengane]).

9. For more information on traditional marriage in Gabon, consult *Protocole du mariage coutumier au Gabon* (2003) by Justine and Grégory Mintsa.

10. Honorine talks about this tradition in *Mariage et violence dans la societe traditionnelle fang au Gabon* (2007) on page 62.

11. Metec-M'avié appears to be a fictional village, with the word *metec* in Fang meaning "earth."

12. Although Obame doesn't mention it, Bwiti religious practices are found in parts of Congo and Equatorial Guinea as well, the same countries where the Fang are found although Bwiti is practiced by other ethnic groups as well (such as the Apindji, Myènè, and the Mitsogho, to name a few).

13. According to Obame's book, the initiator (also known in Fang as the *Nima*) does not take the decision lightly as to who will undergo the ritual since because of its hallucinogenic properties, the dose of iboga must be strictly administered to avoid potential health risks or even death. In the spiritual sense, this initiation ritual is considered to be the most effective as a cure as it is believed that it allows an individual to "open the eyes of the heart," which in turn will identify the causes of a misfortune so that the problems or conflict causing an illness or

condition can be eradicated. Faith in the ritual is implied as it is essential in determining its overall success (57–58).

14. The original quote in French reads: "Il faut reconnaître qu'à l'époque le Bwiti était perçu par le blanc capitaliste et colonisateur comme un outil d'émancipation culturelle, religieuse et politique de l'homme noir. Il s'est alors érigé comme un obstacle majeur à l'entreprise coloniale et néocoloniale."

15. Obame explains the debate as to whether or not Westerners should partake in the ritual. According to Obame, some *Bwitistes* say that it is acceptable as long as the Westerner is initiated. Others are against this idea, citing that the white man has not shared with Africans their secrets and advancements in technology, engineering, etc. and thus Africans must keep secrets of their own. The author himself claims that the decision should not be based on skin color but rather on the "sincerity" of the initiate and whether or not his or her decision "comes from the heart" (45–46).

16. Such a ritual is common in African cultures and is not exclusive to the Fang. For example, Werewere Liking rewrites the Bassa version of this ritual into her play *La puissance de Um* (1979).

17. Personal interview with Sylvie Ntsame at her publishing house in Libreville, March 7, 2011.

Chapter Four

Gender and Sexuality in Selected Works of Honorine Ngou

Professor of French at Omar Bongo University and an avid activist for women's rights in her country, Honorine Ngou has a place all her own in the *herstory* of Gabonese literature. Currently known internationally primarily for her novels, *Féminin interdit* (2007) and *Afép: L'étrangleur seducteur* (2010), Ngou started to write creatively relatively late in her career, focusing her earlier works on literary criticism, language studies, and essays in sociology and history. Although she belongs to the Fang ethnic group like her peers Justine Mintsa and Sylvie Ntsame, Ngou seems to place less emphasis on Fang culture in her novels but she has nonetheless written one important and eye-opening sociological study about her ethnic group, *Mariage et violence dans la société traditionnelle Fang au Gabon* (2007), followed up later by a more general study on the oppression suffered by Gabonese women through marriage, *Mon mari mon salaud* (2013).

Ngou's study, *Mariage et violence*, is the only work of its kind featuring riveting accounts told by eighteen Fang women who were between 48 and 88 years old at the time of publication and who were forcibly married according to tradition between the ages of six and twelve. For the most part, Ngou conducted the fieldwork for this project between 1998 and 2005. Despite the oppressive customs to which the women in the study have been subjected, Ngou nonetheless manages to demonstrate the resilience and the defiance of Fang women. The first account, for example, is told by a 55-year-old woman who physically fights back against a husband who has brutally beaten her. She then makes a trip to the capital to press charges against him and the court ultimately decides the case in her favor (46).

Following the individual testimonies, the rest of *Mariage et violence* is organized as a community conversation of sorts with male and female representatives of different professions and ages in society. The study thus continues with an analysis of various viewpoints as the contributors discuss under what conditions and consequences oppressive customs thrive. The conclusion drawn is that many such customs no longer have a place in contemporary society. In the *Invention of Women*, Oyèrónkẹ́ Oyěwùmí brings up a relevant question in this regard—did such customs in reality ever have a place in traditional society? Similar to our inquiries stemming from Ngou's study, Oyěwùmí brilliantly points out: "Scholars have assumed that present-day 'customs' that they encounter are always rooted in ancient traditions. I suggest that their timelessness should not be taken for granted; some of them are 'new traditions'" (xv). This thought is indeed an interesting one to keep in mind and it is pertinent to the analysis found later in this chapter on Ngou's novel, *Féminin interdit*. There are a variety of historical, political, and economic reasons why misogyny has crept into certain Fang traditions when this had perhaps not been the case before, as Oyěwùmí suggests.

Domestic violence continues to affect Fang women today—as it affects all women for that matter—so the last part of Ngou's study is dedicated to this topic of getting to the root of these problems. The ultimate goal of Ngou's work is not to be critical of the Fang per se, but it is simply a social milieu that she knows best. Ngou's work is primarily a study on misogyny and how it leads to violence. Such misogyny, as Ngou rightfully points out, tends to exist universally, even in so-called matrilineal societies in Africa (27).

In *Mariage et violence*, Ngou concentrates on a time period during which forced marriages were the norm in rural Fang society and it is important to remember that often the marriage was "forced" on both man and woman, as Sylvie Ntsame's *Malédiction* aptly shows. Admittedly, some couples who were married under such conditions did eventually find stability and happiness as a couple, but Ngou chooses not to prioritize such cases in her study (19). The fact that Ngou's mother and grandmother are of the same generation as the women who tell their stories in her book (Ngou indicates in the dedication that her grandmother was married off at four years of age) may be the initial motivating factor for writing *Mariage et violence*. It is important to note that Ngou's childhood and upbringing distinguish her from the majority of women writers of her age group whose parents had had access to higher education. Ngou, who was born in 1957, the oldest of eleven children, basically learned French at school starting at the age of four. Ngou's mother never went to school and her father only completed the first two years of elementary school. However, her parents encouraged her from the beginning to pursue her studies and as Ngou's father worked for Europeans in Gabon at the time, he managed to enroll her in kindergarten where she was the only African girl in her class. Full of intellectual curiosity and a fast learner, Ngou excelled at her studies and even willingly accepted being far away from her family and village to attend boarding school for *collège*—the equivalent of middle school in the French-influenced system. Her parents had a true appreciation for her academic success and for her love for her studies, which is why they were perplexed when Ngou expressed an interest in getting married at sixteen years of age. Although they advised against it, her parents ultimately respected her choice. Albert Ngou was a university student in Libreville at the time and Honorine followed him to the capital shortly after their wedding. Ngou continued her studies there and when her husband had the possibility to attend university in France in 1974, she also took advantage of the opportunity, enrolling in *lycée* (high school) in the suburbs of Grenoble where she eventually earned her *baccalauréat*.[1] She accompanied Albert back to Gabon in 1978 where she pursued her graduate studies first at Omar Bongo University, and then in France to complete her doctorate. By 1985, she was appointed as a professor at Omar Bongo University where she became the chair of the Department of French shortly thereafter.[2]

Perhaps this humble earlier period of Ngou's life explains why she today has chosen to live in one of Libreville's poorest neighborhoods, Nzengayong, where she and Albert have opened the bookstore, Le Savoir. As many of the neighborhood's residents have no means to purchase books, Ngou has been known to give her merchandise away (especially textbooks), leading her to organize an ongoing project to expand Le Savoir to eventually include a library and computer center with free internet access available to everyone in the community. This work coupled with her activism in several organizations to improve the status of women in her society attests to Honorine Ngou's dedication not only to writing and research but also to humanitarian causes and the betterment of women's lives in general.

GENDER AND SEXUALITY IN *FÉMININ INTERDIT*

Ngou's most remarkable contribution to Gabonese and African literature may be in the way her works incite discussion and debate concerning how gender and sexuality are constructed. The novel has a way of shaking a foundation of knowledge for both the African and the Western reader. For the African reader, *Féminin interdit* tackles taboos surrounding homosexuality and questions how behavior is determined to be "homosexual" in a given African context. The novel also provokes the question as to whether or not this determination has changed historically especially as a result of the European colonial period. This in turn leads to yet a new question—what is the true source of homophobia in African society?

As for the Western reader, he or she is challenged to change his or her perception of how gender is defined and is forced to stray away from biological evidence that Westerners traditionally privilege when determining someone else's gender. Almost from the very beginning of Ngou's *Féminin interdit*, the Western reader soon sees how one must be "retrained" to consider social practices as a more significant marker of determining gender in African society than biological sex.

In terms of Gabon's literary history alone, Ngou may very well be the only novelist to truly touch upon the subject of a lesbian couple since Angèle Rawiri introduced it in her 1989 novel, *Fureurs et cris de femmes,* in which the reader tries to interpret the nature of the relationship between Émilienne and Dominique. Although one can say that Ngou continues a discussion on gender starting at a point where Rawiri left off, it must be noted, however, that Ngou does much more than her predecessor to break down taboos on the subject matter. As was shown in the analysis in chapter 1, Rawiri allowed her personal judgment to hinder the progression of a discussion on sexuality within *Fureurs*. Rawiri's presentation of homosexuality in her novel (or the possibility thereof) thus only feeds into the taboos of contemporary African society with the relationship of Émilienne and Dominique being presented as immoral and potentially devastating to family and society. Ngou's *Féminin interdit*, however, is much more nuanced. While Ngou does not speak overtly about the possibility of a same-sex relationship—either romantic and/or sexual—between Dzibayo and Suzanne, the suggestion is certainly evident, but readers are free nonetheless to understand the relationship as they wish. Furthermore, Ngou's writing, unlike that of Rawiri, is quite objective and here lies the ingenuity in her work; Ngou manages to alienate no reader while at the same time inviting new discussions that have never been tested quite like this before in African literature. Perhaps this is the preferable approach to advancing a conversation about sexuality and gender in African literature as opposed to Rawiri's judgment-laden style in *Fureurs* or conversely, it may even be more effective than presenting a frank, but shocking story for many African readers such as Berthrand Matoko's *Le flamant noir* (2004). Matoko's novel is based on his own life from his childhood as an effeminate boy in Congo to his lifestyle as a gay man of African descent in Paris. While Matoko's work was praised in Western societies for being the first to tackle such a taboo subject, reaction in his native Congo and elsewhere on the continent was exactly the opposite and Matoko alienated the vast majority of African readers whom he had initially hoped to reach.

As for exploring the notion of gender in *Féminin interdit*, Ngou's inspiration for this may have come first from her own personal experiences and although Dzibayo is a completely fictitious character, the reader does see the connections between the protagonist's childhood and that of Ngou, especially pertaining to the subject of access to education for girls and young women. Ngou found herself criticized well into her adult years for certain choices regarding her own education. In a March 2011 interview, Ngou explained how she sparked much debate in her circle for leaving behind her husband in

Gabon for three years in order to complete her doctorate in France. She was specifically affected by those who said to her, "Tu n'es pas une vraie femme. Tu es une femme-homme" (You aren't a real woman. You're a woman-man).[3] Such a statement reflects a strict adherence to a more stereotypical Western-inspired definition of gender and all that it entails in terms of roles and expectations for men and women in the given society.

It must be noted, however, that the notion of gender in Africa has traditionally been more fluid than the binary systems typically seen historically in Western societies. As gender and sex are inseparable in the West, it is, in fact, Africa's exposure to Western imperialism beginning in colonial times that has led to the exclusion of gender fluidity in modern African society. African feminist scholars such as Ifi Amadiume and Oyèrónké Oyĕwùmí have discussed this topic in great length in the Nigerian context in particular in works such as Amadiume's *Male Daughters, Female Husbands: Gender and Sex in an African Soci*ety (1987) and Oyĕwùmí's *The Invention of Women: Making an African Sense of Western Gender Discourses* (1997). Much broader discussions are found in important collections of essays on the subject such as Oyĕwùmí's *African Gender Studies* (2005) and also in Signe Arnfred's volume, *Re-Thinking Sexualities in Africa* (2004). Amadiume's work in particular is her "reaction to the racism in social anthropology where 'primitive' women stood at the lowest end of the scale" (2). Amadiume emphasizes that "new Western concepts introduced through colonial conquest carried strong sex and class inequalities supported by rigid gender ideology and constructions." Amadiume cites several Western impositions—Christianity, Western education, and new economies and bodies of governance—that violently suppressed indigenous institutions leading to this change in the perception and definition of gender in Africa (119).

There is, in fact, a vacillation between Western and African notions of gender throughout *Féminin interdit* that confuses the reader at times and this is the main subject of the analysis in this particular chapter. *Féminin interdit* begins in a Fang village with the controversial birth of little girl named Dzibayo; the nature of the controversy lies in the fact that her father was wishing for a boy to the point where he is "disappointed and terrified" at the thought of his adolescent wife giving birth to a girl (8). Daughters are described as an "océan d'ennuis" (ocean of troubles) and Dzibayo's father, Dzila, states that having a daughter is like having nothing at all (8). Thus, Dzila gives his daughter what he thinks is a most befitting title; her name literally translates as "is it really necessary to give her a name?" (11).

Within the first few pages of the novel, the reader not only senses how daughters are far less preferred than sons but also how this translates within the culture as women having a much more inferior position in society overall. The name of Dzibayo's fifteen-year-old mother is never even mentioned until much later in the novel and the reader is only given sporadic information about her life. "Elle n'avait jamais été à l'école et voyait sa destinée vouée au martyre et à l'inconfort intellectuel" (7; She had never been to school and she understood that her life would be filled with great suffering and intellectual discomfort). Considering how the society is presented, the reader is not surprised that Dzila holds his wife personally accountable for giving birth to a girl (9, 10, 11) and he even punishes her by not allowing her to go to her own mother for the customary recovery period after a baby's birth (11).

Although these first few pages may give the impression that there is a similar theme here commonly found in other works of African literature in which a female protagonist is consumed by a struggle with her patriarchal society, the story line soon takes an unexpected turn. Although Dzila and his wife grow further apart, Dzila becomes more attached to his daughter and he decides soon after her birth that he will not allow her sex to determine society's expectations for her and he takes her upbringing into his own hands; this means that he is prepared to raise her like the son he had longed for. Amadiume claims that in African societies where gender construction is flexible—such as in Igbo and Nnobi societies of Nigeria—"daughters could become sons and consequently males" for the simple reason that gender was separate from biological sex (15). However, it cannot be said that Dzila and Dzibayo are living in a society that is wholly comparable to that of the Igbo or Nnobi. In Ngou's novel, it is obvious that gender constructions from both African and Western societies co-exist, but Western constructs are nonetheless favored, which may explain why Dzila never goes as far as to say that Dzibayo is his son.[4]

While some of the decisions Dzila makes regarding his daughter's upbringing are questionable and even rather harsh, the reader soon realizes these steps are necessary to undo society's conditioning of gender roles and it is only this that will allow Dzibayo to become independent later in life. While she is still an infant, Dzila sings lullabies to her and pampers her, yet he refuses her any time with her mother except to be breast-fed. He even prefers that her mother let Dzibayo cry for a time before attending to her needs with the aim of making her into a stronger person. "Dzila ne tolérait pas que Dzibayo restât collée à sa mère" (11; Dzila wouldn't put up with Dzibayo being glued to her mother). In order to avoid contact with her mother, Dzila would regularly bring his daughter to the *corps de garde*, the male-centered space at the entry of a Fang village. This meant that Dzibayo already had a distinctly different lifestyle than other baby girls; in fact, her lifestyle was similar to no other child in the village for that matter. Traditionally, children do not spend their days in the *corps de garde* since Fang mothers in the village bring their young children to the fields or to the river while they work. Girls, in fact, continue to stay with their mothers in this manner even as they grow older unless they attend school or marry.

Dzila declares to the other men in the *corps de garde* that Dzibayo would be educated like a boy; she would do daily chores reserved for boys, play soccer, and go to school instead of marrying young. "[Dzila] était heureux de la voir en compagnie des garçons et souhaitait qu'elle eût leur tempérament" (12; He was happy to see her in the company of boys and hoped she would take on their temperament). Furthermore, Dzila forbids his daughter from crying and demands that she defend herself whenever engaged in a physical fight or argument whether with a girl or boy.

What is curious here at this point in the novel is that Dzila's declarations, comportment, and general views about raising his daughter are never the object of any sort of criticism or protest by fellow villagers. They are just accepted by the community. Dzibayo is neither welcomed nor shunned from the *corps de garde*; she is simply present. This provokes notions of the possible acknowledgement of a "third gender" as Oyěwùmí describes in *The Invention of Women*. Does Dzibayo embody an example of "non-Western social categories . . . assimilated into the gender framework that emerged from a specific sociohistorical and philosophical tradition" (Oyěwùmí 11)? Dzibayo's "gender" is never more than superficially discussed by villagers and Dzila never feels like he needs to explain his position, in defiance of Western expectations perhaps. As Oyěwùmí states: "In fact, even the appropriateness of naming [a] 'third gender' is questionable since the Western cultural system, which uses biology to map the social world, precludes the possibility of more than two genders because gender is the elaboration of the perceived sexual dimorphism of the human body into the social realm" (12).

In *Male Husbands, Female Daughters*, Ifi Amadiume also offers an explanation as to why villagers show no hostility or confusion toward Dzila for how he chooses to raise his daughter. Although Amadiume is referring to the Nnobi of Nigeria here,[5] it is interesting to apply this theory nonetheless to Ngou's novel which takes place in a fictitious African country:

> The fact that biological sex did not always correspond to ideological gender meant that women could play roles usually monopolized by men, or be classified as "males" in terms of power and authority over others. As such roles were not overly masculinized or feminized, no stigma was attached to breaking gender roles. (185)

By age six, Dzibayo is enrolled in school. She is one of the few girls in class, however, since the women of the village prefer to keep daughters at their side to groom them for work in the fields, for example, in addition to teaching them how to be wives and mothers later on. Ironically, it is Dzibayo's mother, Ebii (the reader finally learns of her first name at this point) who argues one day with her husband's approach to raising their daughter: "Mais Dzila, Dzibayo est tout de même une fille. Elle doit apprendre à faire des choses comme une fille" (12; But Dzila, Dzibayo is a girl all the same. She has to learn how to do things like a girl). Her pleading has no effect on Dzila who is hailed by the narrator as being "en avance sur son temps" (13; ahead of his time).

Dzibayo excels in school and she dominates all the boys in her class both mentally and physically. But socially, her behavior poses problems for her. After she beats up a male classmate who has attacked her, Dzibayo's teacher asks her, "Quel genre de fille es-tu?" (14; What kind of girl are you?). At recess, children start to avoid her and suspect she may be possessed by an Evu (15), or the vampire-like creature of Fang legends that inspires fear. Although alienated by other children, Dzibayo is not hindered at all at this point in her life from moving forward as her father has planned for her.

The 291-page novel chronicles Dzibayo's life from her birth well into adulthood as the reader sees the obstacles that Dzibayo encounters at various stages in her life due to the gender her father has assigned to her. As she gets older, however, there are times when Dzibayo seeks to experiment with living life as a typical female according to a stereotype that has perhaps been Westernized; she starts to worry about her physical appearance, and she wants to help her mother and other women either in the fields or in the kitchen (19). Obviously, this is displeasing to her father who reprimands her for straying from the *corps de garde* and he threatens to cut her hair short. But what angers Dzila most is when he finds out that his daughter has already learned about marriage through others in the village. "Pour ce père soucieux de l'avenir de sa fille, renoncer à ses études pour le mariage, c'est creuser sa propre tombe" (21; For this father worried about his daughter's future, giving up her studies for marriage, it's like digging her own grave).

It is at this point in the novel that Ngou adds an intriguing character to the story named Eyui (22–25). Living alone in a feces-laden thatched hut located on the path between two villages, an old sickly woman whom everyone else in the village ignores suddenly tugs at Dzibayo's heartstrings. This old woman, Eyui, is constantly crying out for help, but everyone passes by her house without paying attention. Eyui is thought to be a witch (22), a phantom (23), a recluse (25), and most interestingly, "mi-homme, mi-bête" (24; half-man, half-beast). Although the interaction is brief and hardly warm, Dzibayo does manage to leave food for Eyui one day. One week later, however, Eyui perishes as her hut is engulfed in flames (25). Dzibayo is frightened by the sight every time she passes by thereafter, haunted by the lasting image of the menacing yet pathetic woman's face. Dzibayo is convinced that the woman's demise is due to her solitude, and specifically to the fact that she had no children to take care of her (25). But as Hallnaut Engouang points out in his essay in *Regards sur les grands thèmes de la littérature gabonaise*, even traditional society has failed Eyui because it remains inexplicable how the old and decrepit woman could find herself in such a state while living in a communal society in which members always look out for each other regardless of family ties. (101). Engouang questions the relevance of the character who is never mentioned again in the rest of the novel and he claims that including her is perhaps Ngou's way of criticizing the gradual disappearance of the more positive aspects of traditional society (101). However, this character is, in fact, very relevant to Dzibayo's life and the path that her father has chosen for her and thus it is not surprising that Dzibayo is intrigued and even disturbed by her. What other reason could there be for Dzibayo to be touched so deeply by a woman whom no one else cares about, causing her to wonder just how the old woman's situation got to such a point of no return? Is the mere sight of another human being in need enough to profoundly affect Dzibayo or does she see her own future in Eyui's face? For a woman, does becoming "independent" mean eventually living alone and alienated from society? Is this the destiny that Dzibayo's father's plan ultimately holds for her? Would her father's denial of her femaleness as defined by the contemporary norms for their society leave her one day as an unrecognizable creature to whom no one could relate, as a half-man, half beast? The novel thus far is not about advocating for traditional roles for men and women, but it simply presents the problem of society itself and its non-acceptance of changes in the constructs of family and community that could potentially alter a woman's status in society significantly and for the better. In an African society where each individual is considered a unique link in a chain mapping and classifying all ancestors and descendants, where is a place for someone who chooses to live outside this norm? In a society where individualism is cast aside for the benefit of a family or community, can Dzila's plan for his daughter ultimately work?

Rather unexpectedly, Dzila dies early in the novel leaving Dzibayo without her greatest advocate. Dzibayo becomes even more determined to live as her father had wanted, especially after seeing her mother subjected to the brutal Fang rituals of widowhood, much like what has already been discussed in the chapter on Mintsa's *Histoire d'Awu* and *Larmes de cendre*. Dzibayo is especially enraged at her mother for accepting the custom that marries the widow off to a brother-in-law—in this case, it is her uncle Edzima whom Dzibayo finds mean and suspicious and therefore she considers him as a particularly poor choice for her mother (33).

Despite the death of her father, Dzibayo continues to go to the *corps de garde* to do her homework (34) and aspires to go to *collège* or the equivalent of middle school. Her uncle Edzima, who finds Dzibayo too confident, tries to break her spirit by attempting to arrange her marriage to a much older man. However, Edzima quickly retreats when his brother, Dzila, speaks to him from beyond the grave, implying great harm would come to him if he did not leave Dzibayo alone (39). Edzima then precipitously leaves the village to find work in the city, explaining to his new and inherited wife that his life is in danger. Dzibayo is thus spared a life with an older husband (43).

Dzibayo is eventually accepted into a *collège* run by an order of nuns, but the school is far from the village and the school's dormitory has no place for her at first. This challenging situation will serve as proof that Dzibayo can be independent, despite her young age, just as her father had prepared her. The thirteen-year-old changes residences three times before she is finally admitted to the dorm and in one instance where she is housed by a couple, she is forced out when the husband retaliates against her for informing his wife of his sexual advances toward the prepubescent girl. It is suggested in the novel that Dzibayo is able to fend off her aggressor in the first place because of the skills her father had given her to protect herself (75).

Dzibayo not only finishes middle school but continues on to the capital to attend high school and then university. Working in housekeeping at a local hotel to earn extra money for her expenses, she encounters realities in the city that she has never experienced in the village. In fact, she is surprised to see that men in the city eat at the same table with their wives and children (149); in the village, men were served in the *corps de garde* while women and children ate alone afterward. However, there are less pleasant sides of city life that Dzibayo witnesses as well; she immediately notices the number of street children and prostitutes who are trying to earn a living in the capital, and some are victims of human trafficking and sexual slavery. Dzibayo herself must often put up with unwanted solicitation from the male clients at the hotel where she works.

At university in particular, students take notice that Dzibayo is always alone yet she avoids men and they begin to question her sexuality: "C'est une lesbienne ou elle est juste misandre?" (174; Is she a lesbian or does she just hate men?). Dzibayo does meet a Frenchman, Jules Dessanges, whom she dates for a short time before realizing that he is involved in a pornography ring; she is able to outsmart him, however, before he drugs her in order to film her in compromising positions (182). Dzibayo tries to report this incident to the police, but she finds no sympathy; the police tell her in no uncertain terms that this is what she deserves for being out all night with a white man (184). Considering this and all other negative encounters with men throughout her life, Dzibayo finally comes to this conclusion: "Cet incident m'a permis d'ouvrir les yeux et de fermer la porte de mon coeur aux hommes, quels qu'ils soient" (186; This incident has made me open my eyes and close the door of my heart to men, no matter who they are).

In the penultimate chapter, Dzibayo leaves for France on a university scholarship and she meets there in one of her classes Suzanne Molet, a young woman who grew up in Mauritius and with whom she gets along wonderfully (200). Although there is an obvious affinity between Dzibayo and Suzanne, Ngou's description of the relationship remains ambiguous as the reader is left to decide whether this is a close friendship or something more. The reader is confused further when the narrator tells us:

> Peut-être avait-elle besoin d'affection sans le savoir. Mais les hommes ne lui disaient absolument rien. Le plan machiavélique de Dessanges n'avait pas arrangé les choses. Il avait même suscité en elle un sentiment réel de misandrie. (202)
>
> Maybe she needed affection without realizing it. But she wasn't interested in men at all. Dessanges' Machiavellian plan hadn't helped in that regard. It had even aroused a true feeling of misandry.

However, the reader notes that Suzanne is dating men and when Dzibayo confides in her friend about a young man, Hémiel, whom she has a met at a party, Suzanne encourages her to have fun and to live "sa vie de femme" (207). Although this phrase can be literally translated as "her life as a woman," it is definitely understood here within this context that Suzanne is expecting Dzibayo to follow a heterosexual norm in society. Although Dzibayo has had no sexual partners whatsoever up until this point, this is not the first time in the novel that she has expressed her doubt about being with men:

> Mais le rendez-vous avec Hémiel la troublait et l'attirait. Depuis son jeune âge, elle n'avait jamais été tenaillée par l'idée d'aimer passionnément un homme. Maintenant, elle semblait être animée par une soif absolue d'aimer et d'être aimée. Elle sentait dans son tréfonds une sorte de trou sentimental qu'il fallait désormais boucher. (207)
>
> But her date with Hémiel both troubled her and excited her. Since childhood, she had never been tormented by the idea of loving a man passionately. Now, she seemed to be driven by an absolute desire to love and to be loved. She felt in the innermost depths of her soul a sort of emotional vacuum that now needed to be filled.

Once again, the ambiguity with which Ngou intentionally writes causes the reader to think and a few interpretations are possible. Does the reader consider this statement innocently from the point of view of a virgin who has suddenly met the man of her dreams or is the situation much more complicated than this? Or should the need to fill an "emotional vacuum" be the center of focus here? If so, the desire to love and be loved outweighs Dzibayo's preferences in terms of a sexual partner; does she desire not the man but rather the heart present before her that happens to belong to a man, especially in light of the fact that she has no affective life to speak of otherwise? This is reminiscent of Rawiri's Émilienne in *Fureurs et cris de femmes* who has sexual relations with Dominique, the only human being exhibiting any kind of affection toward her in an environment filled otherwise with hostility. The opportunity to have sexual relations with Dominique is presented to Émilienne whereas no similar possibility has arisen in Dzibayo's case. Furthermore, Dzibayo has not even entertained the thought of having same-sex relations despite the fact she has reiterated several times that she has no sexual desire for men. This should not be interpreted as a moral judgment but rather a denial on a subconscious level that such a possibility even exists. "Elle ignorait tout de la sexualité" (212; She did not know anything about sexuality).

Dzibayo does eventually have a relationship with Hémiel and it is only when she is pregnant with their second child that she consents to marry him, although she is haunted by her promise to her dying father to never marry before finishing her studies (222). Nonetheless, she proceeds with the marriage plans and they return to Gabon soon thereafter. It does not take long, however, before problems surface. Hémiel's family, who is not keen on the marriage to begin with since Dzibayo is from a different ethnic group, is even more horrified to see Hémiel assuming housework and caring for his children since both husband and wife in this case also work outside the home and thus need to share household and family responsibilities as a modern couple. One of Hémiel's cousins declares, "On dirait que que c'est [Hémiel] qui est la femme, et elle, l'homme" (242; One would think that Hémiel is the woman and she is the man). The family accuses Dzibayo of being a witch and having "eaten" her husband's heart to make him behave as such. Signe Arnfred emphasizes in *Re-Thinking Sexualities in Africa* that women who are as successful as men "are not and cannot be subordinate" (15). According to Arnfred, the problem for Hémiel's family is not that Dzibayo is oppressed, but on the contrary, she is "subject to too little male control" (15). Ifi Amadiume would add that women wielding power such as Dzibayo does tend to be seen as "reclassified" by those adhering to a rigid gender system influenced by the West and it is for this reason that Hémiel's family considers her to be "manlike" (Amadiume 185).

To complicate matters, Dzibayo is soon fired from her first job after refusing the sexual advances of her supervisor. Unemployed and already frustrated at how virtually impossible it is for educated women to truly succeed in her country, she also finds out her husband has a mistress, which explains why he has become more and more distant with her emotionally and physically (270). The couple prepares to divorce and Dzibayo returns to the village to visit her mother who assures her daughter that she will have no trouble finding another man. But Dzibayo refuses such an idea. It is here at the end of the novel that Ngou's character makes a surprising declaration:

> Avec tout ce que je viens de vivre, je préfère élever mes enfants toute seule. Je vais me mettre à mon compte et créer une entreprise. J'envisage de faire venir ma copine Suzanne pour m'aider. À deux nous pourrions y arriver. (280)

> With all I have just gone through, I prefer to raise my children alone. I will be my own boss and start my own business. I plan to send for my friend Suzanne to help me. Between the both of us, we could manage.

Again, Ngou's ambiguity here lends itself to a few interpretations. It is clear that Dzibayo has once again rejected men, but does she really intend to remain alone or will Suzanne fill a void in her life? Obviously Suzanne is not being invited solely as a business partner; their relationship is already too close for that. Dzibayo claims to want to raise her children by herself, but in a traditional African society, no woman truly raises her children alone since children are considered to have many mothers, not just their biological one. In *Re-inventing Africa*, Ifi Amadiume reminds us that African motherhood is indeed a construct that unlike in Western cultures, is a means of women's empowerment (114). A child can thus have many mothers and the community takes general responsibility for the well-being of children. However, Dzibayo proposes a life with Suzanne in the city where such thinking is waning. But just how will it appear to society for Dzibayo to be living with her children in an African urban environment with an adult woman who is clearly an outsider? It is more than a question of whether or not a same-sex couple could be officially considered or accepted as parents by their society. As Signe Arnfred points out: "Heteronormativity being taken for granted has made any kind of same-sex relations invisible" (15).

Thus, it can be assumed that Suzanne is being called upon to accompany her in all her ventures in life, not just in business. The novel concludes with Dzibayo and Suzanne's joyful reunion at the airport. Of course, this ending can be interpreted as nothing more than one best friend helping another, with no romantic undertones whatsoever, and it is for this reason that Ngou's work is so intriguing. Is Ngou suggesting a traditional model such as woman-to-woman marriage as seen in some African societies in Nigeria (Amadiume 1987) and among the Gikuyu of Kenya in which the union is formed for socioeconomic reasons but also with some likely form of emotional commitment (Njambi and O'Brien 2005)?

While it is true that Suzanne has come from a completely different society and spent most of her adult years in France where currently the idea of a same-sex couple as parents may be more palatable than in Ngou's imagined African society, it would be too simple, however, to say that Dzibayo's society is less progressive and more homophobic. In his analysis of French colonial writing concerning homosexuality in Senegal, for example, Babacar M'Baye points out that texts by Westerners in colonial times were contradictory in that some described homosexuals as sexual deviants while others claimed that homosexuality did not exist in Africa at all before it was introduced there by Europeans. Both positions have been conveniently used to prove that pre-colonial African society was backward or immoral (116).

Christian missionaries undoubtedly have played a role as well in propagating homophobia in Africa and have done so since the colonial period. Because missionaries discouraged and even shunned the practice of indigenous religions, certain rituals associated with these religions have also been vilified, including many rituals[6] that early Western anthropologists have claimed to exhibit "homosexual tendencies" thus feeding into this notion of homophobia in African society. Unfortunately, the continued and even growing influence of American evangelicals on African Christian churches today does little to change such thinking.

Finally, the dominance of theories originating in Western universities within departments or programs in LGBTQ Studies have ironically encouraged the idea in Africa that homosexuality is a Western construct and therefore inherently un-African. This is essentially how the discipline of feminist studies also had come to be labeled as "Western" and therefore believed to be inapplicable to African women since the dominant voices in such area studies have been overwhelmingly North American or European and above all, white. However, scholars such as Ayo Coly who discuss homophobia in Africa in their works add much to the current debate. In her essay on homophobic Africa for *The African Studies Review* (2013), Coly reminds us that "homophobic Africa is in fact a European-American-African co-production" (23). She further explains:

> Any attempt to unravel the narrative of African homophobia by pointing to external influences must also take into account the reality of homophobia in contemporary Africa and the agency of African actors in the development of these homophobias. (24)

One of the most intriguing aspects of Ngou's *Féminin interdit*, in fact, is that the reader can observe African constructs of gender and sexuality in direct conflict with Western ones and the characters in the novel sometimes inexplicably switch their adherence from one to the other. Thus, even when the reader tries to avoid interpreting a character like Dzibayo according to a Western "bio-logic" that Oyĕwùmí explains as "the conception that biology provides the rationale for the organization of the social world" (ix) leading Westerners to believe that "physical bodies are always social bodies," leaving no real distinction between sex and gender (xii), it becomes challenging at best since this is exactly what some characters (Dzibayo's mother, her teacher, her in-laws, etc.) are doing.

In her study of the Yorùbá in *The Invention of Women*, Oyĕwùmí identifies assumptions about gender and sex that Westerners have applied resulting in an inaccurate reading of this particular society. These assumptions are interesting to consider when approaching a work such as *Féminin interdit*. Thus, when reading such a novel, a Western reader might have the tendency "to inject Western problems where such issues originally did not exist" (Oyĕwùmí 9). Oyĕwùmí claims that Westerners consider many ideas about gender to be universal, ahistoric, and timeless and this, of course, affects how a Western reader may react to a work of African literature. Westerners tend to believe, for example, not only in pre-cultural categories such as "woman" and "man" characterized by the social uniformity of its members, but they have also internalized the notion that gender is a fundamental organizing principle in all societies with the subordination of women being pervasive (Oyĕwùmí xi–xii). Ngou's *Féminin interdit* challenges both African and Western misconceptions concerning gender and sexuality forcing all readers to consider the impact of these misconstructions on society. A reader of any culture or background effortlessly relates to Dzibayo as a character, however, and this is why Ngou's novel has the ability to potentially change a wide range of attitudes and beliefs.

Ngou's novel follows Dzibayo from childhood into adulthood and among the messages conveyed, one understands the importance of how our lives are profoundly affected by how we are conditioned as children. Gabonese women writers are well aware that the future is ultimately in the hands of the youth, and this may be why Ngou chose such a protagonist who exhibits great moral and emotional strength even as a child.

Although children are not necessarily the intended target audience for *Féminin interdit*, there are many Gabonese women writers who have chosen to publish works for children that also speak to adult readers as well and thus this chapter serves as a transition of sorts from a literary analysis of a work in which the childhood of the protagonist is an important part of the outcome of the novel to the topic of children's literature and its importance in Gabonese literature.

The final chapter, in fact, concludes this study with a discussion of how Gabonese women writers actively promote literature to young readers in their country and one way of doing this is by providing works that speak specifically to youth. Gabon has an incredible amount of works classified as children's literature and both first- and second-generation women writers play a major role in producing these works.

NOTES

1. The diploma granted after finishing secondary school in the French system.
2. Ngou recounted this period of her life during an interview on January 4, 2015.
3. Interview conducted at Le Savoir in Libreville on March 9, 2011.
4. The novel is written in the French language, which only allows for a binary system for defining gender. It must be noted, however, that many indigenous African languages have a third gender category that is readily applied to human beings as the case dictates.

5. Of course, it is best to avoid making sweeping generalizations about the African continent, but I apply Amadiume's words to the fictional village here because her study is not the only one that discusses African gender constructions as being vastly different from Western ones in general and so we know from these multiple studies that this concept applies to more than just two African ethnic groups.

6. In the book *Femmes du Cameroun*, for example, Philippe Laburthe-Tolra gives an excellent history of how the woman-centered ritual known as the *mevungu* among the Beti of Cameroon had been misrepresented as lesbianism by early anthropologists and missionaries. The *mevungu* is a ritual of female empowerment and solidarity that involves the public veneration of the clitoris. See Laburthe-Tolra's "Le mevungu et les rituels féminins à Minlaaba" (233–243) and in the same volume, "Rites et associations traditionnelles chez les femmes beti" (244–275) by Marie-Paule Bochet de Thé to learn more about such women's rituals that suffered from misinterpretation by Western anthropologists.

Chapter Five

Taking Literature to the Schools

Gabon's Children and the Contribution of the Woman Writer

Even from the outside of the École Immaculée Conception in Libreville, one could already hear the welcome songs of the children anxiously awaiting the arrival of Justine Mintsa one afternoon in March 2011 when the author graciously accepted an invitation to discuss her novel for children, *Premières lectures* (1997), with an entire class of *sixième*—some 200 students averaging eleven years in age.[1] As Mintsa made her way through the inner courtyards of the school, students and faculty alike lined her path, energetically applauding the highly esteemed author until she reached the classroom of the *sixième*. There, the children and their teachers rose to greet her as a gesture of respect, the students continuing their songs of welcome until Mintsa was comfortably settled behind the table prepared for her visit.

The children's enthusiasm was palpable. It was not as if this was the first time an author of this stature had been to their class, since the promotion of Gabon's literature by those who write it is not an uncommon occurrence in schools across the country. Thus, the children's excitement was not only for the author and her novel, but also for the chance to discuss their interpretations of the reading in Mintsa's presence. Mintsa spoke briefly about *Premières lectures*—a 41-page text intended for young readers, but one that speaks to every individual, regardless of age. It is the story of a remote African village whose residents do not quite know how to interpret the arrival of Brian, a young British teenager touring the interior of the country.

The villagers first react to Brian with fear, but a blind elder welcomes Brian and assures his own community that no harm would come to them from associating with "le Blanc" (the white boy). At the invitation of the villagers, Brian decides to stay for a couple of weeks. The elder's fifteen-year-old daughter, Obone, takes a liking to Brian and the feeling is reciprocated. The story continues with simple, but meaningful cultural exchanges between Brian and Obone until Brian decides it is time for him to move onward in his journey. The text raises important questions about racism and prejudice, tradition and modernity, interracial couples, and even teen sex in an eloquent, poetic style so typical of Mintsa's writing.

To begin her discussion of *Premières lectures* with the *sixième*, Mintsa first situated the text in a brief introduction. The students were obviously very familiar with the novel, however, and each child had his or her copy in hand. Mintsa's introduction soon led way to student questions. It was moving to witness the genuine reverence for Mintsa from such a young audience as well as the passion for reading that *Premières lectures* inspired, motivating the students to ask Mintsa question after question without the slightest bit of timidity:

STUDENTS. Pourquoi Obone et Brian ne peuvent-ils pas se marier? Pourquoi ce mépris du Blanc? (Why can't Obone and Brian get married? Why is there this distrust of Whites?)

MINTSA. Ils n'ont que quinze ans. Est-ce qu'on se marie à quinze ans, les enfants? (They are only fifteen years old. Do we get married at fifteen, children?)

STUDENTS. Non! (No!)

MINTSA. Quand ils sont majeurs, ils peuvent se marier. Les relations sexuelles précoces sont dangereuses—cela vous perturbe dans les études. On espère qu'ils peuvent se marier plus tard parce qu'il n'y a pas de différences entre les races. "Raciste," cela veut dire que vous connaissez l'autre, et que vous avez des préjugés. Si vous ne connaissez pas l'autre, si vous ne l'avez jamais vu, il ne s'agit pas du racisme. (When they are legal adults, they can marry. It's dangerous to have sexual relations too early. It interrupts your studies. We hope they can get married later because there is no difference between races. The word "racist" means that you know the other and you have prejudices. If you don't know the other, if you have never seen him, we're not talking about racism.)

STUDENTS. Pourquoi doivent-ils cacher leurs sentiments? (Why must they hide their feelings?)

MINTSA. Vous êtes des enfants de la ville et il y a des différences pour les gens au village. Au village, il y a un grand fossé entre les

> parents et les enfants. Un jeune amoureux au village ne montre pas ses émotions. C'est très mal vu. Ne pensez pas qu'au village, on n'a pas de "classe." Il ne faut pas mépriser le villageois. Il a toujours la sagesse. L'analphabétisme et l'ignorance ne sont pas la même chose. (You are children of the city and life is different for those in the village. In the village, there is a wide gap between parents and children. In the village, a young person in love cannot show his emotions. It is perceived badly. Do not think that people in the village have no "class." One shouldn't look down upon the villager. He still has wisdom. Ignorance and illiteracy are not the same thing.)[2]

At the very end of the session, Mintsa is presented with analyses of themes the children have completed as a class as well as the final part of *Premières lectures* which students have rewritten individually according to their own interpretations of the characters. But just before this, a nine-year-old student named Alison who let it be known that she had not agreed with Mintsa's original ending was invited to the microphone to read her version of the new final chapter in front of Mintsa, her own classmates, and teachers. The little girl firmly held on to the multiple pages of her handwritten words as she read them in their entirety in a steady and confident voice with astounding maturity and expressiveness for a student her age. Alison completed her reading with a humble smile of accomplishment as the room burst into applause and cheers, everyone knowing—including Mintsa—that they had just been granted a peak at a future Gabonese novelist-in-the-making. Not only was Mintsa elated and intrigued about the "critiques" she received from the children, but she also thanked them for her reception at their school: "Pour un auteur, c'est un moment privilégié. On écrit pour être lu. Merci pour le grand intérêt porté à cette lecture" (For an author, this is a privileged moment. We write in order to be read. Thank you for the great interest you brought to this reading).

Although one would not expect to hear it after witnessing such an afternoon at Immaculée Conception, almost every conversation with a writer or scholar in Gabon reveals a regrettable detail: "The Gabonese do not read." Of course, this statement has nothing to do with illiteracy. In fact, Gabon has one of the highest literacy rates in Sub-Saharan Africa or anywhere for that matter—the country had an adult literacy rate of 89 percent in 2015, but for youth between the ages of 15 and 24, this figure increases to 98 percent, a figure enviable for any nation.[3]

The Gabonese, however, tend to regard books as useful for research or for the preparation of exams but have not necessarily integrated reading for pleasure and personal development into their culture. This is worsened, as is the case worldwide, by the fact that children and adults alike tend to prefer all that is audio-visual and technological to books (Ngou, "Le livre et la lecture au Gabon" 128). This reality presents yet another obstacle for the promotion of Gabonese literature and its authors. Citing the works of three women writers in particular—Émilie Koumba's *Sally de mes rêves* (1992), Lucie Auleley-Peguy's *Les larmes du soleil* (2005), and Prisca Olouna's *La force de toutes mes douleurs* (2005)—which have all sunk into oblivion despite their numerous merits, Ndemby-Mamfoumby points out: "The Gabonese writer must take responsibility, discover himself, and make himself known to the greater public because he cannot be a critic of his own work" (*Les écritures gabonaises* 34).

Justine Mintsa's *Premières lectures* is now considered a standard reading in school curricula all over Gabon. However, when Mintsa herself was President of the Union des Écrivains Gabonais, she recalls making the rounds to as many schools as possible with fellow members, their mission being evident: "On se battait pour que la littérature gabonaise soit incluse au programme" (We fought so that Gabonese literature would be included in the program).[4] The message that the future of Gabonese literature lies in the country's children has trickled down to a younger generations of writers as well; Edna Merey-Apinda, for example, is the author of several books for children and adolescents. In Gabon's daily newspaper, *L'Union*, one regularly finds articles about Merey-Apinda's frequent interactions with primary and secondary school students especially in regions near Port-Gentil where she resides.[5]

Gabonese women writers are major contributors to a body of literature for children and adolescents in Francophone Africa. Works like Justine Mintsa's *Premières lectures*, Edna Merey-Apinda's *Les Aventures d'Imya, petite fille du Gabon* (2004) and *Garde le sourire* (2008), as well as Alice Endamne's *Super Ashley sauve les fourmis* (2010) all complement works based on traditional African tales appropriate for both children and adults such as Merey-Apinda's *Des contes pour la lune* (2010), Nadia Origo's *Le royaume de Longo: le manifeste du Roi Muntu Nene* (2008) and *Le royaume de Longo: l'ange du Roi Muntu Nene* (2009), and Sylvie Ntsame's *Le soir autour du feu* (2010). None of these authors writes children's literature exclusively, but it is not surprising that these writers dedicate some of their creative talent to such activities since African oralities representing their respective cultures never knew a period where genres for children did not exist. Bellarmin Moutsinga affirms that the Gabonese writer today, in fact, is to be considered a *néo-conteur* (118). Similarly, other African women writers outside of Gabon have crafted works for younger readers as well, such as Franco-Cameroonian author Léonora Miano who published specifically for adolescents her collection of short stories entitled *Afropean Soul* (2008).

Before the 1990s, African Francophone authors wrote books about childhood, which is, of course, different than texts written for children specifically. These works are often heavily autobiographical such as Camara Laye's *L'enfant noir* (1953), Marie-Claire Matip's *Ngonda* (1956), Robert Zotoumbat's *Histoire d'un enfant trouvé* (1971), and Ahmadou Hampaté Bâ's *Amkoullel, l'enfant peul* (1991), which all tend to document a day-in-the-life of an African child. In these works, we read about birthing as well as mourning rituals, the child's introduction to both Western-style and traditional education, initiations into adulthood, marriage as viewed by the community, family relations and interactions, and the infiltration of Western ideas that tend to change these traditional societies sometimes for better but most often for worse. Despite the diversity of the texts, all illustrate Uche Ogike's idea of a "royaume d'enfance" (kingdom of children) through which African writers paint the epic glories of traditional Africa (107).

Subsequently, in the 1990s, the Ivorian author Véronique Tadjo revolutionized African Francophone literature by publishing with Nouvelles Éditions Africaines in Abidjan some of the first books devised specifically *for* children. One of the most critically acclaimed and well-known among Tadjo's children's books is entitled *Mamy Wata et le monstre* (1993) for which she received the UNICEF award the same year of publication as well as inclusion on the list of the 100 Best African Books of the 20th Century.[6] Since the emergence of so-called children's literature in Francophone Africa, we have also seen literature for adolescents specifically. In terms of Gabonese women writers, Edna Merey-Apinda has been the most prolific in both of these categories. This chapter intends to look at some of the most intriguing examples of literature for children and adolescents created by Gabonese women writers.

JUSTINE MINTSA'S *PREMIÈRES LECTURES*

Although Justine Mintsa's *Premières lectures* is narrated by a fifteen-year-old village girl, the novel's primary goal is not to recreate Ogike's image of a *royaume d'enfance*, but rather to have the village serve as a terrain of reconciliation between the traditional and the contemporary and the African and non-African. Youth are clear mediators between these worlds; although they are still guided by their elders, there are times nonetheless when Obone and Brian respectfully challenge this authority. Thus, Mintsa's ultimate message to children is not necessarily to provoke outright rebellion but rather to instill an awareness in youth of transitions that are inevitable and to provide them with models on how to approach changing times in a thoughtful, intelligent, and responsible manner as future leaders who will be replacing their elders.

Education and reading of course, are of the utmost importance in this preparation.

There is no lack of credible, positive role models in *Premières lectures*. Obone's parents lead humble, but productive lives. Her blind father spends his days making rattan baskets that her mother will eventually sell at the marketplace in the city along with her homegrown vegetables. Obone remarks that because of all of her responsibilities, her mother is consumed by work and left with no time to "dream":

> Il faut qu'elle s'occupe de tout. Elle doit aussi tout prévoir. Je ne l'ai jamais surprise pensive. Elle est toujours en éveil. Elle ne rêve jamais. (8)
>
> She has to take care of everything. She has to foresee everything. I've never caught her in a pensive moment. She is always alert. She never dreams.

Obone's father is one of the wisest men in the village, but he is obviously limited by his disability. Yet, his blindness seems to have enhanced his other senses, allowing him to "see" differently and oftentimes, better than others gifted with sight. For example, he of course cannot see that Brian, the foreign visitor, is white and thus treats him like any other individual he has encountered, despite the fact that the other villagers have fled to their houses at the site of the "fantôme" (15–17). After Obone warns her father that Brian is white, he is at first startled, but then quickly rationalizes that as he had not perceived anything different about Brian before learning this detail, he must therefore be like any other man, despite the color of his skin:

> Puisqu'il avait survécu à ce premier contact, donc rien ne pouvait plus lui arriver. Rassuré par cette conclusion, il reprit la main du Blanc dans les siennes et lança, triomphant "Mais Obone, qu'importe qu'il soit Blanc?" (18–19)
>
> Since he had survived this first contact, it was unlikely that anything could happen to him. Reassured by this conclusion, he took once more the hand of the white boy in his own and shouted triumphantly: "But Obone, what does it matter if he's white?"

The words of Obone's father, as well as his blindness, often inspire her to draw parallels from which any reader can learn. In this manner, *Premières lectures* functions as any other example of African storytelling whereby there is always a moral or a lesson to be learned:

> Du coup, le Blanc me fit penser à mon père. Lui aussi était aveugle; mais aveugle à la lumière de notre langue. Tout comme il aurait pu tuer mon père sans défense, nous aussi on pouvait planifier sa mort en sa présence sans qu'il

> en eût le moindre soupçon. Je réalisai que tout le monde pouvait être en position de faiblesse à un moment de la vie. (17)

> Suddenly, the white boy reminded me of my father. He was blind as well; but blind to the light of our language. Just as easily as he could have killed my defenseless father, we in turn could have also been plotting his death in his very presence without him suspecting a thing. I realized that everyone in life was capable of being in a position of weakness at one point or another.

The theme of "otherness" comes up frequently in *Premières lectures*. In fact, Mintsa obviously writes Brian's character as an English boy unable to understand French to teach children that ethnicity along with cultural and linguistic diversity applies to both Africans and non-Africans. Through the few number of visits to the city that the villagers have taken, they have made an association between the French language and whiteness. So Brian appears as an anomaly: "Quel était ce Blanc qui ne savait pas parler français? Était-ce un faux Blanc?" (20; Who was this white boy who didn't know how to speak French? Was he really a white person?). Furthermore, the fact that Brian is ignorant of the French language gives Obone confidence. He is dependent upon her to teach him not only how to communicate but also how to act appropriately within her community. She becomes "son livre de la brousse" (23; his book about the country's interior):

> Même dans mes rêves les plus fous, je ne pouvais pas imaginer que moi, une jeune fille noire, puisse parler le français mieux qu'un Blanc! Je dûs me rendre à l'évidence: j'étais plus savante qu'un Blanc! J'étais plus savante qu'un homme! J'étais supérieure à un homme blanc! (22)

> Even in my wildest dreams, I couldn't imagine that I, a young black girl, could speak French better than a white boy! I had to face the facts: I was more skilled than a white! I was more skilled than a man! I was superior to the white man!

Mintsa succeeds in providing a positive image in written literature of Obone overcoming obstacles that the double-bind of being African and female present not only in a Western-influenced world but also within her own male-dominated African society. Furthermore, in a contemporary world where African children are bombarded with media images from Europe and North America, *Premières lectures* offers a character to whom African children can readily identify.

Despite frequent discussion in the text about "sameness," Mintsa chooses not to paint a utopian world for her young readers but rather a realistic one in all its inconsistencies. Thus, the message conveyed is to refuse prejudice and racism either as victim or perpetrator and to recognize subtleties that threaten the possibility of true equality. There are two situations in the text that merit further analysis in this regard.

It is true that throughout the course of the novel, Obone and Brian share their cultures, traditions, and even bits of their respective languages with each other, and as Brian is in the village, he is an eager learner (21) who does not seek to impose his language onto Obone:

> J'apprenais un peu de français à Brian. J'avais vraiment bien fait d'aller à l'école et d'étudier. Curieusement, lui, ne cherchait pas à m'apprendre sa langue. Et je trouvai cela normal. (23)
>
> I was teaching Brian some French. I had really made a wise choice by going to school and studying. Curiously, he wasn't looking to teach me his language. And I found that to be quite normal.

Mintsa is clearly saying then that it is *not* normal that Western nations through colonialism and neo-colonialism have imposed their languages onto Africans and others who find themselves in the so-called developing world, a category uniquely defined by the most dominant political and economic powers. However, the consequences of colonialism, geopolitics, and the fact that the world is divided into "developed" and "developing" countries mean that these exchanges in the text are nuanced very differently for Obone and Brian and this is beyond the control of the two adolescents. Obone struggles to learn French at first; in class, she draws parallels between her lack of comprehension and her father's blindness:

> Je crois que [mon père] ressent la même chose que moi devant certains mots qui n'évoquent aucune image dans ma mémoire, ni aucune idée dans ma pensée. Il arrive même que des phrases entières soient fermées à ma compréhension. À ces moments, tantôt, j'ai l'impression de rôder autour d'une case où il se passe de bonnes choses mais qui m'est fermée. (8)
>
> I believe that my father feels the same thing I do faced with certain words that evoke no image in my memory, nor any idea in my thoughts. It even happens that entire sentences remain closed to my comprehension. At these moments, sometimes, I have the impression of roaming outside of a hut where good things are happening inside, but for me, I am locked out.

Obone perseveres and learns "le français des livres" (book French) as opposed to her parents whose knowledge of French is limited to a vehicular language they have learned by working in the marketplace (23). During a theatrical production of Shakespeare's *Othello* to which Brian has also invited her family and teacher, Obone surprises herself with her competency in French that allows her to fully understand Othello's tragic end, even moving her to the point of tears (34). Realistically, however, Obone has no choice but to master French if she wants to succeed in the goals she has set for herself or at the very least, to be able to manage personal affairs at an administrative level within her own country where the official language is French. As she is the one in the marginalized position, she is obliged "to look upward—colonized people must know themselves and the colonizer" as Chandra Mohanty explains (511). It is through this only that Obone can hope to "engage in work to transform the use and abuse of power" (Mohanty 511).

For Brian, however, his stay in Obone's village is a mere vacation. Of course, he is eager to learn about her village, but his journey is obviously one of personal enrichment—his future career goals are not necessarily dependent on this experience, nor is he obliged to learn her language to succeed in life. It is not by chance that Obone mentions that it is obvious that Brian has never worked in the fields because of the softness of the palms of hands (20). Through Brian, Mintsa introduces a new form of "blindness" in the story—one caused by privilege. Mohanty claims that within the space of privileged communities, "privilege nurtures blindness to those without the same privileges" (510). Just as Mintsa remarks that for Obone's father, "les Blancs n'avaient jamais fait partie de sa réalité" (17; Whites had never been part of his reality), the same can be said of the Western societies that Brian represents—that Africans had never been part of their reality in terms of economic, political, and cultural equality.

Of course, it may be said that each respective community represented by Obone and Brian is blind to the other, albeit for different political and economic reasons. However, one comparison is particularly revealing: Obone's life experience thus far has allowed her to become engaged in the theatrical production of Shakespeare. Brian, however, remains helplessly lost when Obone's grandfather tells traditional stories around the fire at night. Obone finds it impossible to even try to find the sufficient words to translate the magic and emotions of the *contes*, but more importantly, Obone's world remains too foreign for Brian to relate. Obone's teacher, Maître Koumba, cannot help but notice the disparity between the experiences of the two young people as evidenced in the remark he makes to Obone:

> C'est très bon. Tu es maintenant initiée. Tu vois, si Brian avait dansé l'autre soir au village, il serait entré en transe. Pour l'instant, il reste un non-initié. Il a vu notre magie sans y entrer. Toi, tu as vu la sienne, tu y es entrée et tu en es sortie. (34)
>
> That's very good. You are now initiated. You see, if Brian had danced the other night in the village, he would have entered into a trance. For the moment, he remains uninitiated. He saw our magic without entering into it. As for you, you saw his, you entered into it, and you came out of it.

An additional discussion concerning "otherness" is presented through the personal relationship between Obone and Brian. Obone's father's beliefs expressed throughout the text about the sameness of Africans and whites are contradicted by the way in which he and others view interracial couples. As an adolescent, Obone's parents do not permit her to go off alone with boys from the village for fear she will end up pregnant and unable to finish school. However, her parents consider Brian to be an exception of sorts:

> Pour mes parents ainsi que pour tout le village, c'était un homme blanc, c'est-à-dire, un être mi-humain, mi-fantôme. Un revenant à la recherche de la connaissance, et qui, en absence du sexe opposé de sa propre race, avait refoulé en lui un type d'émotion. Il n'y avait rien à craindre. (23)

> For my parents as well as for the entire village, he was a white man. That meant a being that was half human, half phantom. A ghost looking for knowledge, and who, in the absence of someone of the opposite sex of his own race, had repressed this type of emotion. There was nothing to fear.

The villagers see Brian as merely an "Other." He is so unlike them, in fact, that there is no point in them voicing judgment on the acceptability of interracial relationships; such interactions simply do not exist. Obone's father describes them as "unnatural" (38), and attempts to prove his theory through an analogy, that animals in the forest do not mate with fish or birds (38). Neither Obone nor Brian agrees with this reasoning, but they have little power at this stage in their lives to change it.

After increasingly tender moments between the two, however, Obone eventually decides she can no longer be alone with Brian (41). Ironically, it is precisely because Obone is open to a relationship with Brian that she must separate herself from him. As he is no longer an "Other" in her mind, she realizes she is capable of loving him and thus worries about jeopardizing her future. "Mes études avant tout" (41; My studies before anything else).

As illustrated by Mintsa's aforementioned Libreville school visit, *Premières lectures* is a text that motivates children to read and to formulate their own philosophies on the world. As the level of formal education is the only factor that differentiates Obone from her father, Mintsa seems to suggest that it is through education and reading that Obone is able to analyze race relations more profoundly in order to come to the conclusions that she does:

> Quand je ne pense plus aux mots difficiles ni aux choses bizarres comme par exemple l'hiver que je n'arrive pas à me représenter, et que je pense seulement à l'histoire du conte, je réalise avec surprise que tous les hommes sont pareils. (9)

> When I no longer think about difficult words or about bizarre things like, for example, the winter for which I cannot conjure up an image, and I think only about the story itself, I realize surprisingly that all men are the same.

Mintsa emphasizes throughout *Premières lectures* that "le monde du livre" (11; the world of books) is just one aspect of literature that in no way devalues African oral tradition but merely juxtaposes it; written literature represents a new world for Obone to discover. Thus Obone equates the magic of books, theater, and poetry with that of the stories narrated by her grandfather, the songs sung by children, and even by the "music" played by the wind howling through the trees of her village (11). Her traditional education coupled with her Western-inspired schooling enables her to see and hear stories all around her.

EDNA MEREY-APINDA'S *IMYA, PETITE FILLE DU GABON,* AND *DES CONTES POUR LA LUNE*

Shortly after Edna Merey-Apinda emerged onto the literary scene in 2004 with the publication of her novel *Imya, petite fille du Gabon*, the daily national newspaper in Gabon, *L'Union*, named her "la benjamine des écrivaines gabonaises" or the "baby sister" of Gabonese women writers (8 January 2005). There are, in fact, two distinct generations of Gabonese women writers and Merey-Apinda, born in 1976, is the leader of this second generation. As an author and avid reader, Merey-Apinda has a profound respect for all writers but notably for the first female authors from her country who were born in the 1950s and 1960s—Angèle Rawiri, Justine Mintsa, and Chantal Magalie Mbazoo-Kassa, among others. Although Merey-Apinda follows in their footsteps, she is a creative writer in her own right, contributing to a national literature like few before her at her age. Just as her "older sisters," Merey-Apinda promotes reading throughout the country, especially in elementary, middle, and high schools in her hometown of Port-Gentil. She also holds in high esteem her peers who comprise the second generation of writers in her country among whom she is the first. She has no doubt inspired them in their writing, but through various forms of social and print media, it is also evident that she showers her peers with constant support and encouragement, never missing an opportunity to promote new works by Gabon's young authors.

Merey-Apinda's career has proved prolific; *Imya* was quickly followed up three years later by a collection of short stories entitled *Ce soir je fermerai la porte* (2007), a serious look at complex mother-daughter relationships that sometimes run into troubled waters. In the same year, Merey-Apinda published her novel for adolescent readers, *Garde le sourire*, inspired by her own often lonely experience when she was away at boarding school in the south of France. With child readers still very much in mind, *Des contes pour la lune* (2010) is an homage to African traditions and customs that simultaneously reinvents the ancient art of African storytelling for a contemporary society in a globalized world. Most recently, Merey-Apinda published a collection of poignant, contemporary short stories, *Ce reflet dans le miroir* (2011) that tackles, among other subjects, the controversial 2009 presidential elections in Gabon, and her latest novel, *La nuit sera longue*, appeared in 2014 and deals with the devastating effects of alcoholism. These two latest works demonstrate the maturity and depth of a more experienced and sophisticated writer and it is after considering this impressive list of works written in the span of just ten years that one truly begins to understand why she has earned the title that *L'Union* aptly bestowed upon her in 2005, in addition to other accolades received.

Merey-Apinda wrote *Imya* with a child audience in mind, but in reality, the text speaks to all who read it. Evoking Merey-Apinda's Myènè roots, but transcending time and culture all the same, *Imya* conveys a special message to children to remind them that it is ultimately up to them to preserve precious traditions when they in turn become leaders of society. For adult readers, however, we come to the rather sad conclusion that we have forever lost the power and optimism to perceive the world the way only children can and this reality prevents us from fixing—or at the very least ameliorating—many of the world's conflicts and problems. Merey-Apinda's 80-page text is thus reminiscent of Antoine de Saint-Exupéry's *Le Petit Prince* (1945) and in terms of Gabonese literature, it is in the same creative spirit as Justine Mintsa's *Premières lectures*.

When Merey-Apinda wrote *Imya*, she had been away from Gabon for three years for her studies, and the work thus became a journey home by way of writing. It was also a quest to discover her roots; Merey-Apinda considered her education to be very Westernized and she did not have any experience to speak of in her ancestral village since both her grandparents and parents were from the city. While she has always been grateful for the opportunities for advanced education she received in both Gabon and France, Imya's story represents nonetheless the childhood of which Merey-Apinda had always dreamed or rather, the magical childhood that adults often invent for themselves in their imagination.

Imya begins with a prologue that foresees a different life for the little girl in the village who is destined to leave her home for better opportunities in the city—not because she necessarily wants to, but because she will be left with little choice otherwise. As Imya and her father watch the departing boat that will bring its travelers back to the city, she wonders when she too will leave one day (7). The story already suggests that this is about much more than one girl who leaves her village, however, and it brings to light the problem of a mass exodus from the village toward the African city due to a lack of infrastructure. Indeed, 87 percent of Gabon's population today lives in urban areas so Merey-Apinda is bringing to light a very serious problem that affects Gabon directly.[7]

Each week, the boat reappears on the banks of the river, bringing villager-turned-city-dweller back for a visit, or on occasion, there are other more pressing issues that warrant the trip, such as a single man's search for a wife in the village. But those who depart are decidedly more numerous than those who arrive and the reader will soon realize throughout the book that the villagers are disappearing; the boat carries them away for medical attention, for employment, or for education.

After this first telling glance out onto the river through Imya's eyes, the reader is brought back to the banks of the village named Viani renowned for its beauty and hospitality (8). While the names presented throughout *Imya* may give away its Myènè roots for those in the know, Merey-Apinda's story is very much about the many endangered villages representing a multitude of ethnicities that dot the entire continent.

Imya is divided into a series of chapters that may be considered stories within a story, all serving to introduce the characters, their daily lives, and the philosophies of the community. The first chapter, "La vie dans un petit village paisible" (life in a tiny peaceful village), does indicate, however, that we are indeed in Gabon, on the banks of the famed Ogooué River of western Central Africa and the reader's attention is immediately drawn to the ancient Okoumé tree that stands in the center of the village. The personified tree has witnessed the slave trade, but also more recent tragedies such as mass deforestation (9). Imya, whose name means "knowledge" in Omyènè, is in good company in the village, surrounded by her parents as well as elders such as Onéro the chief, Oma the great wise man, Oyembo the tam-tam player, Ikamba the storyteller, and Ma-Ziza, the traditional healer. Thus, this first chapter pays homage particularly to women and mothers who are essential in handing down traditional values and customs without forgetting others who play an equally crucial role in preserving and passing on from generation to generation a people's history, knowledge, and culture. Although the reader soon discovers that there is at least one person in every family who has had to leave for the city for one reason or another, the narrator emphasizes that the remaining villagers are happy in Viani despite the difficult conditions of living there due to a lack of infrastructure—namely schools and hospitals among other modern services and conveniences.

In the second chapter, it is learned that little Imya has become quite a storyteller with a huge following of children as well as the chief himself. Her talent has rivaled that of Ikamba the storyteller, much to his dislike. The actual stories that Imya tells are an important element of the work and Merey-Apinda uses the third and fourth chapters specifically to introduce simplified and more universally relatable versions of spirits that commonly exist in many African cultures; some names are invented, others are recognizable. Tongo, the phantom on stilts who captures disobedient children at night (22), was a figure introduced to Merey-Apinda by her father when she was a child.

The well-known Mamiwata, the compassionate yet potentially destructive goddess of the water who allows no abuse of rivers or seas, appears in some form in many oral stories across the continent and she is also included in *Imya*. But there is also Eréré, the spirit of the great trees who oversees the state of the forest, and Owongo, the goddess of fertility who preserves the richness of the soil (26).

Chapters 5 through 10 indicate the subtle changes taking place in the village as reflected in the words and actions of its youngest members while they play. These seemingly harmless games cause the village elders to chuckle and play along with the children at first, but by the end, these same elders question their own power, influence, and wisdom in a rapidly changing society. For example, Ikamba is devastated when he realizes the children no longer are mesmerized by his stories and they are actually displeased with the negative messages and pessimistic lessons they seem to convey to this new generation, preferring instead Imya's more timely and optimistic narratives (38). In another instance, Imya and her female friends are playing house, defining women's roles as they understand them to be. In their games, the girls do imitate tasks traditionally performed by women such as cooking, cleaning, and childcare. However, their conversations reflect a deep knowledge about the behaviors and reactions of men; one child warns her friend, for example, to improve her cooking to avoid a co-wife in the future (36), but there is also an entertaining moment where the girls pretend to prepare a meal for the village, but find they cannot complete the task because, as they discuss with one another, the men were too lazy to go out fishing that morning. Playing along and telling the girls he is hungry, the great wise man is told firmly by the girls that only the children will be fed that day, and each man will be given a single grain of rice as compensation for his laziness (36). The wise man laughs along lightheartedly with the girls, calling them "coriace" (tough). The chief's youngest daughter does not appreciate that he is humoring them and reminds him: "les temps changent" (37; times are changing).

Although it is implied that these gradual changes are worrisome, Merey-Apinda does attempt to demonstrate that the two generations are or should be, at least, interdependent. Ikamba experiences waves of emotions upon realizing that Imya is nudging him out in the village as the favorite storyteller, including disappointment, anger, jealously, hopelessness, and insecurity. Just when the reader may be convinced that there is no longer any need for the old storyteller, there is a surprising encounter between Ikamba and Imya. When Ikamba fakes illness to avoid the humiliation of showing himself in the village where no one appreciates his stories any longer, Imya is the one who comes to visit to cheer him up. Ikamba asks Imya to tell him one of her stories to make him feel better and also to perhaps recapture some of the magic the young girl has for storytelling. Ironically, Imya tries to tell Ikamba two of his very own stories, indicating that Imya indeed did not develop a talent all on her own, but it is the result of the traditions and wisdom by which she is surrounded (47). Nonetheless, Imya manages to gently tell the elderly Ikamba that the reason they no longer appreciate his stories is because they lack magic and dreams (77) and thus they tend to be interpreted by children as a mere list of rules with no inspiration. Ikamba cannot deny that growing older has caused him to be cynical and thus he is devoid of these positive perceptions of life that come so easily to children.

Toward the end of the text, the children gather to express their fears about what they had been overhearing from adults in the village. One of the children, Ogoula, adds:

> [Pépé] a dit à mon papa que le village va se vider petit à petit. Il dit que, bientôt, il n'y aura plus personne ici. Tout ça parce que les enfants doivent aller à l'école et que les hommes de la ville viennent chercher toutes les femmes du village. (75)

> [Grandpa] said to my dad that the village will empty little by little. He says that soon there will no longer be anyone here. All of this because children have to go to school and men from the city come to look for wives in the village.

It is true that Imya leaves the village under one of these circumstances; her aunt finally convinces Imya's mother that the little girl must go to the city for school. The year indicated is 1980. On the last page of the text, Imya is excelling in school. Just as the reader expects a pleasant ending, he or she is suddenly plunged twenty-two years ahead in time to 2002, the time Merey-Apinda is supposedly writing *Imya*. Here we find a very different world. Viani no longer exists, the majority of its residents having left for the city. Fortunately, Ikamba had written down his stories to pass onto children thanks to his daughter, but this is one of the last remnants of the village's rich culture. Oyembo the tam-tam player is retired. The chief and the wise man are both deceased. The focus then switches to the wise man who had requested before his death to be buried at the foot of the okoumé tree at the center of the village:

> Il paraît même que depuis, son esprit habite le grand arbre auquel il a demandé de chanter encore et encore, inlassablement, pour rappeler à lui les descendants de cette terre laissée à l'abandon. Son chant est très triste. Si vous passez un jour au large de Viani, vous entendrez l'arbre centenaire se plaindre de la poussière et des herbes folles qui le recouvrent aujourd'hui. (80)

> It seems that since his death, his spirit inhabits the great tree, the one he has asked to sing to again and again, tirelessly, to remind him of the descendants of this abandoned place. His song is very sad. If you pass by Viani one day,

> you will hear the hundred-year-old tree complain about the dust and the wild grass covering it today.

Merey-Apinda's ending chosen for *Imya* shows the complexity of a situation with which African children in particular are confronted. The reader could not have imagined that the situation could become so dire in such a short time; the tone of the story's conclusion is dramatically different from the more hopeful one that begins the work, even though the emptying of the village is a consequence that is clearly alluded to early on. What can one make of the fact that we have been unable to find harmony between traditional and modern lifestyles and that the two seem mutually exclusive? Individuals certainly cannot be held accountable for abandoning the village for the reasons cited—better health care, opportunities for employment, access to education, etc. Unlike adults who have already failed to preserve these precious villages, will African children be able to conceive of a solution to save them and realistically, who is ultimately responsible for this lack of infrastructure that causes the problem? Given the image of the okoumé tree with its deep roots nonetheless abandoned and now haunted by the spirit of the wise man, the work's initial message appears to convey to children that they must fight to preserve rich traditions. But is there also a suggestion that the problem is much broader in scope? Obviously, the abandoning of villages is yet one more tragedy that the okoumé tree has witnessed, with implications for the continent as potentially devastating as slavery and deforestation.

Like *Imya*, Merey-Apinda's *Des contes pour la lune* places traditional African storytelling at the heart of the work—perhaps even more so than in *Imya*. Targeting approximately the same age group as *Imya*, *Des contes pour la lune* begins with an introduction in the form of a conversation between the moon and her friend, the horned owl. The four stories that follow are part of that conversation. Here, Merey-Apinda adheres to a common practice in African oral literature by which protagonists are often animals or another entity of nature like the moon, sun, or stars and are personified (this is why, for example, that the moon is referred to as "she"). This technique adds a more magical feel to the stories, although the messages conveyed are very applicable to the lives of the ordinary man, woman, or child. While Merey-Apinda is obviously inspired again here by African oral literature, what she offers is not an exact replica. *Des contes pour la lune* is a work for a contemporary society with real world problems of the here and now and it is more relevant perhaps to a universal audience than *Imya*, which seems very specific to Africa. The horned owl, for example, tells his stories on a night when "il ne se passait rien de grave sur la terre" (10; not much was happening on the earth) and "l'aide alimentaire était arrivée en pays affamés, les cessez-le-feu avaient été respectés, des anges bienheureux s'étaient invités dans les rêves des enfants malades" (10; food aid arrived to all the famished countries, cease-fires were respected, and luck-filled angels entered into the dreams of sick children),[8] realities that certainly go beyond the continent. The premise of the aforementioned conversation between the moon and the horned owl was the moon's interest in hearing stories that reminded her of a time when all animals lived in peace. The horned owl reminds his friend that such places still exist in the minds of children: "que seuls les enfants sont capables de les voir dans leurs rêves, car eux seuls sont assez malins pour les imaginer" (10; only children are capable of seeing them in their dreams, because they alone are clever enough to imagine them).

The four tales in Merey-Apinda's work allow children to see that life is not always how we envision it to be, but despite initial disappointment, good things may come even in a form that is completely unexpected. In any case, there is always something to be taken away from any given experience and the overall message is that we must all have faith in humanity. Sometimes such messages manifest themselves in the tales in a more intimate setting between two beings, but for other stories, Merey-Apinda is clearly referencing a broader political situation. "Le bal des lucioles" (The Festival of Fireflies), is a story of a beautiful firefly who, after an initial disappointment, finally finds her love, the grasshopper, and thus the most beautiful night of her life was not exactly the one she had spent so much time preparing for (11–24). However, in "Longue nuit dans la forêt des abeilles" (Long Night in the Forest of the Bees), the reader suspects that the tale of the celebrated monkey kingdom that will soon be led by a most unlikely candidate, Lucci the slug, is really a story about the eventual rise of the global south and the expected resistance and shock of the world's fading superpowers. In this instance, it turns out that the scenario presented is only Woulia the chimpanzee's nightmare for now, but it was an image that was so real that when the chimpanzee finally awakes, he does so with a new appreciation of the creatures he had deemed insignificant before falling asleep (25–37).

The final two tales presented in *Des contes pour la lune* approach personal subjects such as marital infidelity, starting over, and commitment to friendship but also serious environmental issues such as poaching and preserving the environment and endangered species. These particular tales—"Un Noël dans la forêt des colibris" (A Long-Winded Christmas in the Forest of Hummingbirds) and "La comptine des animaux" (The Animal Nursery Rhyme) are filled with nuances that gently teach children about the misfortunes that will eventually affect them as adults either in their personal life or as global citizens.

One commonly hears that oral literature is the African child's first textbook and while this is true, the same can be said for all children regardless of culture, gender, or social class. When a book is read over and over again to a two- or three-year-old child, the child may turn the pages and give the impression he or she is "reading" the story, but actually the child has memorized the text before actually learning to read it. This does not mean that the message conveyed is any less powerful. While the African reader may have a different appreciation of *Des contes pour la lune* based on his or her reverence of storytelling so deeply embedded in the culture, there is an additional message for the Western reader beyond those presented in the individual tales. One of the reasons why Merey-Apinda's work is noteworthy is the mere fact that it challenges the notion of some Westerners that African literature is only what is recent and new. In 1967, some time before Robert Zotoumbat and Angèle Rawiri had written their respective works, Gabonese writer, ethnographer, and missionary André Raponda-Walker pointed out in his celebrated collection of tradition tales, *Contes gabonais*: "Of course, written literature in Gabon does not exist because writing was unknown before the arrival of the Europeans. But there was a spoken-word literature, transmitted orally from generation to generation" (11).[9] African storytelling is an art so old that its origins are often unknown, but one thing is certain—it predates the Western novel by centuries. The rewriting of oral tales in Gabonese literature in the form of stories or texts aimed specifically for children but that address all of us nonetheless certainly reminds us of this history.

It is appropriate to end this study with an analysis of selected examples from children's literature to show the breadth and depth of women's writing in Gabon. Spanning a wide range of subjects, Gabonese literature written by women offers something to readers of all ages, origins, and cultures. The reliance on oral tales in children's literature is a way of bridging old and new ways of literary expression while preserving rich traditions of African storytelling that continue to appeal to children today and promote a general love of literature beginning at a very young age. For Gabonese women writers who have made tremendous efforts to promote their literature throughout their country, the production of children's literature is yet another means by which their literature can become more visible while ensuring a wider readership for years to come.

NOTES

1. Gabon's school system adheres to the French structure of education. Thus, *sixième* corresponds to the first level of *collège*, or middle school, the equivalent of sixth grade in the American system.

2. Partial transcript of Mintsa's discussion with Immaculée Conception's *classe de sixième* that took place March 8, 2011, in Libreville.

3. These statistics represent UNICEF's findings on Gabon. Complete statistics may be viewed at: www.unicef.org/infobycountry/gabon_statistics.html (valid as of June 19, 2016).

4. Taken from a March 8, 2011, personal interview with Mintsa.

5. See the section "Littérature" of the November 18, 2011, edition of *L'Union* for the article "*Ce reflet dans le miroir* d'Edna Merey-Apinda présenté aux lycéens" written by Fidèle Afanou Edembe.

6. The project known as the 100 Best African Books of the 20th Century was officially launched in February 2000 at the Zimbabwe International Book Fair by Dr. Ali Mazrui after no African books whatsoever appeared on the Modern Library Board's List of 100 Great English Books of the 20th Century, excluding works even by African Nobel Laureats Wole Soyinka, Naguib Mahfouz, and Nadine Gordimer. Mazrui collaborated with the Pan-African Writers Association and the Pan-African Booksellers Association to compile books in three categories: children's literature, creative writing, and scholarly writing.

7. This statistic is confirmed by many online sources: Tradingeconomics.com, *World Data Atlas*, IndexMundi.com, and *The World Factbook*, among other sources. This was verified in June 2016.

8. All translations for *Des contes pour la lune* is from Beth Johnston's published English translation, *The Moonlight Tales*.

9. The original quote in French that I have translated here reads: "Bien entendu, il n'existe point de littérature gabonaise écrite, puisque l'écriture était inconnue avant l'arrivée des Européens. Mais il y avait une littérature parlée, transmise oralement de génération en génération."

Conclusion

Affirming One's Place in African Literature: Gabon's Second Generation of Women Writers Forges Ahead

This book presents only part of a potentially much larger discussion on Gabonese literature and thus it has a very specific purpose—to bring to the forefront the unique accomplishments and contributions of Gabon's first generation of women writers who until now have remained seemingly invisible compared to some of their peers in other African Francophone countries for numerous reasons outlined throughout this study. It is an understatement, in fact, to call these authors mere contributors to Gabon's national literature and it is more appropriate to say rather that they have led the way, starting with the country's very first novel, Angèle Rawiri's *Elonga*. Would there have been no Gabonese novel without women? Of course, there would have, as the number of successful male novelists in the country[1]—Laurent Owondo, Maurice Okoumba Nkoghe, Auguste Moussirou-Mouyama, Jean Mathieu Angoue Ondo, Eric Joël Békalé, Jean Divassa Nyama, Janis Otsiemi, and Jean-René Ovono Mendame, among others—can attest. But the fact that no other country can boast a first novelist who is female sets Gabonese literature apart from the rest and this uniqueness has had a positive impact on its trajectory ever since. Gabon also has a very promising second generation of women writers who continue to make their country's literature known and they, too, are making a name for themselves in African literature.

The aim of this book is also to ensure that Gabonese literature remains outside of the "empty canon," as Irène Assiba d'Almeida has defined it. Gabon's writers—and especially its women writers—have often found themselves within this "empty canon" through no fault of their own. Already a lack of infrastructure in a country with a particularly small population led to Gabonese authors publishing their first works relatively late compared to writers in other African countries. In Gabon today, there is still no extensive highway system linking all cities, towns, and villages and no reliable transportation or courier services yet exist to facilitate the distribution of books there. But even internationally, publishers and booksellers have made few efforts to promote Gabonese literature and they have made this decision without even considering—or even investigating—its merits; if they had, we would have likely seen a very different outcome. These realities explain why Gabonese authors are motivated to correct this situation, making both individual and collective efforts to do so.

But oversights and errors made by researchers in the very fields that should be promoting Gabonese women's writing have unfortunately also contributed to this problem of invisibility. Although Angèle Rawiri knew none of the obstacles that plagued other pioneering women writers from other African countries and *Elonga* was well received in Gabon, she struggled to be known outside her country and her work attracted too little critical attention, especially outside of Europe. Ironically, even a discipline such as African Studies has not been able to escape the dominance of Western influence despite the inclusion of many more African scholars conducting research in North America and Europe over the last twenty to thirty years. Oyèrónké Oyěwùmí concurs: "In African Studies, historically and currently, the creation, constitution, and production of knowledge have remained the privilege of the West (x)." The oversight of Gabonese literature by North American scholars specifically has ultimately hurt Gabon's writers who have thus had to overcome many more obstacles than their African neighbors in order to gain similar recognition.

This book seeks not only to demonstrate how Gabon's women writers have defied invisibility despite numerous hurdles, but it also presents a discussion about the authors and works that are particularly unique and innovative for their time, writers and texts known for "firsts." It should not be assumed that those omitted from this study have nothing to offer in this regard or that they are lacking in quality. Considering many Gabonese women writers are prolific, it is impossible to include everything in one book and there is no shortage of texts to be analyzed.

One of the first generation writers whose novels are notably absent from the literary analyses here is Chantal Magalie Mbazoo-Kassa. Although her critical work, *La femme et ses images dans le roman gabonais* (2009), is cited throughout this study, there is no chapter devoted to her two novels, *Sidonie* (2001) and *Fam!* (2003). Mbazoo-Kassa was born in 1967 and is considered to be Gabon's third female novelist after Angèle Rawiri and Justine Mintsa. After having pursued advanced studies in France first in journalism and then in literature, Mbazoo-Kassa returned to Gabon in the late 1990s to teach at the École Normale Supérieure, but currently she spends her time working between publishing (continuing her activities at La Maison Gabonaise du Livre) and as an advisor on the President's Council on Communication."[2] Éric Joël Békalé places Mbazoo-Kassa and her accomplishments as a writer "dans le groupe de tête des femmes écrivains au Gabon" (54; in the leading group of women writers in Gabon), and he considers the time she spent away from her country to have had a major impact on her work. Békalé claims: "This is why she ventures to show multiple negative images of Africa in the grip of corruption at the hand of its elites not to mention the poverty of its populations as well as all other flaws that also serve as a hindrance to development" (54–55). This is especially well illustrated in Mbazoo-Kassa's second novel, *Fam!*, the title of which ironically translates as "man" in the Fang language even though the pronunciation is reminiscent of the French word for "woman" or "femme." *Fam!* describes the many faces of corruption, both males and females who are living—and ultimately destroying—the fictitious African nation called Sy and its "peuple de maboules heureux" (48; population of happy lunatics). Every citizen is held accountable in *Fam!*, but especially the elite—from political leaders and their twisted mentalities to the women who are convinced they are acting like feminists: "la femme en voulant à tout prix égaler l'homme, s'aliène profondément au detriment de la fameuse liberté tant recherchée" (83; wanting to be equal to men at any cost, woman profoundly alienates herself, well out of reach of this much-touted freedom that she wants so much). Mbazoo-Kassa states in no uncertain terms in her novel that the people have the government that they deserve (110) and thus it is not so ironic that *Fam!* ends with the "Grand Créateur" or the "Great Founder" declaring, "Je suis l'otage de mon propre système" (161; I am the hostage of my own system). In *Fam!*, the reader also notices similarities to other works by Gabonese women writers; Mbazoo-Kassa also infuses Fang words and phrases as an attempt to decolonize the Francophone novel like Sylvie Ntsame, she rewrites versions of traditional funeral rituals similarly to Justine Mintsa, and she is critical of corruption and sees it as the primary factor hindering development much like Rawiri does in her novels. Therefore, it would be an interesting project to formulate a comparative analysis between *Fam!* and various other works of Gabonese literature. Furthermore, an analysis of both *Fam!* and Mbazoo-Kassa's first novel, *Sidonie*—a reference to a euphemism commonly used in Central Africa when talking about HIV/AIDS, the underlying subject of the novel—would complement any study about the introduction of African feminisms in literature. HIV/AIDS is yet another taboo subject that has only surfaced in African literature recently. Angèle Rawiri's *Fureurs* brought up this topic only briefly at the end of the 1980s, becoming a precursor to later works in which main characters are victims of this disease, as ones sees in Mbazoo-Kassa's *Sidonie*.

Also among novels by Gabon's first generation of woman writers not included for in-depth analysis in this study is Justine Mintsa's *Un seul tournant Makôsu* (1994). Although Mintsa earned international acclaim for *Histoire d'Awu*, this was not her first novel; *Makôsu* actually marked the beginning of her literary career. However, Mintsa's novel has encountered similar problems in terms of documenting its original publication date, just as we have witnessed with Angèle Rawiri's first two novels *Elonga* and *G'amèrakano*. Mintsa published a second edition of *Makôsu* with L'Harmattan in 2004—leading many to believe (including Alain Mabanckou) that this was the novel's very first printing. *Makôsu* is a semi-autobiographical work about the establishment of a second national university in a provincial capital in an African country, undoubtedly the Masuku campus, better known as the University of Science and Technology in Franceville, Gabon. Mintsa's novel centers around a young family who moves from the capital so that the husband, appointed as Vice-Chancellor (9) can oversee the building of the new campus. The Vice-Chancellor's wife is the narrator of the story and she opens with a letter to a faraway friend explaining she is sending along her diary documenting her experiences. It is thus the diary entries that become the novel itself. Wrought with emotions of every kind, this is much more than a story about a university; the writing of this novel was also cathartic for Mintsa because it allowed her a means of talking about a very painful event in her own life, the death of her son in an auto accident. From the turmoil and social unrest associated with building a new scientific university in a developing country to the emotional and mental strength of a couple in the middle of such a project while also dealing with joy and tragedy in their own personal lives, *Makôsu* is an essential text to include in any comprehensive study of Mintsa's career.

The last chapter of this study ended with analyses of some of the works of Edna Merey-Apinda, the leader of Gabon's second generation of woman writers. However, the importance of this second generation cannot be emphasized enough as they continue this strong tradition of women's writing in Gabon, and indeed, these authors are clearly up to the task. This too is an aspect particular to Gabonese literature since it is rare to see a second generation of African women writers as strong as the first as there are usually ebbs and tides in terms of literary production as witnessed in the case of Cameroonian literature, for example. However, Gabon's women writers have been consistently prolific from the beginning and its second generation perhaps even more so. While it was mentioned in the introduction that Alice Endamne thought that this interest in writing among young women was due to the particularities of a girl's upbringing and education in Gabon, Miryl Eteno pointed out an additional factor, claiming that this second generation of writers who are for the most part in their thirties almost all were forced to study abroad during the 1990s due to chaos in Gabon's education system leading to countless strikes and disruptive demonstrations that had devastating consequences on students who could not finish semesters of study at the time. Eteno claimed that when these young women eventually returned home to Gabon, they resented the fact they had missed so much during their absence and this in turn motivated them to express all of the associated emotions in writing.[3]

Not only do these young authors produce individual works, but they have come together to produce magnificent anthologies of short stories that attest to their collective literary strength. *Les lyres de l'Ogooué* (2012) and *Le plus beau des noms* (2015), both edited by Edna Merey-Apinda, are tremendously rich and would make for an excellent starting point for any reader or researcher who seeks to know more about Gabon's newest young women writers. Many of the authors included are already well established. Miryl Eteno and Charline Effah have each contributed to both anthologies. Eteno—who is Myènè and a native of Lambaréné now living in Libreville—has also written two collections of short stories, *Frasques* (2010) and *Les doux murmures de mon enfance* (2012). Like Mintsa, Eteno found writing to be therapeutic and her first collection of short stories helped her emerge from a dark period of her life after the untimely death of her father. Both collections are inspired by her life's journey and the individuals who have helped shape it with *Frasques* in particular allowing her to express what feminism means to an African woman. Effah, who currently lives and works in Paris is now gaining much acclaim for *N'être* (2014), the work that follows her first novel, *Percées et chimères,* published in 2012. Both of these novels deal with complex mother-daughter relationships and they are particularly insightful when paired in an analysis with Merey-Apinda's *Ce soir je fermerai la porte* (2007).

Also featured in *Les lyres de l'Ogooué* are three more proven writers—Nadia Origo, Pulchérie Abeme-Nkoghe, and Mélissa Bendome. Nadia Origo's formal education as a geographer surfaces in her two semi-autobiographical novels, *J'ai résolu de . . .* (2008) and its sequel, *Le voyage d'Aurore* (2010) in which Aurore, a Gabonese university student and member of the environmental organization Forêt-Source, sets out to do fieldwork in the province of the Ogooué-Ivindo with a mission to help populations make use of their resources without further harming the environment. In the end, however, Aurore returns to Libreville with other assessments of and expectations for both the capital and the village as she comes to the realization that a lack of development is a problem for both albeit for different reasons. Origo's writing of geography and ecology into the novel is indeed very innovative and certainly incites a timely debate about many issues. These two novels in particular are thus bursting with originality. These, coupled with her latest novel, *Le bal des débutants* (2013), that thrusts out into the open the horrifying issue of ritual crimes in Gabon and elsewhere, distinguish Origo as a major Gabonese writer.

After writing a book geared toward children and three well-received collections of poetry, *La vie est un bouquet de fleurs* (2006), *Le chant des blessures* (2007), and *Croissant de soleil* (2010), Pulchérie Abeme-Nkoghe decided to test her talents as a novelist, recently publishing *Chambre 117* (2013), tackling the difficult subject of child sexual assault. Mélissa Bendome likewise has published a novel of note, *Les mains ordinaires de Nane* (2010) which is her exploration of village life through the eyes of her young female protagonist, Etouka, who merely wants what is best for her family. Etouka's experiences with urban life remind readers of Merey-Apinda's Imya. Like Nadia Origo who asserts that African villages would not be endangered if problems in infrastructure could be corrected, Bendome's novel also shows the richness of traditions that have been lost in a transition from rural to urban life as populations try to reconcile both traditional and contemporary worlds.

Finally, it is worth mentioning the three youngest up-and-coming novelists among Gabon's women writers: Elisabeth Aworet, Muetse-Destinée Mboga, and Staël Mavioga. These authors born in 1985, 1986, and 1998, respectively, have already published well-received collections of poetry and considering that many of Gabon's women writers arrived at the novel by way of poetry or novellas, one can expect great things to come from these three authors. Aworet is already the author of two substantial collections of poetry, *Pourquoi je pleure* (2011) and *L'aquarium* (2014), the latter being especially sophisticated and heartfelt for such a young writer. When I met Aworet in Gabon in January 2015, she told me of her plans to soon publish her novel. Happily, *Le regard de Kooga* is due to appear before the end of 2016 with Éditions Odette Maganga in Libreville. In addition to her contribution to the aforementioned anthology, *Le plus beau des noms*, Muetse-Destinée Mboga has published a collection of poetry, *Muendu murime: Le voyage du coeur* (2012), and most recently, a collection of six short stories, *Demain, je m'en vais, je meurs* (2014). Mboga's poetry pays homage to her father but also touches upon the theme of exile and immigration. Like Mboga's first work, *Demain, je m'en vais* is also an exploration of human experiences and emotions as well as a thought-provoking journey with relatable characters who are dealing with the consequences of their life choices, for better or for worse. Mboga also is hard at work on her own first novel. And the new "benjamine" or "baby sister" of Gabonese women writers is Staël Mavioga who was still in high school when her first collection of poetry, *Premières images de ma vie*, was published in 2015 to the delight of her mentors in Port-Gentil and Libreville.

While reading Elisabeth Aworet's *L'aquarium*, my attention was drawn to one of her poems in particular entitled "Aux lecteurs" (To my readers) in which Aworet humbly states: "je n'ai pas choisi la poésie, c'est elle qui m'a choisie" (77; I did not choose poetry, it's poetry that chose me). Being fortunate enough to work with Gabonese women authors over the past several years, it is evident to me that for most, writing is not only a passion, but a calling of sorts, lending assurance that there is still an incredible amount of literature yet to come from Gabon's most gifted women writers.

NOTES

1. For the most complete listing of Gabonese authors, male and female, who have published up to and including the year 2010, please see Eric Joël Békalé's *50 figures de la littérature gabonaise*.
2. The official title Mbazoo-Kassa holds is "Conseillère du Président du Conseil National de la Communication."
3. Eteno made these comments in a personal interview with her in Libreville in January 2011.

Bibliography

Abeme-Nkoghe, Pulchérie. *Chambre 117*. Paris: Edilivre, 2013.
———. *Croissant de soleil*. Libreville: Editions Ntsame, 2010.
———. *La vie est un bouquet de fleurs*. Paris: Éditions Publibooks, 2006.
———. *Le chant des blessures*. Condé sur Noireau: Éditions Acoria, 2007.
Aidoo, Ama Ata. *Changes: A Love Story*. The Feminist Press, 1993.
———. *The Dilemma of a Ghost*. Accra: Longmans, 1965.
Akomo-Zoghe, Cyriaque Simon-Pierre. *Parlons fang: Culture et langue des Fang du Gabon et d'ailleurs*. Paris: L'Harmattan, 2010.
———. *L'art de conjuguer en fang*. Paris: L'Harmattan, 2009.
Alexandre, Pierre. "Introduction to a Fang Oral Art Genre: Gabon and Cameroon mvet." *Bulletin of the School of Oriental and African Studies of the University of London*, vol. 37, no. 1, 1974, pp. 1–7.
Amadiume, Ifi. *Re-inventing Africa: Matriarchy, Religion, and Culture*. London: Zed Books, 1997.
———. *Male Daughters, Female Husbands: Gender and Sex in an African Society*. London: Zed Books, 1987.
Ambourhouet-Bigmann, Magloire. "Où est le roman gabonais?" *Africultures*, vol. 36, Mar. 2001, pp. 18–19.
———. "Naissance d'une littérature." Ngou, *Notre librairie*, pp. 37–39.
———. "Une littérature du silence." Ngou, *Notre librairie*, pp. 45–46.
Arnfred, Signe, editor. *Re-Thinking Sexualities in Africa*. Uppsala: Nordic Africa Institute, 2004.
Auleley-Peguy, Lucie. *Les larmes du soleil*. Libreville: Éditions Abdon Makaya, 2005.
Aworet, Elisabeth Aïcha Nguidjombi. *L'aquarium*. Libreville: Éditions Odette Maganga, 2014.
———. *Pourquoi je pleure*. Libreville: Éditions Odette Maganga, 2011.
Bâ, Amadou Hampâté. *Amkoullel, l'enfant peul*. Paris: Actes Sud, 1991.
Bâ, Mariama. *So Long a Letter*. Translated by Modupe Bode Thomas. Portsmouth: Heinemann, 1989.
———. *Une si longue lettre*. Dakar: Nouvelles Éditions Africaines, 1986.
Barbier, Jean-Claude, editor. *Femmes du Cameroun*. Paris: Karthala, 1985.
Beauvoir, Simone de. *Tout compte fait*. Paris: Gallimard, 1972.
———. *La femme rompue*. Paris: Gallimard, 1967.
———. *Le deuxième sexe*. Paris: Gallimard, 1949.
Békalé, Eric Joël. *50 figures de la littérature gabonaise de 1960 à 2010*. Achères, Éditions Dagan, 2013.
Bendome, Mélissa. *Les mains ordinaires de Nane*. Paris: Edilivre, 2010.

Beyala, Calixthe. *The Sun Hath Looked Upon Me*. Translated by Marjolijn de Jager. Portsmouth: Heinemann, 1996.

———. *Your Name Shall Be Tanga*. Translated by Marjolijn de Jager. Portsmouth: Heinemann, 1996.

———. *Tu t'appelleras Tanga*. Paris: Stock, 1988.

———. *C'est le soleil qui m'a brûlée*. Paris: Stock, 1987.

Bikene Bekale, Béatrice. "De la dimension historique des personnages féminins dans le roman gabonais." Ndemby-Mamfoumby, *Les écritures gabonaises*, pp. 81–100.

Bikindou, F., and L. Baker. "Angèle Rawiri Ntyugwétondo: Première femme-écrivain du Gabon." *Amina,* vol. 224, Dec.1988, pp. 12–16.

Binéné, Pascal Mulangu. "L'impossible aboluité du pouvoir." Binéné et al., *Regards*, pp. 9–74.

Binéné, Pascal Mulangu, et al. *Regards sur les grands thèmes de la littérature gabonaise.* Vol. 1. Paris: La Doxa Éditions, 2010.

Bjornson, Richard. *The African Quest for Freedom and Identity: Cameroonian Writing and the National Experience*. Indiana UP, 1991.

Bochet de Thé, Marie-Paule. "Rites et associations traditionnelles chez les femmes beti." Barbier, *Femmes du Cameroun*, pp. 244–275.

Boukandou, Annie-Paule. "Personnages et discours féminin dans le roman gabonais." Ndemby-Mamfoumby, *Les écritures gabonaises*, pp. 101–124.

Brière, Eloise, and Rangira Gallimore. "Entretien avec Calixthe Beyala." Gallimore, *L'œuvre romanesque,* pp.189–204.

Cazenave, Odile. *Rebellious Women: The New Generation of Female African Novelists*. Lynne Rienner Publishers, 1999.

———. *Femmes rebelles: naissance d'un nouveau roman africain au féminin*. Paris: L'Harmattan, 1996.

Cazenave, Odile, and Patricia Célérier. *Contemporary African Francophone Writers and the Burden of Commitment*. U of Virginia P, 2011.

Chevrier, Jacques. *Litératures francophones d'Afrique noire*. Aix-en-Provence: Edisud, 2006.

———. *L'arbre à palabres: Essai sur les contes et récits traditionnels d'Afrique noire*. Paris: Hatier, 1986.

———. *Littérature nègre*. Paris: Armand Colin, 1974.

Clerc, Jeanne-Marie, and Liliane Nzé. *Le roman gabonais et la symbolique du silence et du bruit*. Paris: L'Harmattan, 2008.

Coly, Ayo. "*African Studies Review* Forum: Homophobic Africa?" *African Studies Review*, vol. 56, no. 2, Sept. 2013, pp. 21–30.

———. *The Pull of Postcolonial Nationhood: Gender and Migration in Francophone African Literatures*. Lanham, MD: Lexington Books, 2010.

d'Almeida, Irène Assiba, editor. *A Rain of Words: A Bilingual Anthology of Women's Poetry in Francophone Africa*. Translated by Janis A. Mayes. U of Virginia P, 2009.

———. *Francophone African Women Writers: Destroying the Emptiness of Silence*. UP of Florida, 1994.

Dembé, Irène. *La femme poison*. Libreville: Éditions Abdon Makaya, 2011.

Diallo, Nafissatou. *De Tilène au Plateau: Une enfance dakaroise*. Dakar: NEF, 1975.

Dingome, Jeanne, editor and translator. *African Ritual Theatre: The Power of Um and a New Earth by Werewere Liking*. International Scholars Publications, 1996.

Dolisane, Cécile Ebossè. "Pour une poétique de l'hybridisme: le genre dans la prose rituelle de Werewere Liking." *Francofonía*, vol.18, 2009, pp. 9–20.

Edembe, Fidèle Afanou. "*Ce reflet dans le miroir* d'Edna Merey-Apinda présenté aux lycéens." *L'Union*, 18 Nov. 2011, p. 4.

Effah, Charline. *N'être*. Paris: Editions La Cheminante, 2014.

———. *Percées et chimères*. Saint-Maur-des-Fossés: Jets d'encre, 2011.

Emecheta, Buchi. "Feminism with a small 'f'!" Peterson, *Criticism*, pp. 173–185.

Endamne, Alice. *Afropean*. Translated by Cheryl Toman. CreateSpace Independent Publishing, 2015.

———. *Garçons et filles*. Saint-Maur-des-Fossés: Jets d'encre, 2010.

———. *Super Ashley sauve les fourmis*. One Child Publishing, 2010.

———. *C'est demain qu'on s'fait la malle*. Saint-Maur-des-Fossés: Jets d'encre, 2008.

Engouang, Hallnaut Mathieu. "La mort comme raison d'une écriture." Binéné et al., *Regards*, pp. 93–141.

Essono, Fortunat Obiang. *Les registres de la modernité dans la littérature gabonaise: Maurice Okoumba Nkoghe, Laurent Owondo, et Justine Mintsa*. Vol. 2. Paris: L'Harmattan, 2006.

Eteno, Miryl. *Les doux murmures de mon enfance*. Saint-Maur-des-Fossés: Jets d'encre, 2012.

———. *Frasques*. Paris: Edilivre, 2010.

Fondation Mebege-Libreville, creator. *Quelques maîtres-mvett*, 2010.

Fouda, Vincent Sosthène. *Le peuple Ekang: Ou comment être Bëti?* Montreal, 2007. Booklet.

Francis, Gladys. "Women's Transgressional Writings in Gender and Body: (Con)texts in Gabonese *Afra* Writings." *Women's Studies*, vol. 38, 2009, pp. 872–887.

Gallimore, Rangira Béatrice. *L'œuvre romanesque de Calixthe Beyala: Le renouveau de l'écriture féminine en Afrique francophone sub-saharienne*. Paris: L'Harmattan, 1997.

Gyasi, Kwaku. *The Francophone African Text: Translation and the Postcolonial Experience*. New York: Peter Lang, 2006.

———. "The African Writer as Translator: Writing African Languages through French." *Journal of African Cultural Studies*, vol. 16, no. 2, 2003, pp. 143–159.

Hitchcott, Nikki. *Women Writers in Francophone Africa*. Oxford: Berg, 2000.

Ikonne, Chidi, Emilia Oko, and Peter Onwudinjo, editors. *Children and Literature in Africa*. Ibadan: Heinemann, 1992.

Kalondji, Christine. *Dernière genèse*. Paris: Saint-Germain-des-près, 1975.

Kalu, Anthonia, Juliana Makuchi Nfah-Abbenyi, and Omofolabo Ajayi-Soyinka, editors. *Reflections: Anthology of New Work by African Women Poets*. Lynne Rienner Publishers, 2013.

Kanor, Fabienne. *Anticorps*. Paris: Gallimard, 2010.

Kéita, Aoua. *Femme d'Afrique: La vie d'Aoua Kéita racontée par elle-même*. Paris: Présence Africaine, 1975.

Kesteloot, Lilyan. *Histoire de la littérature négro-africaine*. Paris: Karthala, 2001.

Koumba, Émilie. *Sally de mes rêves*. Paris: Africa Editions, 1992.

Kuoh-Moukoury, Thérèse. *Rencontres essentielles*. 1969. MLA Texts and Translations Series, 2002.

Laburthe-Tolra, Philippe. "Le mevungu et les rituels féminins à Minlaaba." Barbier, *Femmes du Cameroun*, pp. 233–243.

Larrier, Renée. "Reconstructing Motherhood: Francophone African Women's Autobiographies." *The Politics of (M)othering*. Edited by Obioma Nnaemeka. Routledge, 1997, pp. 193–206.

Laye, Camara. *L'enfant noir*. Paris: Plon, 1953.

Liking, Werewere. *La Puissance de Um*. Abidjan: CEDA, 1979.

L'Union. "Edna Merey-Apinda, la benjamine des écrivaines gabonaises." 8 Jan. 2005, No. 8707, section 1, p. 1.

Lyonga, Nalova. "African Women and Feminist Theory." *Defining New Idioms*. Edited by Eckhard Breitinger. Amsterdam: Rodopi, 1996, 153–66.

Mabanckou, Alain. "Une nouvelle voix gabonaise." *Jeune Afrique.com*, 30 July 2015, www.jeuneafrique.com/mag/247957/culture/une-nouvelle-voix-gabonaise.

———. "SOS: pays africains cherchent désespérément des écrivains." *Congopage Blog*, 17 April 2006, www.congopage.com/SOS-pays-africains-cherchent.

Mabik-ma-Kombil. *Ngongo des initiés en hommage aux pleureuses du Gabon*. Paris: L'Harmattan, 2003.

Matip, Marie-Claire. *Ngonda*. Paris: Bibliothèque du Jeune Africain, 1958.

Matoko, Berthrand Nguyen. *Le flamant noir*. Paris: L'Harmattan, 2004.

Mayes, Janis A. "Reverberations of African Culture and Women's Creativity in Poetry." d'Almeida, *A Rain of Words*, pp. xxxi–xxxvii.

Mba Abessole, Paul. *Aux sources de la culture fang*. Paris: L'Harmattan, 2006.

M'baye, Babacar. "The Origins of Senegalese Homophobia: Discourses on Homosexuals and Transgender People in Colonial and Postcolonial Senegal." *African Studies Review*, vol. 56, no. 2, Sept. 2013, pp. 109–128.

Mbazoo-Kassa, Chantal Magalie. *La femme et ses images dans le roman gabonais*. Paris: L'Harmattan, 2009.

———. *Fam!* Libreville: Maison Gabonaise du Livre, 2003.

———. *Sidonie*. Paris: Alpha-Omega, 2001.

Mba-Zué, Nicolas. *L'œuvre de Sylvie Ntsame: Entre multiculturalisme et quête identitaire*. Libreville: Éditions Ntsame, 2011.

———. "De la société précoloniale à la société moderne." Ngou, *Notre librairie*, pp. 40–45.

———. "Une littérature en quête d'une identité." Ngou, *Notre librairie*, pp. 46–49.

Mboga, Muetse-Destinée. *Demain, je m'en vais, je meurs*. Paris: La Doxa Éditions, 2014.

———. *Muendu Murime: le voyage du cœur*. Saint-Maur-des-Fossés: Jets d'encre, 2012.

Merey-Apinda, Edna. *The Moonlight Tales*. Translated by Beth Johnston. CreateSpace Publishing, 2016.

———, editor. *Le plus beau des noms*. Paris: La Doxa Éditions, 2015.

———. *La nuit sera longue*. Paris: La Doxa Éditions, 2014.

———. *Les lyres de l'Ogooué*, editor. Saint-Maur-des-Fossés: Jets d'encre, 2012.

———. *Ce reflet dans le miroir*. Saint-Maur-des-Fossés: Jets d'encre, 2011.

———. *Des contes pour la lune*. Saint-Maur-des-Fossés: Jets d'encre, 2010.

———. *Garde le sourire*. Paris: Le Manuscrit, 2008.

———. *Les aventures d'Imya, petite fille du Gabon*. Paris: L'Harmattan, 2004.

Miano, Léonora. *Afropean Soul et autres nouvelles*. Paris: Flammarion, 2008.

Milolo, Kembe. *L'image de la femme chez les romancières de l'Afrique noire francophone*. Fribourg, Editions Universitaires Fribourg, 1986.

Mindja, Essindi. *Le Mvett: La guerre du fer*. Paris: L'Harmattan, 2009.

Ministère de la Coopération et du Développement. *Contes du Gabon*. Paris: Conseil International de la Langue Française, 1991.

Minko Mve, Bernardin. *Gabon entre tradition et post-modernité: Dynamiques des structures d'accueil Fang*. Paris: L'Harmattan, 2003.

Mintsa, Justine. *Larmes de cendre*. Alger: Tira Éditions, 2010.

———. *Histoire d'Awu*. Paris: Gallimard, 2000.

———. *Premières lectures*. Lomé: Haho, 1997.

———. *Un seul tournant: Makôsu*. Paris: La Pensée Universelle, 1994.

Mintsa, Justine Elo, and Grégory Ngbwa Mintsa. *Protocole du mariage coutumier au Gabon*. Libreville: Polypress, 2003.

Mohanty, Chandra. "'Under Western Eyes' Revisited: Feminist Solidarity through Anti-Capitalist Struggles." *Signs: Journal of Women in Culture and Society*, vol. 28, no. 2, 2002, 499–535.

M'Okane, Faustin Mezui. "L'inceste dans l'espace romanesque de *Mon amante, la femme de mon père* de Sylvie Ntsame." Ndemby-Mamfoumby and Mongui, *Ces espaces*, pp. 133–149.

Monsard, Pierre. "Le conte oral traditionnel." Ngou, *Notre librairie*, pp. 56–60.

Morgan, Robin. "Goodbye to All That." *Rat*. Feb. 6–23, 1970.

Moupoumbou, Clément, and Pierre Ndemby-Mamfoumby, editors. *La mort dans l'espace littéraire gabonais*. Libreville: Éditions Odette Maganga, 2012.

Moutsinga, Bellarmin. *Les orthographes de l'oralité, poétique du texte gabonais*. Paris: L'Harmattan, 2008.

Mavioga, Staēl. *Premières images de ma vie*. Paris: Edilivre, 2015.

Mve Ondo, Bonaventure. Preface. *Mvett Ekang: forme et sens*, by Angèle Christine Ondo. Paris: L'Harmattan, 2014, pp. 7–10.

———. "L'image de la femme dans l'épopée gabonaise." Ngou, *Notre librairie*, pp. 70–72.

———. "Qu'est-ce que le Mvet?" Ngou, *Notre librairie*, pp. 61–66.

Nang Eyi Obiang, Pierre-Claver. "Au rythme des saisons." Ngou, *Notre librairie*, pp. 28–34.

Ndemby-Mamfoumby, Pierre, editor. *Les écritures gabonaises: histoire, thèmes, et langues*. Vol. 1. Yaoundé: Éditions Clé, 2009.

———. "Le roman gabonais en question: histoire, critiques et éléments d'analyse." Ndemby-Mamfoumby, *Les écritures gabonaises*, pp. 19–55.

Ndemby-Mamfoumby, Pierre and Pierre-Claver Mongui, editors. *Ces espaces littéraires sans frontières: de la critique gabonaise aux études francophones actuelles*. Libreville: Editions Odette Maganga, 2013.

Ndinda, Joseph. "Écriture et discours féminin au Cameroun: trois générations de romancières." *Notre librairie*, vol. 118, 1994, pp. 6–12.

Ndong, Rodrigue. "Esquisse d'un profil du 'lecteur modèle' de deux romans gabonais: *Malédiction* de Sylvie Ntsame et *Le passeport* de Peter Ndemby. Ndemby-Mamfoumby and Mongui, *Ces espaces*, pp. 91–100.

Ndong Ndoutoume, Tsira. "Notre littérature est abondante." Ngou, *Notre librairie*, pp. 35–36.

———. *Le Mvett*. Paris: Présence Africaine, 1970.

Nfah-Abbenyi, Juliana Makuchi. *Gender in African Women's Writing: Identity, Sexuality, and Difference*. Indiana UP, 1997.

Ngou, Honorine. *50 contes éducatifs fang*. Libreville: Éditions Odette Maganga, 2013.

———. *Mon mari, mon salaud: Essai*. Libreville: Éditions Ntsame, 2013.

———. *Afép: L'étrangleur seducteur*. Paris: L'Harmattan, 2010.

———. *Féminin interdit*. Paris: L'Harmattan, 2007.

———. *Mariage et violence dans la société traditionnelle Fang au Gabon*. Paris: L'Harmattan, 2007.

———. "Le tribalisme: le virus qui tue la paix." Libreville: Multipress, 2003. Booklet.

———, editor. *Littérature gabonaise*. Spec. Issue of *Notre librairie* 105, vol. 2, 1991.

———. "Le livre et la lecture au Gabon." Ngou, *Notre librairie*, pp. 126–129.

Nguema, Zwe. *Un Mvet par Zwe Nguema*. Paris: Armand Colin, 1972.

Nguimbi, Arnold. "De la mort du maître à la mort symbolique de l'école: pour une pratique stylistique dans *Histoire d'Awu* de Justine Mintsa." Moupoumbou and Ndemby-Mamfoumby, *La mort*, pp. 130–149.

Njambi, Wairimu Ngaruiya, and William E. O'Brien. "Revisiting 'Woman-woman marriage': Notes on Gikuyu Women." Oyěwùmí, *African Gender Studies*, pp. 145–165.

Nnaemeka, Obioma. *The Politics of (M)othering*. Routledge, 1997.

Ntsame, Rose Nguéma. *La condition de la femme au Gabon: Essai sur l'évolution de la condition de la femme Fang*. Bordeaux II, Bordeaux, France, 1981. Dissertation.

Ntsame, Sylvie. *Femme libérée, femme battue*. Libreville: Éditions Ntsame, 2010.

———. *Le soir autour du feu*. Libreville: Éditions Ntsame, 2010.

———. *Mon amante, la femme de mon père*. Paris: L'Harmattan, 2007.

———. *Malédiction*. Paris: L'Harmattan, 2005.

———. *La fille du Komo*. Paris: L'Harmattan, 2004.

Obame, Landri Ekomie. *Qu'est-ce que le Bwiti? Regard croisée sur une religion naturelle africaine*. Paris: L'Harmattan, 2014.

Obiang, Ludovic. *Et si les crocodiles pleuraient pour de vrai*. Libreville: Éditions Ndze, 2006.

Odounga, Didier Taba. "L'expérience de la mort dans *Dommage!* de F. Leckyou et *Larmes de cendre* de J. Mintsa." Moupoumbou and Ndemby-Mamfoumby, *La Mort*, pp. 49–65.

Ogike, Uche. "Children in Francophone West African Novels: The Power of Childhood." Ikonne, Oko and Onwudinjo, *Children and Literature*, pp. 107–126.

Olouna, Prisca. *La force de toutes mes douleurs*. Paris: L'Harmattan, 2005.

Ondo, Angèle Christine. *Mvett Ekang: Forme et Sens*. Paris: L'Harmattan, 2014.

Origo, Nadia. *Le bal des débutants*. Paris: La Doxa Éditions, 2013.

———. *Le voyage d'Aurore*. Paris: La Doxa Éditions, 2010.

———. *J'ai résolu de . . . .* Condé sur Noireau, Acoria Éditions, 2008.

———. *Le royaume de Longo: le manifeste du Roi Muntu Nene*. Paris: La Doxa Éditions, 2008.

———. *Le royaume de Longo: l'ange du Roi Muntu Nene*. Paris: La Doxa Éditions, 2008.

Ormerod, Beverley and Jean-Marie Volet. *Romancières africaines d'expression française: Le sud du Sahara*. Paris: L'Harmattan, 1994.

Ovono Mendame, Jean-René. "*Histoire d'Awu* de Justine Mintsa: Entre soumission et révolte: les paradoxes d'un destin ambigu." *Africultures*, 6 April 2006, www.africultures.com/php/index.php?nav=article&no=4368.

———. "Gabon: Naissance d'une littérature: Chantal Magalie Mbazoo-Kassa, une romancière en pleine croissance." *Africultures.com*, 10 March 2006, www.africultures.com/php/index.php?nav=article&no=4348.

Owondo, Laurent. *Au bout du silence*. Paris: Hatier, 1985.

Oyěwùmí, Oyèrónké, editor. *African Gender Studies: A Reader*. Palgrave Macmillan, 2005.

———. *The Invention of Women: Making an African Sense of Discourses*. U of Minnesota P, 1997.

Petersen, Kirsten Holst, editor. *Criticism and Ideology*. Uppsala: Scandinavian Institute of African Studies, 1988.

Powrie, Phil. "Rereading between the Lines: A Postscript on *La femme rompue*." *The Modern Language Review*, vol. 87, no. 2, April 1992, pp. 320–329.

Raponda-Walker, André. *Contes gabonais*. Paris: Présence Africaine, 1967.

Rawiri, Angèle. *The Fury and Cries of Women*. Translated by Sara Hanaburgh, U of Virginia P, 2014.

———. *Fureurs et cris de femmes*. Paris: L'Harmattan, 1989.

———. *G'amèrakano au carrefour*. 1983. Paris: Silex, 1988.

———. *Elonga*. 1980. Paris: Silex, 1986.

Rawiri, Georges. *Chants du Gabon*. Paris: Edicef, 1975.

Rich, Adrienne. "Compulsory Heterosexuality and Lesbian Existence." Schneir, *Feminism*, pp. 310–326.

Renombo, Steeve-Robert, Pierre Ndemby Mamfoumby, and Nicolas Mba-Zué, editors. *Littératures francophones et comparatisme*. Libreville: Éditions Odette Maganga, 2014.

Saint-Exupéry, Antoine de. *Le petit prince*. Paris: Gallimard, 1945.

Schneir, Miriam, editor. *Feminism in Our Time: The Essential Writings, World War II to the Present*. Vintage, 1994.

Segun, Mabel. *My Father's Daughter*. Lagos: African UP, 1965.

Senghor, Léopold Sédar. "Femme noire" / "Black Woman." Shapiro, *Négritude Black Poetry*, pp. 130–131.

———. *Chants d'ombre*. Paris: Seuil, 1945.

Shapiro, Norman, editor and translator. *Négritude Black Poetry from Africa and the Caribbean*. October House, 1970.

Sharpley-Whiting, T. Denean. *Negritude Women*. U of Minnesota P, 2002.

Sidikou, Aïssata. *Recreating Words, Reshaping Worlds: The Verbal Art of Women from Niger, Mali, and Senegal*. Africa World Press, 2000.

Stratton, Florence. *Contemporary African Literature and the Politics of Gender*. Routledge, 1994.

Syrotinski, Michael. *Singular Performances: Reinscribing the Subject in Francophone African Writing*. London: U of Virginia P, 2002.

Tadjo, Véronique. *Mamy Wata et le monstre*. Abidjan: Nouvelles Éditions Africaines, 1993.

Toman, Cheryl. Afterword. *The Fury and Cries of Women, a novel by Angèle Rawiri*, translated by Sara Hanaburgh, U of Virginia P, 2014, pp. 195–223.

———. *Contemporary Matriarchies in Cameroonian Francophone Literature*. Summa, 2008.

———, editor and translator. *Essential Encounters* by Thérèse Kuoh-Moukoury. MLA Texts and Translations Series, 2002.

Volet, Jean-Marie. *La parole aux Africaines ou l'idée de pouvoir chez les romancières d'expression française de l'Afrique sub-saharienne*. Amsterdam: Rodopi, 1993.

Zeleza, Paul Tiyambe. "Gender Biases in African Historiography." Oyěwùmí, *African Gender Studies*, pp. 207–232.

Zotoumbat, Robert. *Histoire d'un enfant trouvé*. Yaoundé: Éditions Clé, 1971.

Index

About the Author

Cheryl Toman is an associate professor of French and director of the Women's and Gender Studies Program and the Ethnic Studies Program at Case Western Reserve University. She has been the recipient of a Fulbright Fellowship for Research and Teaching and she was a Brown Foundation Fellow at the Dora Maar House in Ménerbes, France. Her first single-authored book is entitled *Contemporary Matriarchies in Cameroonian Francophone Literature* (2008) and she has edited several volumes with the most recent being *Defying the Global Language: Perspectives in Ethnic Studies* (2013). Her essays appear in journals such as *Research in African Literatures*, *Feminist Studies*, *The French Review*, *Women in French*, and *Women's Studies International Forum*, among others. She is also an accomplished literary translator and among her translated works is the first novel written by an African woman, Thérèse Kuoh-Moukoury's *Essential Encounters* (*Rencontres essentielles*) published by the Modern Languages Association. Toman's research focuses on women writers from Cameroon, Gabon, and Mali.